Endorsements for *Search Committees*

"Selecting the right person for an academic appointment has become increasingly challenging in a competitive environment with dwindling resources. In his guide, Dr. Lee provides a clear process for a search, including helpful tools, hints, and warnings, to improve the likelihood of success for the institution. Woven through the guide is an evidence-based rationale for the recommended approach, including vignettes that make the theoretical come to life. This reference is a must for both novice and seasoned search committee members."

—Patricia Maguire Meservey, President, Salem State University

"The book is well organized and referenced, and provides some outstanding tools and ready-to-use templates for HR professionals supporting searches, as well as committee chairs and committee members. Rather than 'guessing,' or simply utilizing the process your institution has had for many years, this book can help any institution build (or reinvigorate) its search committee process!"

—Isaac Dixon, Associate Vice President and Director of Human Resources, Lewis & Clark College

"This is a comprehensive resource and guide to effective recruitment of faculty and staff. Chris has a high level and sophisticated understanding of the higher education community, as evidenced by his ability to delve deeply and broadly into critical nuances and to offer practical advice for every stage of the search process. Throughout, Chris incorporates strategies to promote the development of a strong and diverse pool of candidates—which is foundational to an effective process and to ensure a successful outcome. I highly recommend this book for all HR professionals, especially those charged with providing leadership in the area of recruitment, and for others across campus who participate in any way with the faculty and staff search, recruitment, and selection process."

—Lauren A. Turner, Associate Vice Chancellor of Human Resources and Equal Opportunity and Outreach, University of Massachusetts Lowell; and past National Board Chair, College and University Professional Association for Human Resources

"In my 15+ years in talent acquisition, I have rarely encountered a single resource that provides step-by-step guidance on maximizing your institution's recruitment and selection process. Dr. Lee's book delivers exactly what it promises in the title: a comprehensive guide for search committees that will instantly upgrade faculty, staff, and administrative searches. If you are among the enlightened souls who believe diversity recruitment is not an after-the-fact consideration, but rather a required component of all successful searches, this book will prove invaluable to you. The templates, samples, interview protocols, case studies, exhibits, and other first-class training materials make Dr. Lee's book 'required reading' for all search committee members."

—Glenn R. Powell, Director of Employment Equity, Georgia Regents University

"*Search Committees* is an intelligent guide to identifying well-qualified candidates for various levels within academic organizations—a critical activity for the success of any organization, often taken for granted and not always thoughtfully implemented. Included are useful techniques and strategies for illuminating the complex and sometimes overwhelming search process, including integrating diversity and involving stakeholders. The value of this book is that it can serve as a checklist for techniques that many of us know but fail to use, as well as motivate committees to renovate the search process."

—Cheryl R. Wyrick, Professor of Management and Human Resources and Associate Dean, College of Business Administration, California State Polytechnic University, Pomona

"In the competitive world of identifying and successfully recruiting professional talent for higher education, I consider Dr. Lee's book a must-read before any serious search is undertaken. The release of this second edition further confirms why Dr. Lee's methodical approach to finding, accessing, and securing talent is so indispensable to building a professional staff."

—Elaine M. Lemay, Executive Director of Human Resources, Samuel Merritt University

"I saw Dr. Lee speak at a CUPA-HR conference in the early 2000s and was immediately impressed with his knowledge of the subject matter of higher education searches. There was such a dearth of information on the subject that I, as a busy HR administrator of a higher education research organization, was thrilled to have access to a bounty of high quality material that I could actually reproduce to train with! Thanks to Dr. Lee, my campus has some of the very best material for our search committees. Our searches are lawful, cast a wide net, and are fair and equitable. Our committees are thankful for the ability to understand each of their roles along with comprehension of how critical the choice is to the institution to reach and choose the most qualified applicants. I highly recommend that those with responsibilities to conduct searches, in whatever capacity, be it as an administrator or a member of a committee, take advantage of this marvelous book and the companion webiste. It may be one of the best choices you make in your career."

—*Sandra Schoelles, Director of Human Resources Office of Sponsored Programs, SUNY, Buffalo State Campus*

"In this in-depth practical playbook chock-full of useful scenarios, examples, templates, and tools, Dr. Lee masterfully captures the essence and art of the higher education search committee process. This is a 'must-have resource' for all CHRO's and higher education HR professionals responsible for leading, managing, and recruiting an equitable 'meritocracy' in higher ed institutions."

—*Brian K. Dickens, Associate Vice President for Human Resources and Payroll Services, Texas Southern University; and National At-Large Board Member, College and University Professional Association for Human Resource (CUPA-HR)*

"The work of selecting new faculty, staff, and administrative colleagues is very challenging. Often, it is performed by committees made up of deeply concerned individuals for whom human capital issues are not part of their daily work. That's why this book is so important. Dr. Lee demystifies the work of selection committees—both for those who are asked to serve on them and for the candidates with whom those committee members will interact. Ensuring that new employees are a good fit within an academic institution is a tough job, and the market for highly skilled talent is extremely competitive. It's important that committees work quickly and diligently to ensure their institution will have the broadest candidate base from which to select. This book will help selection committees avoid the pitfalls that can slow their progress. Dr. Lee has done a fine job of making smart selection processes accessible to committee members and the employers who rely on the fruits of their work."

—*Cheryl Crozier Garcia, Professor of, Human Resource Management and Program Chair, MAHRM Program, Hawaii Pacific University*

"Dr. Lee has written a comprehensive manual that provides human resources professionals with invaluable knowledge on how to conduct efficient and effective searches for their institutions. Filled with cutting-edge and practical techniques, this book will help colleges and universities identify the best and brightest talent available."

—*Jaffus Hardrick, Vice President of Human Resources and Vice Provost of Access and Success, Florida International University*

"For an institution to achieve its goals, it is critical that every position be filled with the best possible candidate that fits the institution's needs. Yet most higher education search committees, who will recruit, interview, and recommend the candidates, are often assembled with little training or experience. This seminal book explains the best practices for managing the search process to get the desired results. It should be required reading for department chairs, deans, search committee chairs, and anyone fortunate enough to be filling a faculty or administrative position in higher education. *Search Committees* will save the university time and money and will undoubtedly produce more satisfactory results."

—*Betsy V. Boze, President, The College of The Bahamas*

"Whether you are chairing your first search committee or your tenth, you will learn something important from this book. Emphasizing how to hire strategically and diversely, Dr. Lee gives detailed advice and proposes sound practices. Who knew, for instance, that the cost to hire a faculty member for 30 years comes to about $3 million, a fact that should give committees pause as they decide whether an applicant should be offered an interview? *Search Committees* will be of tremendous benefit to anyone involved in the academic search process, from board chairs to HR professionals and faculty members."

—*Carol M. Bresnahan, Vice President for Academic Affairs and Provost, Rollins College*

"In order to best educate our students and prepare them for a global economy, they must learn from faculty, administrators, and staff that represent a diverse range of life experiences, race, gender, ethnicity, sexual orientation, background, and worldviews. Attracting and hiring a diverse and highly qualified workforce is critical to our mission as higher education professionals. After having served as a diversity representative on hiring committees, I understand how difficult it is to recruit, hire, and retain great candidates who also increase the diversity of our campuses. Dr. Lee really understands the importance of diversity in the hiring process. In addition to including an entire chapter on diversity in the hiring process, there are many vignettes and tips to reinforce this throughout the book. It should be read and discussed by everyone who cares about increasing diversity in a higher education environment."

—Laura E. Saret, Professor of Management Emeritus, Oakton Community College

"This is a relevant, up-to-date guide with a plethora of practical information from sourcing and evaluating candidates to interview questions. The appendices offer a wealth of information and the Diversity Tips and Diversity Topics are invaluable. This book offers a complete 'soup to nuts' approach that is comprehensive and just right on target. Even those who think that they are pros, having led searches for years, will benefit from what this book offers."

—Tamara D. Spoerri, Director of Human Resources, Bowdoin College

SEARCH COMMITTEES

SEARCH COMMITTEES

A Comprehensive Guide to Successful Faculty,
Staff, and Administrative Searches

SECOND EDITION

CHRISTOPHER D. LEE, PhD, SPHR

Foreword by Edna B. Chun

Published in association
with CUPA-HR

College and University Professional
Association for Human Resources

STERLING, VIRGINIA

Published by Stylus Publishing, LLC
22883 Quicksilver Drive
Sterling, Virginia 20166-2102

Library of Congress Cataloging-in-Publication Data

Lee, Christopher D.
    Search committees : a comprehensive guide to successful faculty,
staff, and administrative searches / Christopher D. Lee, Ph.D.,
SPHR ; foreword by Edna B. Chun.—Second Edition.
        pages cm
    Includes bibliographical references and index.
    ISBN 978-1-62036-199-3 (cloth : alk. paper)—
    ISBN 978-1-62036-200-6 (pbk. : alk. paper)—
    ISBN 978-1-62036-201-3 (library networkable e-edition)—
    ISBN 978-1-62036-202-0 (consumer e-edition)
        1. College teachers—Selection and appointment—United
States 2. College administrators—Selection and appointment—
United States. 3. Universities and colleges--Professional staff—
Selection and appointment—United States.
    I. Title.

    LB2332.72.L44 2014
    378.1'2--dc23
                                                        2013049717
13-digit ISBN: 978-1-62036-199-3 (cloth)
13-digit ISBN: 978-1-62036-200-6 (paperback)
13-digit ISBN: 978-1-62036-201-3 (library networkable e-edition)
13-digit ISBN: 978-1-62036-202-0 (consumer e-edition)

Printed in the United States of America

All first editions printed on acid-free paper
that meets the American National Standards Institute
Z39-48 Standard.

Bulk Purchases

Quantity discounts are available for use in
workshops and for staff development.
Call 1-800-232-0223

First Edition, 2014

10 9 8 7 6

For

*Sophia and Grace, who almost grew up while I was
developing the materials for this book,
Maureen, who was tolerant and patient with my
running and hiding away to write,
Amber for "whatever";
my friends at Georgia Highlands who encouraged me,
the HR gang at Bates who cared for me, and Donna and
my colleagues at the VCCS who supported me;
and, finally . . .
Mom, if you are looking down here and counting, this is book number three.*

~cdl

Contents

Exhibits

Vignettes

Foreword

WHY ARE SEARCH COMMITTEE PROCESSES so essential to the future success of higher education? In a rapidly changing global environment, talent is the most significant strategic asset of our colleges and universities. Talent is the source of innovation, knowledge, and creativity—the backbone of institutions of higher education that drives the creation of sustainable competitive advantage.

As Alvin Evans and I argue in *The New Talent Acquisition Frontier* (Stylus, 2013), the practices of talent management require a strategic and systematic approach that brings the knowledge, capabilities, and organizational intelligence colleges and universities need to advance research, prepare students for participation in a global society, streamline and optimize administrative systems, and build an inclusive organizational culture.

From this perspective, the search for talent is a continuous process, not a one-time event. In difficult budgetary times, we know that each hiring opportunity is precious. Department heads in academic departments and nonacademic units alike face the challenge of meeting their defined educational and administrative objectives with a constrained complement of staffing and budgetary resources. Tenure-track lines for new faculty are limited but essential in order to strengthen disciplinary expertise, provide new research streams, and expand curricular offerings for both graduate and undergraduate students. Positions in facilities, human resources, information technology, student affairs, and other administrative areas provide the necessary organizational infrastructure to address faculty, staff, and student needs.

The search committee is the channel through which colleges and universities attract, identify, evaluate, and recommend talent. Yet, too often, search committees lack the tools, guides, necessary preparation, and competencies for highly specialized sourcing, recruiting, and evaluation processes. When an institution does not have a systematic process for guiding search committees, the potential for missteps, inconsistencies, inequities, and questionable practices increases.

Dr. Lee's book addresses a long unmet need in higher education for a concrete, approachable resource that will assist search committees in building the knowledge base, skills, and competencies for the search process. In essence, this guide provides a prescription for conducting a successful search from start to finish that will help institutions avoid costly mistakes; decrease the potential for challenges to the validity of the search; use limited resources effectively; and ensure a fair, balanced, and rigorous search process. Dr. Lee illustrates this progressive pathway with engaging vignettes and practical exhibits that will answer many of the questions that typically arise in the course of a search.

Often search committees ponder questions like, "What do I do if I have two identical candidates, one who is qualified and one who is diverse?" Or "Does the hiring manager really have the right to bring additional candidates into the pool besides those whom the committee recommended?" Or "Should we rank order the candidates, and what happens if the appointing authority makes a different selection?" Committees sometimes struggle with the criteria for evaluating candidates and developing behavioral-based questions that reflect demonstrated experience rather than simply reflecting the candidate's viewpoint. Among other considerations, the composition of the search committee must reflect the needs of a representative bureaucracy, in terms of both the constituencies the position serves and the emerging demographic diversity of student populations. This book answers these questions and provides a concrete frame of reference with illustrative examples for approaching these issues.

Since attracting a diverse and talented complement of new scholars, administrators, and staff is one of the most important roles of a search committee, Dr. Lee stresses the importance of creating a true meritocracy by overcoming preconceived notions, and the tendency to select similar others, by focusing on objective criteria. In a similar vein, Alvin Evans and I have also emphasized the importance of integrated diversity and HR efforts in recruitment and hiring processes that build a high-performance workforce.

Yet diversity efforts can be thwarted in the search committee process if adequate care is not taken to advise the committee of the importance of a balanced pool, define job requirements to attract a broad talent base, implement good faith efforts to meet affirmative action goals, and develop rigorous and fair evaluation criteria with structured interview questions. Dr. Lee provides diversity tips, vignettes, and an introductory "Diversity Advantage" chapter that reinforce these concepts and provide concrete examples. As a result, this book will resonate with chief HR

officers (CHROs) and chief diversity officers (CDOs) as well.

Given the pivotal importance of the search committee in the viability and success of institutions of higher education, this book's wide dissemination to search committees, human resources professionals, diversity officers, department heads, deans, and hiring officials will enhance immeasurably the ability of higher education institutions to conduct successful searches that identify, attract, and retain talent. An additional benefit is access to Dr. Lee's website on search committees (www.SearchCommittees.com), which provides additional guidance, webinars, and strategic advice on search processes. From the perspective of a practitioner in the field, I am delighted that this resource is now available to deliver the needed information, exhibits, templates, and tools to provide systematic guidance to search committees in the search process.

Edna B. Chun, DM
Associate Vice Chancellor for Human Resources
University of North Carolina at Greensboro

How to Use This Book

Why You Should Buy This Book

Few higher education professionals receive training on the search committee process, even when they are expected to serve on or lead committees. This book provides advice, training, and a step-by-step guide for conducting a rigorous, thorough search. Following the expert model presented in this book will virtually guarantee successful searches. Additionally, this guide provides advanced diversity selection techniques not commonly found in many resources inside or outside of higher education.

Who Should Read This Book

Committee Chairs. This book guides committee chairs through the selection process step-by-step, provides them with case studies offering practical tips and cautions against common pitfalls, and advises them when to seek HR assistance.

Administrators. Find the best faculty and staff by following a proven model. Handy templates, checklists, and suggestions are available as needed.

Human Resources Professionals. This comprehensive text provides expert advice, professional insight, sample resources, and invaluable tips for every search phase. This desktop reference guide and library of information will make you a subject matter expert so you can train, equip, support, and monitor searches effectively.

Committee Members. This book is a reference manual with suggestions, how-to guides, answers to questions, legal facts, and sensible solutions that clear up myths and misperceptions about best practice approaches to a professional search.

What Is in This Book

This book contains four major components:

1. An expert step-by-step search model
2. Dozens of templates, samples, tools, plus a bank of interview questions
3. Diversity recruitment and selection protocols and techniques
4. Resource guide with advice, case studies, examples, and training materials

The content areas include the following:

- How to build a successful search
- Recruiting guide
- How to design a diverse selection process
- Minority recruiting resources
- Interview guide
- A bank of interview questions
- Additional screening methods
- Sample forms, templates, checklists
- A glossary of terms
- Legal, ethical, and regulatory issues
- Search committee bibliography

There are 34 exhibits included that are meant to be copied and used as training handouts or as handy reference and resource materials that provide guidance at various stages of the search process. You can use the over two dozen vignettes included as training case studies or as expert advice that illuminates key concepts that are helpful for improving the quality of the search process.

How to Read This Book

Read this book by following the search process as it unfolds from beginning to end in an orderly fashion. Later, use it as a desktop reference by skipping to the stage of the process in which you are interested, want advice, or need a resource. Share individual tools and instruments with colleagues who need an expert resource on a particular topic, such as writing an advertisement, developing better interview questions, or making an offer. The best use of the book would be for HR professionals to buy needed copies and give one to each hiring manager or search committee chair as he or she embarks on the search. For HR professionals, this is a desktop reference guide for all things related to the employment process in higher education.

Website and Other Resources

The website, www.SearchCommittees.com (an ever-growing resource on this subject), is designed to train, equip, and empower search committees. Many resources in this book are used with this site's permission.

Introduction

A FTER DECIDING ON ITS PURPOSE, the most important decision any organization ever makes is determining who will join the organization. The selection process is both an art and a science. The science involves doing the right things—using the best tools, methods, and techniques. The art of selection deals with hiring the right person—qualified candidates who live and breathe your organizational mission, vision, and values. In higher education, colleges and universities expend significant time, attention, and resources to do this well. These wise investments yield significant advantages in retention and quality. When the process works, a commensurate return on investment manifests itself in the form of the finalist succeeding within an organization for years to come. Likewise, when an organization makes poor selection decisions, costs to the institution can be considerable in terms of both finances and intangibles (see Vignette A: *The Cost of a Bad Hire*). Deciding whom to select is often a multi-million-dollar decision (see Vignette B: *The $3 Million Decision*).

The academic tradition of using the shared governance process as a framework for selecting faculty and staff is worth preserving because it yields great benefits. These include a higher-quality candidate, greater diversity, and a better organizational fit—and, therefore, greater retention. Better candidates are identified when an institution takes the time to get a 360-degree look at the requirements for a position and then recruits and selects candidates according to this clear vision. Bias is reduced through a carefully chosen committee whose members have a multidimensional and multicultural view of candidate capabilities. Retention improves when the rigorous process finds well-qualified candidates who match both the position and the institution. This occurs because candidates get a sneak preview of community life and culture by interacting with a wide variety of community members. They are then able to make more informed decisions about accepting any offer of employment.

Practice of the art of selection varies significantly across colleges and universities in the United States and abroad. Nonprofit organizations, professional associations, and even some churches use search committees for hiring. This second edition of an award-winning resource offers a best practice model for such search and selection processes (Lee, C. D. 2001). It contains tools, techniques, examples, and advice as well as a model framework to enable campuses to select the best possible faculty and staff with greater efficiency, effectiveness, and probability of success. The framework and associated steps can be tailored to how a particular campus works. Finally, readers get expert advice and assistance on each step in the selection process as well as special topics to enhance how effectively a search committee works.

Definitions and Models

Using the search committee process to select faculty and staff varies significantly, as does the vocabulary used to describe it. Therefore, the following definitions are provided for clarity:

Search Committee: a group of individual stakeholders from various areas and levels within an organization whose members come together in a structured and coordinated manner to screen, evaluate, and recommend potential candidates for employment.

Selection Committee: search committees that are empowered to make the final hiring decision instead of recommending candidates for hiring.

VIGNETTE A
The Cost of a Bad Hire

Conducting a search involves many costs. They are felt most poignantly when a search ends without a selection or when the wrong person is hired. Financial costs include direct expenditures and indirect costs. Indirect costs are significant, but are often hidden or embedded in members' time or in the support functions such as the HR department or equal opportunity professionals who are assigned to monitor the process. When the wrong person is hired and then leaves within a short period of time—or worse yet, the person stays and performs marginally for a long period, there can be a cost—a tangible negative effect on colleagues and students. A bad hire includes direct, indirect, and intangible costs. Examples follow:

Direct Costs
advertisements, candidate travel, meals, printing and copying, background checks, relocation expenses, severance payments, legal fees, etc.

Indirect Costs
recruiting efforts, search committee time, HR staff labor costs, lost productivity, training and professional development costs, etc.

Intangible Costs
poor morale in the department, emotional toll on colleagues, reputation of the institution, negative impact on students, etc.

Bad hire costs are underscored more for high-profile or sensitive positions. A president who starts, charts a new course, then leaves within two years, causing the institution to bounce from one strategic direction to another, is an archetypical example of a costly, damaging hire. An unpopular faculty member who negatively affects hundreds of students and calls into question the quality of instruction at an institution is another example. When a staff member is hired without a thorough background check, and then newspapers report that he or she was previously found guilty of a crime that embarrasses the organization, is an all too common occurrence according to media that report such incidents. These are all examples of the negative effect of not being thorough and careful in the selection process.

VIGNETTE B
The $3 Million Decision

The salary of a college professor over a 30-year career can easily exceed $3 million. This seemingly large amount is actually a conservative estimate that includes salary, benefits, retirement, life insurance, health care, disability, tuition reimbursement, and other resources. It does not factor in relocation costs, recruitment incentives, office space and supplies, professional development funds, lab facilities, support staff, and related costs. In short, the process of making a selection decision should not be taken lightly. Its importance cannot be underestimated if for no other reason than the large financial investment that is funded by student tuition, federal and state resources, grants, or donations. Good advice for committee members when making close calls about whether candidates should be asked for an interview is to consider whether they're willing to wager $3 million on that decision.

Screening Committee: a group of stakeholders whose members evaluate the written materials of applicants to identify a group of semifinalists or finalists who will be evaluated further during the selection process. Screening committees are not necessarily involved in the actual interview process as a group, though individual members may participate in the interviewing or selection process as a member of a search or selection committee.

There are important differences in the roles and functions of search, selection, and screening committees, which include the following:

- Search and selection committees sometimes define a position.
- Search and selection committees may participate in recruitment.
- Screening committees are most useful when a group of subject matter experts is charged with culling the number of applicants down to a more manageable number for consideration by a search committee or hiring manager.
- Screening committees prove particularly useful when the search committee does not have enough technical expertise to evaluate the applicants' competitiveness (e.g., selecting a chief information officer or a faculty member in a newly created program).
- Screening committees can expedite a search since they are typically smaller in size and usually from a single department. They organize and meet more easily and are likely to reach consensus faster due to their members' similar ways of thinking and working.
- Sometimes the HR department acts as a screening committee and conducts an initial screen of applicants by eliminating those who do not meet the minimum requirements for a position (e.g., lack of appropriate degree, experience, identified competencies, etc.; See Vignette Q: *HR Prescreen or Minimal Qualifications Screening*, p. 63).
- When screening committees are used, there is little diversity of thought in the process. The likely limitations can be counterbalanced by ensuring that the search committee to which the screening committee gives its results is as diverse as possible.
- Screening committees are a valuable and efficient use of time and resources when there are multiple searches for similar positions in a given time frame.
- A best practice approach for both search and selection committees is to include at least one member from outside the hiring department to broaden the perspective about the position and the institution.
- A selection committee example is when all faculty members of a department select a department head.

How these committees function when they are used on a given campus varies significantly. These committees often act singularly or in combination, or their elements are used differently in various environments (see *Alternative Search Models*, p. 149). Nonetheless, the previous functions can be adapted for any campus community. The most important advice is to determine which model(s) will work for your campus and establish them in policy. Considerable frustration and failure are by-products of committees unclear in their purpose, process, and *charge*. Clarifying roles and functions of committees is an important initial step in designing successful campus search committee processes.

An Investment of Time

As noted earlier, colleges and universities invest a significant amount of time and resources in the selection process. Table I.1 provides a general estimate of the time it takes to recruit and select for various positions. These estimates are based on historical patterns across institutional types. In addition, they are affected by the time of year a search begins, the availability of faculty participation between semesters and in the summer, the workload of committee members, the urgency of the hire, the relative availability of applicants based on the labor market for a particular position, plus various other institutional factors. This table provides a broad estimate for those unfamiliar with the search committee process while acknowledging that each of the estimates can be expedited or prolonged depending on the efficiency and effectiveness of conducting a search.

While the estimates might seem high and unnecessary for those not sensitive to academic traditions, they do reflect the nature of the search committee process in higher education. On a positive note, there are many ways to expedite the search and selection

TABLE I.1
Typical Time Frame for Conducting Searches

Position	Recruiting & Advertising Time	Selection Time	Delay Before Reporting to Work	Estimated Total Time
Faculty	2–6 months	2–6 months	*	4 or more months
Directors & Department Heads	4–8 weeks	4–6 weeks	4–8 weeks	3–4 months
Academic Department Chairs	2–6 months	2–6 months	*	Semester
Deans	4–8 weeks	4–8 weeks	*	Semester
Vice Presidents & Provosts	4–8 weeks	2–3 months	*	6 months
Presidents	4–8 weeks	2–6 months	1–6 months	6–12 months

* The delay varies depending on the time of year the selection is made. Faculty and academic leaders selected in December may not report until the following fall semester, as much as nine months later.

process, and there are many occasions when it is prudent to do so (see *Expediting the Search*).

Building a Successful Search, Step-by-Step

To ensure a successful search, there are tried-and-true elements of the process that must be completed. At each step, there are critical components that must be included and deployed in the proper order to buttress the building block approach to a successful search. Skipping or eliminating steps is perilous. A quote about the search committee process from Julie A. Sweitzer and Carol Carrier in *The Search Committee Handbook* (Marchese & Lawrence, 2005, p. 18), speaks volumes: "Expediency rarely leads to excellence."

Furthermore, experience shows that when searches fail, the majority of errors were made in the initial stages. Laying the groundwork effectively reduces the risk of costly and time-consuming adjustments later in the process. We can avoid being placed in the difficult position of having to reopen a search due to process problems or administrative mistakes. The challenges of an inadequate candidate pool whose members lack diversity or having preferred candidates who do not accept employment offers can be avoided. Mistakes come from poor planning, bad search design, improper preparations, and lackadaisical execution. Each of these and other search committee mishaps, shortcomings, and failures can be prevented.

As outlined in Table I.2, three leading search committee sources describe the various steps and stages of the search and selection process. This book follows the www.SearchCommittees.com model, which offers a more detailed, discrete delineation of steps. This classical approach provides a better comprehensive resource for colleges and universities to follow for conducting a model search as well as a quick reference guide when seeking expertise on one search process element. Information, advice, and useful tools or samples are provided for each of the 16 steps noted in the www.SearchCommittees.com model. Thus, this book is a guide for human resources (HR) professionals responsible for supporting committees, a useful and practical tool for search committee chairs responsible for leading the process, a reference guide for committee members, and an instructional manual for administrators charged with appointing committees and receiving their recommendations.

Expediting the Search

Many tasks can be completed differently to expedite a regular search. The time-savers involved do not have a negative impact on the search's rigor. The key factor is to use any or all of the following techniques in the correct combination and degree when appropriate for unique situations. Building in additional safeguards to ensure a quality search is also an option.

TABLE I.2
Typical Steps in Search Committee Process

Steps	www.SearchCommittees.com	*The Complete Academic Search Manual (Vicker & Royer, 2006)*	*The Search Committee Handbook (Marchese & Lawrence, 2005)*
1	Approvals		
2	Organizational Analysis		The Vacancy: An Organizational Opportunity
3	Building the Foundation		
4	Defining the Position	Profile & Position Descriptions	The Job: Identifying Preferred Qualifications
5	Forming, Orienting, & Charging the Committee	Preparing the Search Committee	The Committee: Composition, Charge, & Ground Rules
6	Recruiting	Recruiting Candidates	The Search: Recruiting a Candidate Pool
7	Advertising		
8	Screening & Evaluating Candidates & Materials	Evaluating Résumés	The Screening: Identifying Talent Among Applicants
9	Preparing for Interviews	Preparing to Interview	The Interviews: Knowing & Courting Candidates
10	Interviewing	Campus Interviews	
11	Additional Screening Methods	Evaluating Finalists	
12	Background & Reference Checks		Making the Appointment
13	Making a Recommendation		
14	Making the Offer	Negotiating & Making the Offer	
15	Closing the Search		
16	Welcoming Colleague to Campus	Extending Hospitality to the New Hire	

The following are suggestions that can help to expedite searches:

- Complete approvals via electronic means instead of campus mail, or announce the expedited nature of the search to all decision makers at once through a single e-mail asking for support.
- Shorten the advertising period, with length depending on the type of position.
- Use online media rather than printed. Online ads can be placed immediately; print generally involves lag time.

- Recruit before posting the job by informing promising candidates that a vacancy announcement is forthcoming.
- Recruit aggressively via phone; have two or more people call numerous potential candidates.
- Start screening applications as they come in rather than waiting until the closing date to review (this is easier if you use an electronic applicant–tracking system).
- Use a screening committee to reduce the candidate pool to a list of 6 to 12 semifinalists,

and then give the list to the search committee for further review and action.

- An appointing authority or hiring manager screens the pool, reduces the pool of candidates to 6 to 12, and then hands over semifinalists to the search committee.
- Reduce the number of search committee members to five. Smaller groups are easier to assemble and can deliberate faster.
- Determine selection criteria and screening instruments in advance; these are chosen by the appointing authority/hiring manager, committee chair, or HR.
- Evaluate all candidates by the prepopulated screening instrument presented to the search committee for its initial review to expedite the members' analysis and deliberations (This initial screening can be completed by the appointing authority, committee chair, or HR—see Vignette Q: *HR Prescreen or Minimal Qualifications Screening*, p. 63).
- Establish a calendar before forming a committee. "We invite you to serve on the search committee for _____ position. Due to time considerations, the committee will meet on the following dates _____ and will interview the week(s) of _____. If you are interested, and are available to serve in this important capacity, we thank you in advance for your consideration."
- Conduct additional screening methods prior to the on-campus interview, reducing the number of interviewees.
- Use telephone interviews, questionnaires, sample writings, submission of portfolios, and so on.
- Use video interviews to reduce the number of candidates invited to campus.
- Abbreviate the interview schedule; schedule a half day instead of a full day, and so on.
- Interview candidates on the same day; rotate candidates through the committees, groups, and individuals involved in the interviews.
- Rank and invite only the top candidate (based on the search committee's deliberation) to campus. If he or she is successful, hire that person without entertaining others further. It is important to note that the best approach with this option is to use it under the following

conditions: (a) your policies allow this practice, (b) this option is selected and approved of before the search commences, (c) it is used in conjunction with multiple screening methods, (d) the campus interview occurs after all telephone/video interviews are completed, and (e) invitations should be sent with the oversight and approval of senior leaders and equal opportunity professionals.

- Schedule the search committee to meet one hour after the last candidate leaves campus to formulate a recommendation rather than waiting until a later time.
- Give a recommendation to the *appointing authority* verbally instead of in writing.
- Schedule the *appointing authority* to meet with the committee immediately following its deliberations.

You can accelerate the time frame with forethought, planning, and coordination. Activities can be completed to enrich search rigor and quality even though the time frame is shortened:

- When fewer stakeholders are involved in the screening stage, involve more stakeholder groups at the interview stage.
- Ask for more information from all applicants up front, including letters of recommendation, portfolios, statements of teaching philosophy, completed questionnaires, and so on. (Use an applicant tracking system to make this easier.)
- Conduct additional screening methods prior to on-campus interviews or while on campus— telephone interviews, questionnaires, writing samples, submission of portfolios, and so on.
- Have candidates complete *work samples* while on campus.
- Schedule the finalist for a second interview; it is easier to bring one candidate back to campus for a second look than to manage a protracted regular search.
- Hire a third-party firm to conduct reference checks.
- Have an HR department consultant attend each committee meeting to offer advice, support, tools, techniques, sample forms, and checklists for completing committee work efficiently and effectively.

A fast search does not automatically mean lower quality, but it does mean working deliberately and efficiently.

While some stages in the search can be completed more quickly, expediency is not recommended during the Laying the Groundwork or Background and Reference Check stages of the search process. Searches fail most at these two process stages, so you should observe due diligence.

To consider using various alternative models for search committees or the techniques offered, create a policy authorizing this practice prior to its first use (see *Alternative Search Models*, p. 149). Most important, the chosen model should be approved before each search; it is not acceptable to start a regular search and then change midstream to an alternative search model. When this happens, it raises legitimacy questions. Finally, a number of affirmative action (AA) considerations may weigh against alternative models or changes in process—depending on how your campus practices the search committee art. Yet, with the appropriate safeguards and prudence, such models can be advantageous in identifying diverse candidates, particularly when intensive recruiting efforts begin by targeting minority candidates.

CHAPTER 1

The Diversity Advantage

MANY INSTITUTIONS FIND IT A CHALLENGE to recruit and select a diverse faculty and staff. The most important advice about diversity recruiting and selection is that it is part of the search process, not an addition to it. Therefore, effective tips and techniques that support diversity are included throughout this book and noted at each stage of the search process.

There are six ways diversity-related materials are incorporated into this resource:

1. This chapter is an in-depth overview of diversity-related subject matter.
2. In-text references are contained throughout the book.
3. Diversity tips are included at the end of several key sections.
4. Diversity-related vignettes are included to explain key concepts.
5. Key diversity topics are presented in bold in the index.
6. A diversity resources bibliography is provided for readers wanting additional or advanced study on related topics.

This integrated approach to delivering diversity-related material reinforces the major premise that a comprehensive, professional search is not possible without certain key elements. Included in these elements are diversity-related techniques. Diversity-related activities, among a few other essential elements, are inherent to a successful search, and thus receive highlighting.

Diversity Creates a True Meritocracy

Emerging evidence argues that true meritocracies exist only where diversity resides (Kaplan & Donavan, 2013). A meritocracy implies that the best candidates are evaluated by achievements, contributions, talents, and potential—not where they went to school, whom they know, socioeconomic status, pedigree, or other nonwork-related criteria. In a meritocracy, all candidates are considered, not a preselected subgrouping based upon some set of consciously or unconsciously chosen criteria.

As an example, we cannot assume that the best scholars in the world come only from schools in Massachusetts. For this reason, we must assume that if we want to find the best biologist, we might have to recruit from other states and even other countries. While some candidates have different or even nontraditional backgrounds, they may contribute at the same or higher level than those candidates previously considered models. We cannot assume a monopoly exists on the ideal description of what produces a great scholar or professional. Many experts argue that some preconceived notions of quality are actually personal preference in disguise (Smith, Turner, Osei-Kofi, & Richards, 2004), so merit-screening of candidates is actually a masquerade.

As an example of how preconceived notions undermine fairness, in the article, "The Impact of Legacy Status on Undergraduate Admissions at Elite Colleges and Universities," the author posits that an applicant's chance of getting admitted increased by as much as 43% on the basis of his or her parents having attended the same highly selective institution (Hurwitz, 2011). Therefore, if one assumes that every candidate who graduated from certain institutions is more capable than any candidate from other institutions, this would be an example of bias that is both unfounded and unfair. Likewise, considerable evidence exists that people refer and hire people similar to themselves, thereby overlooking relevant criteria in deference to familiarity (Rivera, 2012; Topa, Brown, & Setren, 2013). Few informed professionals would argue that traditional hiring practices are bias-free, fair, and reflect a pure examination of objective criteria. However, a meritocracy is built upon this very idea and assumption of fairness—the requirement that the talented are advanced based upon their demonstrated outputs alone.

A true meritocracy asserts that results will speak for themselves and will not be based upon bias or a proprietary view of what is deemed best. In a meritocracy, all candidates' capabilities are assessed fairly against previously defined, job-related criteria. Embracing diversity is an endorsement for a meritocracy if all are given an opportunity to be judged by known, objective criteria alone.

The Business Case for Diversity

A compelling body of literature is emerging that proves diversity makes good business sense. Dr. John Sullivan—whom *Fast Company* magazine deems the Michael Jordan of hiring—in numerous publications and speeches over the past decade has made the following arguments regarding this cause. He states diverse workforces produce the following:

- Increased product sales
- Higher revenue
- Better employee retention
- Better organizational decision making
- Avoidance of blunders due to the multi-dimensional and multicultural perspectives offered
- Products better tailored to customer needs
- Improved customer loyalty because employees look like the communities within which they do business
- Lower legal/Equal Employment Opportunity Commission costs due to fewer complaints based upon *protected classes*
- Better public relations and reputation for corporate and organizational social responsibility (Sullivan, 2000)

Dr. Sullivan's research observations have been supported by countless other authors (Chua, 2011; Global Diversity and Inclusion, 2011; Herring, 2009; Hong & Page, 2004; Page, 2007; Slater, Weigand, & Zwirlein, 2008; Watson, Kumar, & Michaelsen, 1993). The following are some quotes from relevant research reinforcing his point:

> In a study comparing the financial performance of the Diversity, Inc. Top 50 Companies for Diversity to a matched sample, we find evidence that firms with a strong commitment to diversity outperform their peers on average. (Slater et al., 2008)

> Examining Fortune 500 companies, . . . those with the highest representation of women on their board of directors experienced better financial performance on average . . . than those with the lowest representation of women. Similar findings . . . analyzing a statistically significant sample of companies across Europe, Brazil, Russia, India and China, [from a] 2010 report showed that companies with the highest share of women in their senior management teams outperformed those with no women from 2007–2009 by 41% in terms of return on equity. (Deloitte, 2011)

> Task-related diversity was found to be positively related to both quality and quantity of team performance as hypothesized. By demonstrating this positive link between task-related diversity and team performance, this study confirms that diversity presented in team members that are [sic] highly related to tasks facilitates team performance despite many factors influencing team outcomes. This finding is an empirical confirmation of "value-in-diversity" in team settings. (Horwitz & Horwitz, 2007, p. 1005)

> Diversity yields superior outcomes is a quick summary of research that explains how and why diverse groups produce better results. (Page, 2007)

> Diversity is a key driver of innovation and is a critical component of being successful on a global scale. ("Global Diversity and Inclusion," 2011, p. 3)

The conversation about diversity and its positive effects on business has shifted from *if* to *how*. Since conventional wisdom says that diversity strengthens businesses, many for-profit organizations are earnestly working to build diverse and inclusive workplaces to realize a return on their investment. A similar trajectory of the educational case for diversity is emerging.

The Educational Case for Diversity

The tenets of diversity parallel Thomas Jefferson's notion of a broad liberal education. Education provides exposure to variety, diversity, complexity, discovery, and change. An education is not complete without diversity in its fullest expression. This notion is embedded in the mission of most institutions of higher education (see *The Diversity Advantage: Multicultural Experiences as Mission-Essential Criteria*, the following section).

While it might seem unnecessary, there is often the need to prove diversity's positive effect on the educational experience. Examples of the findings from studies that support this idea include:

- Positive impact on the educational outcomes of both minority and majority students
- Positive effect on student development
- Positive effect on college satisfaction
- Increase in intellectual engagement and growth of students
- Increased student retention and persistence
- Greater success for women graduate students correlated with presence of women faculty
- Diverse organizational climates increase student-centered practices in the classroom
- Better preparation of students to live and work in a global society

Countless articles and an emerging body of research are validating what has been widely believed for centuries—that diversity is inherent to a quality education (American Council on Education & American Association of University Professors, 2000; Board of Regents of the University of Wisconsin System, 2010; Gurin, 1999; Lee, J. A., 2010; Milem, 2003; Smith et al., 1997). The educational benefit of diversity is the topic of many policy debates and has been politicized to a large degree in contemporary society. Suffice it to say, an education without diversity is not an education at all.

The Diversity Advantage: Multicultural Experiences as Mission-Essential Criteria

Many colleges and universities have some element of diversity or multiculturalism embedded in their mission statements. The following are a few excerpts from some of the country's leading institutions (Macalester, Bowdoin, and Amherst Colleges, and Yale, Columbia, Duke, and Georgetown Universities, respectively):

- ". . . high standards for scholarship and its special emphasis on internationalism, multiculturalism, and service to society"

- ". . . tolerance of and interest in differences of culture and belief"
- ". . . in order to promote diversity of experience and ideas"
- ". . . to attract a diverse group of exceptionally talented men and women from across the nation and around the world and to educate them for leadership in scholarship, the professions, and society"
- "It seeks to attract a diverse and international faculty and student body, to support research and teaching on global issues, and to create academic relationships with many countries and regions."
- ". . . to promote a deep appreciation for the range of human difference and potential"
- ". . . founded on the principle that serious and sustained discourse among people of different faiths, cultures, and beliefs promotes intellectual, ethical and spiritual understanding. We embody this principle in the diversity of our students, faculty and staff."

If one institutional purpose is to advance diversity or multiculturalism, it would seem reasonable, appropriate, and necessary that the institution promote, implement, and sustain such elements. Thus, candidates who would bring diverse or multicultural assets to the college or university should be given special consideration—if not an advantage—in the selection process. This would become a diversity advantage for any individual who came from a multicultural background, had a multicultural education, had multicultural professional experiences, conducted multicultural research, or who otherwise brought a multicultural perspective to the workplace. Experts call the facility to interact effectively with people different from oneself *cultural competence.*

If the institution educates students from many backgrounds, this diversity advantage would also support the education of a diverse student body. This diversity advantage could be factored into the screening and evaluation of all applicants (O'Rourke, 2011). This advantage should be given to all qualifying candidates—regardless of their appearance. Candidates who are non-native-born Americans fit this example. Minority group members would likely qualify, provided they can prove that they have lived, worked, and interacted with multicultural populations or can provide a multicultural perspective (minority and majority cultural experiences). Similarly, majority candidates or any candidate who grew up in racially segregated communities, attended largely monocultural schools, did not interact with others outside of a certain socioeconomic strata, or had never been involved in social, professional, or civic activities working with other populations different from their own likely would not be an organizational fit because they would not possess the necessary cultural competence to work with and relate to all of their students and colleagues (see *Evaluating Organizational Fit: Why You Should and Must*, p. 107).

Candidates who speak second languages, who have researched different groups, who have worked in homeless shelters for immigrants, or who demonstrate through verifiable experiences that they have acquired multicultural perspectives would be ideal employees for institutions valuing their diversity mission. Minority candidates who have successfully worked and studied in majority organizations, exhibit cross-cultural characteristics, and offer multicultural perspectives would also be well qualified. While the concept of diversity advantage may seem far-fetched, it is wholly reasonable when organizations are true to their mission and purposes. Where multiculturalism does not provide an outright advantage, it should at least be considered as an advantageous organizational criterion (see *Evaluating Organizational Fit: Why You Should and Must*, p. 107; *Evaluating Organizational Fit: Defining and Documenting Fit*, p. 108; and *Organizational Fit Criteria*, p. 109).

How to Incorporate Diversity Into the Search and Selection Process

Effective search strategies already inherently support diversity because a fair, comprehensive, professional search is naturally inclusive. Here is an overview of how and when diversity-related strategies can be incorporated into the search committee process.

Policy

Employment policies should include effective recruitment and networking techniques, equal opportunity considerations, and Affirmative Action (AA) guidelines. Additionally, policies that advocate for diversity and provide guidelines and incentives for diversity

selection need to be documented, especially if diversity is considered essential to the institution's mission, is a part of a strategic plan, is a stated organizational goal, or is a part of a major institutional initiative. Furthermore, *opportunity hire* policies and protocols have been shown to have a positive effect on the selection of diverse faculty (Smith et al., 2004).

Organizational Analysis

Such analysis identifies the unique characteristics of the work environment and organizational needs. Here, for example, diversifying an all-female staff of advancement officers or a predominantly male math department might be uncovered and discussed.

Defining the Position

If the position serves diverse clientele—and almost every position does—highlight the need for cultural competence, familiarity with gender issues, or knowledge of the literature on multicultural counseling techniques as a part of employee responsibilities. When defining a position, it is important that a full analysis is conducted and a 360-degree view is considered—to include diversity and multicultural factors.

Completing a Labor Market Analysis

A thorough market analysis for particular skills should indicate the relative availability of candidates with the background sought (e.g., years of experience, degrees, certifications). The analysis should describe the demographic makeup of target populations (e.g., number of practicing civil engineers, availability of certified counselors, or number of female medical school graduates in the past five years). This information is vital when recruiting and advertising for any position. The availability of minority candidates is inherent to such an analysis.

Forming the Committee

The chief advantage of a search committee is multiple perspectives where greater expertise in decision making exists. A diverse search committee makes a true multidimensional and multicultural analysis of candidate application materials possible. Excellence cannot be achieved without different points of view, resident multiple intelligences, and different experiences and expertise. These elements also help to mitigate any natural bias found in individual decisions.

Charge

The *appointing authority* must articulate his or her advocacy for diversified selection. For example, the absence of women in the school of engineering or the absence of assistant professors in the sociology department should receive appropriate attention.

Training and Orienting the Committee

Many different training topics support professional searches. Training for search committees should include developing selection criteria development, eliminating bias in decision making, identifying and recruiting minority candidates, and other diversity-supportive topics.

Recruiting

Recruiting and networking must include searching for minority candidates and expanding the reach to identify candidates whom the institution has not traditionally engaged. This activity cannot be overstated. Different kinds of recruiting methods, techniques, and locations must be used to change the composition of recruiting pools from those that the organization usually produces (see Vignette K: *Minority Recruiting: The Wrong Bait, the Wrong Technique, and the Wrong Pond*, p. 45). Every search aims to identify the best possible candidate, and this is only possible by searching far, wide, and into every possible community.

Advertising

Advertising must include announcements in minority journals and publications. Some experts indicate that there are nearly 500 higher education–related sources available. Consult your HR staff, equal opportunity professional, chief diversity officer, or an advertising agency to identify new sources. Committees should never say they do not know where to find minority candidates. Additionally, the obligatory AA and equal opportunity statements found in most advertisements often seem artificial. Progressive organizations take the time to develop an accurate, welcoming statement that reflects their campus cultural values (see *Equal Opportunity Statements*, p. 54).

Selection Criteria

Selection criteria should follow the elements highlighted in organizational analysis, position description, positional advertisement, and *committee charge*—all of which may already support diversity. The organizational analysis might indicate a preference for candidates with experience working with students from backgrounds served. Position descriptions might indicate needed foreign language skills. Advertisements could indicate a preference for candidates with experience studying abroad. The *charge* from the *appointing authority* can advocate for a candidate familiar with instructional techniques for differently abled students. (See the *Diversity Advantage: Multicultural Experiences as Mission-Essential Criteria*, p. 10.) Even in the absence of *cultural competence* as a selection factor, clearly defined criteria are the best defense against bias. When criteria are clearly defined, they create a standard for selection that prevents arbitrary, preferential, or ad hoc criteria.

Evaluating Candidate Materials

Because individuals bring preconceived notions to the process, exercising extra care ensures that bias does not undermine candidate evaluation. Unconscious preferences, subjective criteria, or emotional judgments cloud decision making when objective criteria are not used. The fairest evaluation is based upon previously defined criteria noted in the organizational analysis, position description, positional advertisement, and *committee charge*. Some examples of bias used at this stage are based upon a person's gender, surname, address, alma maters, or professional affiliations.

Interviewing

Similar to evaluating candidates' written materials, committees must be trained to keep bias from influencing the evaluation of candidates in person. Research indicates that people prefer and hire people like themselves (Rivera, 2012; Topa et al., 2013). Therefore, we all must work hard to eliminate unintentional bias from our decision making. Training is one method and group decision making is another; see the section titled *Avoiding Bias in Interviews*, p. 95, and Vignette P: *Eliminating Bias From Selection*, p. 62. Additionally, questions related to diversity can be asked during the interviewing process to ensure that candidates have a multicultural perspective or *cultural competence*.

Additional Screening Methods

With a little imagination, diversity-related criteria can be incorporated into statements of philosophy, questionnaires, *work samples*, portfolios, and other screening methods. Ask professor candidates to submit a statement of teaching philosophy that includes their perspectives on teaching minority students, students with disabilities, or students for whom English is a second language. Inform instructor candidates in advance that students with learning disabilities will be reviewing their syllabi or attending their demonstration lecture. Questionnaires asking student affairs candidates about experiences with multicultural counseling techniques are a strong example of incorporating diversity selection techniques into the search committee process. Additionally, asking all candidates to include examples in their portfolios of experience with multicultural populations can be instructive.

Evaluating Organizational Fit

Identify, document, and agree upon institution-specific (*organizational fit*) criteria (see *Evaluating Organizational Fit: Why You Should and Must*, p. 107; *Evaluating Organizational Fit: Defining and Documenting Fit*, p. 108; and *Organizational Fit Criteria*, p. 109). Objective, documented, and agreed-upon criteria help to reduce bias—esoteric or unconscious—that surfaces in discussions about *organizational fit*. The potential bias based upon appearance dilutes when real, relevant, institution-specific criteria are transparent and elevated in importance. Only then is a deeper analysis of candidates possible. Tendency to pick only those like us is mitigated when using previously defined, documented, objective criteria.

Reference Check

If the institution values candidates who can relate to students from all walks of life, references about the candidate's experience and success working with people from different backgrounds is a truth-teller. Reference checks are an effective means of verifying one's *cultural competence*—diversity or multicultural experiences.

Recommendations

Recommendations that include the strengths and weaknesses of candidates against a full range of previously agreed-upon criteria—such as multiculturalism, interpersonal skills, or ability to get along with others (including those not like themselves)—enables the *hiring authority* to select candidates likely to succeed and get along with a wide range of faculty, staff, and students.

Making the Offer

When making an offer, it is reasonable to consider factors important to the candidate, if they are known. It is appropriate to mention the hiking trail and similar outdoor opportunities near campus for candidates who like camping, just as it is to mention the African American art collection housed in the local museum to candidates expressing such an interest. For candidates concerned about practicing their religion, giving them information on where the local mosque, synagogue, or church is located is simply smart business. Being sensitive to these needs and interests during the offer makes the candidate feel valued and welcomed.

Welcoming Colleagues to Campus

Employment literature is filled with examples of recruiting and selection successes and retention failures. The sought-after ethnic studies scholar leaves after her first year because she does not feel that she belongs on campus, a result of how she was received and treated by her colleagues and community. Retention challenges are as likely to occur with women and minority candidates as they are for candidates from distant places or small towns, or those who take a new and cutting-edge approach to this discipline (see Vignette Y: *The One[s] Who Got Away*, p. 139). Nothing seems truer than the infamous line from The Doors' song "People Are Strange" (1967): "faces look ugly when you're alone." The key observation is that any and all differences seem to be exaggerated when one is new to a community. Committees should be aware of this fact and react appropriately.

Smart search committees make strategic attempts to seek out the most diverse candidate pool possible. Proper planning and a strategic approach will yield untold benefits. Yet, as indicated, minority recruiting and diversity selection techniques are inherent to a professional search, not something that is added to the process.

Diversity Success Does Not Require Extra Effort

It is fallacy that producing a diverse search requires unnecessary additional effort. This matter is properly viewed not as extra but as appropriate. For example, a networking hiring manager seeking to recruit would not call the same seven places he or she has always called to announce a vacancy. Instead this manager could call four of the tried-and-true sources and three new ones. Ideally, the new sources (like the old) would be well researched and chosen based upon the particular position in question—not one's personal network of family, old friends, and favorite colleagues. The idea that seven familiar contacts are the best contacts for all scholars, for all positions, and all of the time flies in the face of reality and is antithetical to the concept of meritocracy. Recruiting and selection require right, fair, and appropriate effort.

PART ONE

Laying the Groundwork

CHAPTER 2

Approvals

IN MOST ORGANIZATIONS the authority to hire is reserved to a small group of executives or department heads with budget authority. There are two independent but intertwined process elements—one is approval for the position, and the other is approval of funding resources. Approval to create the position is usually granted through HR or the provost's office, while position funding comes from the finance office or provost/vice president of academic affairs office, depending upon how an institution is structured. The difference between the two approvals becomes apparent during budget cuts when hiring is frozen due to limited resources.

Searching to fill the position should commence only after all approvals are granted. Stories abound of academic departments completing a search only to be told that there is insufficient funding to make a valid offer. Sometimes funds are available, but the institution will not commit to a tenure-track position, but would approve of a lectureship or temporary appointment. Some institutions even use the approval process for vetting the need for different positions. Therefore, written justification for a position is usually standard for the approval process.

Most organizations manage their approval process by using forms that serve two primary purposes. First, they document approvals. Second, they announce to everyone in the hiring process that a search is now under way. Next, some campuses require the consent of the equal employment opportunity (EEO)/AA/ diversity officer at the search's onset. Having this office endorse the form also prompts the *appointing authority* and/or the search committee chair to become aware of and follow the institution's diversity or AA policies and plans.

The forms used to gain search approval have different names, including:

- Position requisition
- Request to hire
- *Request to recruit*
- *Position authorization*
- Position budget request
- Authority to hire

Regardless of the institutional nomenclature, the purposes and processes of these forms are similar. The search committee should receive both verbal and documented permission to commence a search.

Approval Forms: Paper and Electronic

An organization may have different types of approval forms. Since the search and selection process varies by type of position, it is prudent to have different forms for different positions. As an example, with a temporary or part-time staff position, the authority to hire may be given to department heads with budget authority, and they may bypass a formal search. At the opposite end of the employment spectrum is a tenure-track faculty position that obligates the institution for upward of 40 years. As such it requires not only a full search, but also considerable ongoing resources. The former may require a simple signature without justification, while the latter might require a half-dozen signatories depending upon institutional governance and fiscal procedures. Appendices A and B provide examples of two different approval forms.

The advent of online *applicant tracking systems*— computer systems that collect and route résumés and CVs via the Web—include the use of electronic approvals. These electronic approvals can be obtained in a matter of minutes versus days. Paper forms require individuals to be on campus to receive the forms, sign, and then send them via campus mail to the next signatory. Electronic approvals allow busy executives—and others—to green-light positions any date and time using the Internet or e-mail.

CHAPTER 3

Organizational Analysis

AN ANALYSIS OF INTERNAL FACTORS should be undertaken to ensure that every position is necessary and, if so, that the institution is ready to conduct a search. Some work can be completed in ways that eliminate the continuing need for a particular position, such as distributing it among coworkers, abolishing it through the use of technology, having vendors provide it, or outsourcing it. If a position is still needed, this internal examination can include whether to make an interim appointment, internal promotion, leave the position vacant until the next fiscal year due to budget limitations, or change it to a part-time or academic year position. Consider the departmental or institutional initiatives, goals, or strategic aims affected by filling this position. Items like these should be considered before any search, and then used to guide it.

Like a missing puzzle piece, a position vacancy exists within the context of a team, a department, and an organization. It interacts with other positions, and how it interconnects with others is a major consideration. Job requirements will naturally evolve over the time since the position was last vacant. Pausing to reflect upon the needs of the department anew is valuable because it enhances decision making and prevents mistakes. Use Exhibit #1: *Organizational Analysis* as a starting point for any such internal examination.

At the conclusion of the analysis, the organization can then chart the best course, having armed itself with proper information and appropriate decisions. If a position is needed and a search is warranted, the next step is to define the position's expectations clearly. All future actions and considerations are driven by the decisions or assumptions made at this stage.

Diversity Tip: As noted in chapter 1, the organizational analysis highlights the need to recruit, select, and appoint professionals who have values, employment experiences, or backgrounds that support the organization's educational mission or strategic goals. This opportune time should reinforce the organization's commitment to its principal goals wherever its mission statement already highlights diversity and multiculturalism as necessary for education.

EXHIBIT #1
Organizational Analysis

Before commencing any search, answering the following questions will ensure that the search is grounded in the right ideas. It is prudent to consider departmental, institutional, and environmental factors that affect the new position and the team the new hire will join. The process of answering these questions will either prevent a fruitless search or ensure that the search you undertake is grounded in the right considerations.

- Did organizational issues prompt the vacancy (e.g., change of leadership, change of work requirements, frequent turnover, downsizing, etc.)?
- What would happen if this position were not filled/refilled?
- Could this be a half-time, part-time, seasonal, academic year, or temporary position?
- Is it the right time of year to search for this particular kind of position?
- Can some or all of the work be automated, outsourced, or distributed among others?

(continues)

(*continued*)

- Should an interim or acting appointment be made before a regular search?
- Could there be an internal search only?
- What changes have occurred with this position over time, such as new or different duties and greater responsibility?
- Are the title, classification, and compensation still accurate for this position?
- What has changed in the department/college/university?
- What has changed in the general workplace or in society that influences how this position works (e.g., changes in technology, computer and security requirements, labor shortage in this discipline/field, changes in legal requirements, etc.)?
- What institutional initiatives, goals, or strategic aims are affected by or could be affected by this position?
- Are there diversity considerations for this position (e.g., no men on staff, generational factors, etc.)?
- What unique characteristics did the incumbent have that are likely not to be replaced?
- Are there internal candidates who can be promoted or trained for this opportunity without a regular search?
- Does the organization have an affirmative action plan or other employment strategy that affects how the recruitment is conducted?
- Have all appropriate stakeholders had a voice in the position analysis?
- Should we consider waiting six months before filling the position to review and analyze whether the work can be eliminated, reshaped, absorbed, or reorganized?
- Is there a sufficient budget to conduct a successful search (e.g., advertising, recruiting, travel budgets, etc.)?

_____

Adapted from Lee & Bradley-Baker, 2012.

CHAPTER 4

Building the Foundation

Every search can be successful with a few key elements in place. Laying the groundwork for a successful search involves several preparatory activities to build this foundation. While the temptation exists to rush or skip process elements, this is a recipe for failure. A quality outcome needs as firm a foundation as any other structure. Fortunately, the foundation does not need rebuilding every time; the institution can do one, and then use it for many years to come.

Many foundational elements are cemented in policy guidelines. Used properly, they can prepare the search committee for success and prevent fundamental mistakes. Many of these activities are completed by the *appointing authority* or hiring manager and the HR staff, but it is the *appointing authority* that ensures that they are completed to satisfaction. Additionally, many of the by-products of the groundwork are communicated to the search committee chair and the search committee during the committee's *charge*. As such, these activities are often completed before the search committee meets for the first time.

Elements of Building the Foundation

Building the foundation for a successful search involves the following:

- Defining the position
- Classifying the position
- Establishing a competitive hiring range
- Completing a labor market analysis
- Reviewing employment policies
- Incorporating diversity considerations
- Creating a recruitment strategy
- Establishing a time frame

Defining the Position
Every position is unique. Thus, selection decisions are based upon the vision and description of how it will operate. Faulty descriptions send the search off in the wrong direction. Where to recruit, where to advertise, selection criteria, selection methods, and how to evaluate candidates are all tied to position elements. Before a search begins, the department needs a crystal clear view of the position requirements.

Every vacancy creates an opportunity to hire for the current needs of the department, while also considering changes to the position and department over time, changes in technology, or other dynamics like regulatory changes. This fact cannot be underestimated, making the step of *defining the position* deserving of greater attention; therefore, chapter 5, in its entirety, is dedicated to this topic.

Classifying the Position
Subtle changes alter duties enough to affect a title and other position characteristics. An associate professor who chairs the honors program committee and the honors program director who is tenure-eligible hold two fundamentally different jobs. Similarly, the titles of coordinator and manager communicate entirely different ideas. Classification determines who might be interested in the job and the pay. Understanding subtle differences for each profession leads to announcing a position effectively and recruiting the right candidates.

Establishing a Competitive Hiring Range
A competitive salary compared to similar positions at peer institutions must be established to attract good candidates. Additionally, the hiring range must be balanced favorably with that of internal persons doing similar work. The HR department (and provost's office for academic positions) should have credible data to establish a competitive pay range acceptable to most candidates. Knowing how the institution's *total compensation* compares with the market before the search begins is critical to a successful search. It correlates directly with how easy or hard you might have to

recruit to find candidates who meet requirements and are willing to work for the offered wages. (See chapter 16, *Making an Offer*, and *Benefits Briefs: Recruiting With Total Compensation*, p. 148.)

Completing a Labor Market Analysis

Data must be gathered to determine the relative availability of targeted candidates before the search—whether looking for assistant professors of sociology or a director of financial aid. The analysis tells how aggressively the institution should recruit and how competitive the candidate's future pay must be. Supporting data can come from state and federal departments of labor, professional associations (including minority professional associations or affinity groups within associations), graduate schools (and minority graduate schools), employment and temporary agencies, national publications (and minority publications), research institutes, licensing and certification bodies, and various other public and private organizations that are associated with particular professions. See Vignette AA: *An Eminent Scholar, Industry Star, and Superhero Required: A Labor Market Analysis Case Study*, p. 151, for an explanation about how to employ this technique.

Obviously, if there are many English professors in the market and few who teach physics, then English professor wages are likely to be lower and recruitment easier due to supply and demand. There is no substitute for making data-driven decisions about recruitment and advertising, and the labor market analysis provides insight. This is a prime opportunity for the hiring manager to partner with HR and compare information to better analyze market conditions.

Diversity Tip: Numerous data sources on minority candidate market availability should be pursued. Along with reviewing segmented data about minority populations available from general market sources, data from minority professional associations or affinity groups within majority associations, minority graduate schools, minority publications, and similar resources should be analyzed. Building this into searches is no different from finding an information technology professional with a background in a particular piece of software, if needed, or targeting candidates with particular language skills or professional experiences.

Reviewing Employment Policies

Collective bargaining, faculty legislation, promotion policies, limit of budgets or travel, relocation policies, and equal opportunity policies all affect the employment process. Committees should receive a briefing on employment-related policies and practices in advance since following them is crucial. Do the institution's policies allow for interim appointments or create an advantage for internal candidates? If so, is there a defined process for these to occur with appropriate oversight to ensure that minority and women candidates are given equal opportunity to receive plum interim assignments as well? A good practice for committees is to receive an overview of these at their first meeting offered by the committee's ex officio member. (See Vignette D: *Ex Officio Members Supporting and Monitoring the Search*, p. 30.)

Incorporating Diversity Considerations

Does the institution have an AA plan or diversity initiative? Does it alter recruitment practices if there are no men in the English department? Are there advertising requirements in certain publications? What recruiting activities have already located diverse candidates? How is *diversity* defined? Does the inclusion of international candidates meet recruitment goals? Are trailing spouses or minority candidates eligible for *opportunity hire* policies or protocols? Many more related questions have both strategic and operational implications. *Appointing authorities* and committee chairs should ensure that these are addressed in a positive manner. Having an HR professional, equal opportunity officer, or *diversity advocate* attend the committee's first meeting to outline such matters is best for an inclusive search. (See *Orienting the Committee*, p. 28, and Vignette E: *The Role and Advantage of Diversity Advocates*, p. 31.)

Creating a Recruitment Strategy

Advertising is necessary, but not sufficient to cultivate the best pool of diverse, qualified applicants. Recruitment is necessary. Recruitment is an active outreach process that identifies and targets ideal candidates. Where to recruit, who should be involved, when recruiting starts, what resources or tools are available to those who are recruiting and networking—all of these should be addressed. Can the HR department or equal opportunity office help? To cultivate a rich pool

VIGNETTE C
How to Prevent a Failed Search

Many of the common pitfalls that undermine a successful search can be avoided by laying the groundwork for a search properly and following some key advice. Simple guidelines such as being crystal clear in defining the position and ensuring that the committee is properly trained are mandatory. Here is a quick reference list of tips, suggestions, and highlights that have proven to be effective in preventing failed searches:

- Host a meeting of the committee chair, *appointing authority*, and HR representative to discuss conduct of the search.
- Seek assistance from the experts (e.g., HR representative, *diversity advocate*, equal opportunity professional, ad agency executive, search firm consultants, etc.).
- Learn and follow the institution's employment policies.
- Identify and use the institution's resources that are designed to support searches.
- Assign an ex officio member to support the committee's efforts (include a *staff assistant* as needed).
- Assign a diversity advocate.
- Define the position properly.
- Classify the position correctly.
- Establish the right hiring range up front.
- Ensure that HR completes a labor market analysis to ascertain the relative availability of desired candidates, including minority candidates.
- Ask the *appointing authority* to prepare a written charge and deliver it at the first meeting.
- Train and orient the committee.
- Discuss common bias and decision-making tendencies and agree upon how the committee will police itself to mitigate these.
- Align the committee's efforts with the committee's charge.
- Recruit aggressively in addition to advertising.
- Ensure that networking includes minority candidates.
- Ensure that there is agreement with the selection criteria prior to screening any applicants.
- Identify any organizational fit criteria in advance and agree upon their use.
- Use proven techniques and follow established protocols (e.g., use screening instruments, select interview questions from a questions bank, follow agreed-upon selection criteria, etc.).
- Use multiple screening methods (see chapter 13, *Additional Screening Methods*).
- Ensure that every candidate gets a *benefits briefing* so that each is aware of and appreciates your total compensation package prior to making an offer (see *Benefits Briefs: Recruiting With Total Compensation*, p. 148).
- Ensure that you are well prepared and know how to deliver an enticing employment offer. Have an HR representative participate as needed.
- Assign a liaison to ensure that the chosen candidate makes a smooth transition (and relocation, if necessary) to campus.

There are a lot of details in the search committee process, and the details matter. You can use this checklist of tips and advice to ensure that you are mindful of the typical mistakes that can sometimes derail the search process. Many of the elements described are illuminated in the pages and chapters that follow.

of applicants, an organization must not assume that the right candidates are looking for a job right now or that they will find the institution. Wise organizations establish recruitment protocols that guide the actions of stakeholders (see *Sourcing*, p. 39).

> **Diversity Tip**: No recruitment strategy or protocol would be complete without considering how an institution actively networks to identify minority candidates. This is especially important if the pool of recruits from which the institution typically draws does not normally produce minority applicants (see *Yield Ratio*, p. 137). A well-designed recruitment strategy is a prerequisite to a diverse applicant pool (see Vignette K: *Minority Recruiting: The Wrong Bait, the Wrong Technique, and the Wrong Pond*, p. 45).

Establishing a Time Frame

The *appointing authority* should give the committee a targeted deadline by which its activities should be complete. This deadline should be aggressive yet reasonable enough given the organization's needs. Committees that do not work within a deliberate time frame risk letting good candidates escape. The best candidates have options and may accept another offer while a committee takes extra time to complete its work. A target completion date also signals to those who are invited to serve on the committee the time commitment to which they are agreeing.

Preventing a Failed Search: A Building-the-Foundation Summary

The sum total of these activities ensures that all of the basic prerequisites for a successful search are complete. Together with other activities, they reduce the possibility of failed searches (see Vignette C: *How to Prevent a Failed Search*). Most of the activities to lay the groundwork belong to the HR department's domain and represent the service support model that HR should develop and use to support its institution's search committees. Advertising and delivering these services enhances HR's image within the institution. The best part about the process of laying the groundwork is that its design has to be completed only once; its framework can be used over and over again for all successive searches.

Failed searches can be avoided if extra efforts and precautions are taken early in the search process. Failed searches include not finding enough qualified candidates, having the chosen finalist fail to accept an offer of employment, or when an administrative mistake derails the committee's actions. These can be prevented 95% of the time. Committees must deliberately design a process in advance and ensure that everyone is in agreement about executing the search plan. Use this resource book as a quality assurance guide.

CHAPTER 5

Defining the Position

THE MOST IMPORTANT STEP in the search committee process is to properly define the position for which you are engaging in a search. Despite the importance of this step, it is often overlooked, skipped, or completed haphazardly. Many hiring managers dust off the old job description—or even worse, the old job advertisement—and start the hiring process. How a position is defined has a profound impact on the search. An imperfectly defined position leads to an imperfect hire. If it is merely good enough, your selected candidate will also likely be merely good enough. It is regrettable—and avoidable—to select a candidate who is a great match with the position for which you advertised, recruited, and then selected, but the person is not a great match with the position you truly wanted but did not describe accurately.

Doing a sloppy job at this stage leaves the success of both the search and the candidate to chance (see chapter 4, *Building the Foundation*). The position will be used for all of the following purposes in the life cycle of a position:

- Create a job description or position profile.
- Establish a salary range.
- Create advertisements.
- Determine the recruitment strategy.
- Develop selection criteria.
- Develop interview questions.
- Determine *work samples* for the interview/selection process.
- Validate candidates' experience and potential for success in this position.
- Determine what training, support, or professional development activities are needed.
- Evaluate a candidate's performance.
- Determine whether the candidate has met the standards for promotion/tenure.
- Other . . .

Since every position exists within the context of the organization it serves, no two positions are the same. An assistant professor at a community college is very different from one at a research university. An assistant professor in a lab sciences or engineering department will have very different duties from those in political science or sociology. Nursing professors in the same department will be very different as one may be responsible for leading accreditation efforts, while another coordinates clinical placements with area hospitals, and still another may have the collateral responsibility for advising the National Student Nurses Association. Acknowledging the uniqueness of each position is necessary and serious.

Defining the position is one of the key activities that search firms do when they are engaged to lead a search. They know that getting this part right dramatically increases the chances of a good outcome. Shortcuts here undermine the effectiveness of a search.

There are many methods of defining a position; typical ones include:

- Complete a *Position Analysis Questionnaire* (see Appendix C).
- Complete a *task inventory*.
- Observe the work and document findings.
- Interview stakeholders.
- Solicit written suggestions or input from stakeholders (See Exhibit #2: *Gathering Input to Define a Position: Sample Letter and Questions*).
- Benchmark your position against others at peer institutions.
- Seek the advice of experts (internal and external).
- Use the government data source O*Net (http://online.onetcenter.org) to compare against a repository of thousands of positions.
- Confirm the *essential functions* of the job (see Exhibit #3: *Identifying Essential Functions*).
- Analyze and compare advertisements for similar positions.
- Seek advice and assistance from your friendly HR manager.

EXHIBIT #2
Gathering Input to Define a Position
Sample Letter and Questions

When defining or redefining a position, it is always wise to get input from all stakeholders. Their insight into the nature and requirements of the position, as well as the needs and priorities of the work unit, are invaluable. However, to gather useful information that is actionable, a series of questions should be offered instead of an open-ended inquiry. Questions help to structure the process and focus the responses of the various stakeholders. The following is a sample letter and a few open-ended questions that could be used to help define or redefine a position:

Dear Colleagues:

As you know, the _____ position has become vacant due to the departure of _____ . This vacancy is a unique opportunity for the department to look at what is most important to us right now. With consideration of University Goals 2025 and our department's desire to focus more on _____ [e.g., research/service-learning, etc.], I write to ask for your input in defining the most important priorities for this position in the next few years.

Please respond by answering the following questions or sending your comments to me via e-mail no later than _____. I will compile your responses and synthesize them with the stated requirements for the position and with the guidelines identified by the provost's office. Then I will create an up-to-date position profile. This position profile will be used to draft an advertisement and to delineate selection criteria for the search committee.

Thank you in advance for sharing your input about this critically important position. The new _____ will be a valued colleague who will help the department achieve its goals of increasing _____ and providing invaluable service to the university.

Sincerely,

Diego Rivera
Department Head

Position Definition Input Questions

1. What are the three to five major duties/requirements of the _____ position?
2. What are some of the unique elements of this position that differ from those of similar positions?
3. What are the major priorities of the _____ position?
4. What are the three things the new incumbent must accomplish in the first six months to be successful?
5. What is the most important skill the new incumbent must have to perform this job well?
6. What known and unexpected challenges could possibly derail the success of the new incumbent?
7. If you could change, add, or delete one duty related to this position, what would it be?
8. Please provide any other general criteria you think are important for defining this position accurately.

EXHIBIT #3
Identifying Essential Functions

All job descriptions should include a job's *essential functions*. Identifying these functions is a requirement of the Americans with Disabilities Act (as amended) and is critical to the search for qualified job applicants. The following considerations in and basis for identification of *essential functions* are by no means exhaustive. The institution's HR office or attorney should be consulted for further guidance.

Some considerations in identifying essential functions are:

- Whether functions are limited in number
- The frequency or regularity with which they are performed
- Whether the former incumbent actually performed the functions
- Whether the new individual in the position will be expected to perform the functions
- Whether removing any of the functions would change the job

A function is essential if

- The position exists to perform it
- The number of other employees available to perform it is limited
- The person performing the function is hired for his or her ability to perform it

Essential functions are identified on the basis of

- Employer's judgment
- Job description
- *Position announcements* and advertisements
- Proportion of time spent performing the function
- Work experience of incumbents and individuals in similar positions
- The nature of the job

Beyond meeting the requirements of the law, identifying *essential functions* helps hiring managers gain a greater degree of clarity about what the position requires. This information is useful in delineating the requirements for the position, compared to factors that are preferred, although not essential, but that make one candidate more competitive than another.

Regardless of the method, the key factor is that you make a deliberate and concerted effort to be precise. This investment in effort will yield tangible returns.

The by-product of a well-defined position is a *position description* (also called a job description), which simply documents the position requirements. A good description entails the three major categories of work activities: responsibilities, duties, and tasks.

Responsibilities

These include all of the required activities—expressed or implied—that the individual is to perform to complete the work in a given function, position, sphere of operation, or profession, including the expected duties, tasks, and miscellaneous assignments that produce workplace outcomes.

Duties

These are tasks or activities in a given functional area. Examples include: complete monthly financial reports (account for all funds; balance statements; research variations; verify all transactions; document results), teach a course (design, develop, and deliver instructional materials, etc.), or provide customer service (determine customer needs; identify products for customer; sell appropriate products; service products provided that meet customer requests).

Tasks

These are required individual work activities of a general or specific nature (e.g., reconcile accounts, deliver lectures, meet with clients, etc.). Care must be taken to ensure that you document a holistic view of each position, since many decisions will be based upon this description.

Diversity Tip: Responsibilities, duties, and tasks include the requirement to work with multicultural populations (e.g., students, employees, communities the institution serves, international populations, etc.), thereby creating a diversity competency requirement for a position. This requirement could become a selection criterion. Research has shown that such variables increase the probability of minority candidate selection (Smith, Turner, Osei-Kofi, & Richards, 2004).

CHAPTER 6

Forming, Orienting, and Charging the Committee

Forming the Committee

FORMING A COMMITTEE is similar to making a good soup or salad. Different ingredients in just the right mix and amount create a satisfying whole. Therefore, committees should broadly represent the college or university and provide a multidimensional perspective to the value, role, and function of the position in question. Some call this process *diagonal selection*, wherein there are various representatives from across the organization and at different levels who can help you get a 360-degree view of the position and its requirements (see Exhibit #4: *Forming a Committee Checklist*).

The size of a search committee typically varies from five to nine members. However, when hiring presidents and other senior administrators, it is not uncommon to see search committees with 11 to 15 or more members. With presidents, provosts, and other senior positions, there usually are many stakeholders, such as alumni, foundations, boards, community members, and members from state educational organizations. The level and type of the position being sought is a good indicator of the amount of time and resources to be invested in seeking a good candidate as well as the number of people who actually serve on the committee. Additionally, ensuring diverse representation on any committee increases the likelihood of committees making diverse selections.

Other ways of ensuring that the various constituents and stakeholders have some influence over the search process is by getting them involved on a *screening committee* or as participants in the interview process in some facet such as a town hall meeting or reception. This in turn manages the size of committees.

In addition to regular members, *ex officio members* are normally appointed to monitor the activities of search committees (see Vignette D: *Ex Officio Members Supporting and Monitoring the Search*). Ex officio members do not vote and their status follows the Latin interpretation: *by virtue of their office/position.* They can be members of the human resources department or equal employment opportunity/diversity and inclusion office; members of the institution's diversity, equal opportunity, or similar committees; members of the provost's staff; or interested stakeholders who seek to support the institution's diversity efforts. The last are often referred to as *diversity advocates* (see Vignette E: *The Role and Advantage of Diversity Advocates*). These advocates serve valuable roles in communities that are not as culturally diverse, or in those that are not as knowledgeable as they desire to be about engaging in contemporary hiring practices that provide for state-of-the-art equal opportunity selection.

Ex officio members advise, train, monitor, and support committees in addition to helping them with legal and equal employment opportunity–related issues. Additionally, certain types of ex officio members provide necessary administrative and logistical support to coordinate committee activities. These members are sometimes referred to as *staff assistants.* Finally, Vignette F: *Appointing Authorities as Committee Members* provides some advice on the implications of having the *appointing authority* serve as the chair or as a member of a search committee.

Orienting and Training

Orienting the Committee
Orienting and training the committee are essential ingredients to a successful search (LaCorte, 1998). The first meeting of a committee is the ideal time to orient the members to the task. A best practice and proactive approach to this orientation is for an HR representative, equal opportunity professional, *diversity advocate,* or the ex officio member of the committee

---

EXHIBIT #4
Forming a Committee Checklist

Here are some typical criteria to consider when appointing a committee:

- Committee chairpersons should hold peer or senior positions to the vacant position (e.g., vice presidents should chair vice president committees, directors or above should chair director searches, a tenured faculty member should chair a tenure-track search, etc.).
- Members should include peers, supervisors, and customers of the position.
- Diversity in all forms, including in terms of gender, race, age, status, and perspective.
- Sufficient technical expertise on the committee to properly decipher each applicant's professional credentials and experience.
- Size of the committee should correlate to the importance or impact of the position.
- Is there someone available who has performed similar work or held positions before?
- Is there someone who has supervised said or similar positions in the past?
- Is the committee balanced otherwise (a balance of skill, experience, perspectives)?
- Invite students, alumni, community members, graduate students, consultants, HR professionals, or colleagues from other institutions. Experts from professional associations, vendors, consultants, and other external professionals can be used to review résumés when you do not have enough in-house expertise.
- Does each committee member have enough time to devote to these duties, given the expected time frame for the search?
- Ensure that members' superiors are informed and approve of members' service on the committee.
- Include an HR or EEO/AA/*diversity advocate* member.
- Are there ex officio (by virtue of office) members?
- Is the *appointing authority*/hiring manager chair of the committee? (See Vignette F: *Appointing Authorities as Committee Members.*)

---

to provide the orientation. This should include the following:

- College/university goals and initiatives
- College/university employment policies
- Diversity/AA/EEO considerations
- Overview of the search process and best practices
- Committee member responsibilities
- Legal issues
- Other institution-specific content

This orientation prepares the committee to execute its responsibilities. The orientation should take no more than 15 minutes during the first committee meeting. Failure to prepare the committee adequately will yield inconsistent results, increase confusion,

extend the time needed to complete a search, affect the quality of the hiring decision, and possibly result in a failed search. Many organizations require training and orientation before an individual is eligible to serve on a committee. Another way of delivering training and orientation is to use an online learning module.

Training the Committee
Training involves actual techniques that can be used to screen and evaluate candidates. These include how to screen written materials, conduct interviews, host candidates, and other tips for performing efficiently and effectively. The expert advice of an HR professional stepping in at this point is a priceless resource for any committee. As an example, according to the Society

VIGNETTE D
Ex Officio Members Supporting and Monitoring the Search

Ex officio is a Latin term that means by virtue of office or position. Ex officio search committee members are nonvoting members who support the process. Generally, they provide four types of support and have two separate and distinct position types that provide such services. Ex officio members provide training and advice on the search and selection process; monitor the process to ensure compliance with legal and institutional mandates; share diversity and inclusion expertise to support fair and diverse selections; and give administrative and logistical support to the committee.

Many colleges and universities appoint individuals from the HR department or diversity and inclusion/equal opportunity office to serve as ex officio members of every search committee to support and monitor the committees' activities. They can provide advice and counsel as well as training on policies and procedures, laws and regulations, and other institutional criteria relevant to the search process. Separately, such professionals might include *staff assistants* who are appointed to support the committee with the administrative and logistical requirements of a search, such as arranging meetings, meeting rooms, audiovisual equipment, candidate travel, meals, reimbursements, and related matters.

However, HR departments and inclusion/equal opportunity offices are wholly separate activities. *Staff assistants* are generalists and might include an administrative assistant who supports junior searches or a vice president who serves ex officio in support of a presidential search, while HR professionals are specialists who have developed particular expertise in the employment or diversity process to serve in this role. To make matters more confusing, for some searches and in some organizations, ex officio members might provide all four types of support. Also, there may be multiple ex officio members who participate in various parts of the search process. It is not uncommon to have an HR officer to advise and support the committee, a diversity officer to monitor the committee, and an administrative assistant to handle the logistical details.

The need for such support is apparent. In addition to the importance of every hire—see Vignette B: *The $3 Million Decision*, p. 2—there is considerable complexity in the search process. In addition to the support of diversity goals, there may be other institutional factors that bear upon a search committee's work, such as strategic plans or other initiatives. Ex officio members may serve as ambassadors, institutional representatives, or experts on these matters as well, depending upon their position. An associate provost who is a *diversity advocate* might also be responsible for advocating for the organization's research agenda.

HR professionals' guidance is indispensable because many federal and state EEO laws affect the search committee's work. Violations or lack of compliance can expose the institution to significant liabilities. Therefore, ex officio members also have a monitoring role to keep the organization out of hot water. Finally, coordinating the activities of the many stakeholders involved in the search committee process is administratively intense. Coupled with the fact that most committee members are volunteers, it is incumbent upon the *appointing authority* and the HR officer to ensure that the committee has the administrative support it needs to do its work.

VIGNETTE E
The Role and Advantage of Diversity Advocates

Diversity advocates are usually volunteers who support their institution's diversity efforts by providing training and support in cultural diversity and equal opportunity selection techniques to search committees and other groups. The typical advocate is a faculty or staff member who serves on a committee that is appointed by a president/provost to advise leaders on building a diverse and inclusive community or developing programs and recommending strategies and policies that advance the mission and goals of the institution. These responsibilities are important in that most institutions of higher education have some element of diversity and multiculturalism in their educational mission. Members of HR departments or diversity and inclusion office staffs may also serve as *diversity advocates* by virtue of their positions.

Diversity advocates are uniquely qualified individuals who are carefully selected because of their often positive worldview or set of beliefs that make them open to being challenged about the behaviors and attitudes that may adversely affect others. These professionals tend to be comfortable and feel good about their own group membership and are proud of their own identity. This allows them to have a healthy respect for the heritage, culture, and personal history of others. This positive orientation to difference helps put others at ease and makes others more comfortable when discussing sensitive topics.

What makes them effective advocates for the search process is that they are usually trained to work with search committees and to support the selection process. Their training typically includes (a) advanced education around issues of working with difference, diversity, equity, and inclusion; (b) legal and ethical issues related to employment matters; and (c) actual techniques for supporting unbiased and equal opportunity selection procedures. Their specific activities related to search committees include the following:

- Provide training on how to create an environment that allows differences to be discussed in a healthy manner.
- Provide techniques for posing and discussing sensitive matters.
- Provide information that helps to reduce bias in thinking, decision making, and behavior.
- Support and monitor the activities of the committee to help ensure that preconceived notions and stereotypical biases do not appear at any step of the selection process.
- Ensure that no decision is based solely on gender, religion, creed, race, age, or physical disability, or other *protected class*, including reverse discrimination.
- Ensure that any and all personal concerns by any committee member regarding personal biases and prejudices are addressed properly.
- Ensure that every recruiting, advertising, and networking avenue is explored to maximize the diversity of the potential candidate pool.
- Ensure that all institutional rules, regulations, and bylaws regarding diversity and inclusion are upheld each step of the process.

Diversity advocates are key members of a search committee and a campus community since they help institutions achieve their educational missions by ensuring that diversity, multiculturalism, equity, inclusion, and other worthy community values are used in a proper manner in the search and selection process.

VIGNETTE F
Appointing Authorities as Committee Members

A question that often arises in forming search committees is whether an *appointing authority* should sit on committees or should such authority just react to recommendations from committees it appoints. There is no universal answer to this question, and there are a number of contrasting principles involved. Some of the factors that affect this situation include the type and level of the position, the institution's policies and traditions, the administrative style of the *appointing authority*, the prerogative of the administrator, the makeup of the committee, and the fact that the *appointing authority* is often the sole person responsible for the success or failure of the new hire.

Nonetheless, some patterns can be illuminated that may help the stakeholders involved make the best choice. The more senior the *appointing authority*, the less likely it is that he or she will serve on the committee. In addition to being busy, this individual will have capable subordinates who are seasoned enough to manage a search. The *appointing authority*'s technical expertise may or may not be needed to guide the committee's efforts or inform its decision making.

Whatever the case, the *appointing authority*'s presence on the committee presents several challenges—namely that this individual might dominate the committee in such a way that it merely rubber stamps his or her preferences. One of the tenets of the search committee process is that of shared governance. If the *appointing authority* does not want or expect the full measure of what a search committee offers, he or she should forgo the use of a committee or otherwise design a search process accordingly. One example is to use the "Advise and Consent" search committee model (see *Alternative Search Models*, p. 149). In this model, the leader screens applicants, and then uses a search committee only to help interview candidates.

Similarly, the mere presence of the *appointing authority* might mute many members' opinions, which largely undermines the value of a committee if its members are reluctant to offer their perspective. The voting process can be tricky as well. Either way, the search committee's role in making a decision or recommendation should be stated clearly in the *charge* to the committee so that the members are not surprised or offended when the *appointing authority* asserts his or her prerogative to make a decision.

---

for Human Resource Management (SHRM), upward of 61% of résumés contain some falsehoods (Burke & Schramm, 2004). Committee members should be taught how to spot common résumé errors; see Exhibit #10: *How to Evaluate Résumés and CVs*, p. 67. The ex officio HR representative can also provide the committee with sample forms, templates, question banks, and other helpful resources. The training, orientation, and resources prepare the committee well.

Here are some how-to examples you can discuss:

- Conduct a search (for committee chairs).
- Conduct an effective search committee meeting.
- Avoid common search pitfalls (e.g., trying to clone the last incumbent, failing to use a multiple screening method, taking too long or unnecessary delays in the process, etc.).

- Recruit and network in support of the search, including minority recruiting.
- Develop selection criteria.
- Eliminate bias from decision making.
- Screen résumés and CVs.
- Draft effective interview questions.
- Conduct an effective telephone or video interview.
- Evaluate presentations.
- Conduct reference checks.
- Serve as an effective institutional ambassador.
- Document a search.

While many members who serve have prior experience, this does not mean that their experience serving was based upon sound practice. Nor does it mean that they should bypass a refresher course, since many committee members serve on search committees less often than once a year. A short, 10- to 15-minute presentation, accompanied by samples, templates, and checklists from the HR department, can go a long way toward training and preparing search committees. This book was designed to serve as a how-to manual for search committee chairs.

Charging the Committee

The *appointing authority* should provide the committee with his or her expectations of the committee's performance and results. This discussion, commonly referred to as a *charge*, should ensure that the committee understands its tasks, timeline, budget, and other factors, including the kind of finalists the *appointing authority* wishes to consider. Many hiring officials will have a vision that might be hard to articulate succinctly, so the *charge* should comprise both a written document and professional, verbal dialogue. A written *charge* is a valuable reference tool the committee has for use later when it needs a reference point upon which to anchor its decisions, or when hiring deliberations stall (see Appendix E: *Charge for Dean of Research*).

The *charge* is usually given at the committee's first meeting. Committee members can ask clarifying questions and otherwise deepen their understanding of position requirements and organizational needs. It is also an opportune time to reinforce the institution's commitment to diversity. In ideal situations, the search committee should meet before the recruiting period has elapsed so the *appointing authority* can solicit their assistance in recruiting applicants, since committee members—as a result of the *charge*—now have a full understanding of the candidate type desired.

The *charge* should highlight the committee's purpose and the manner in which work is to be completed. It is a professional faux pas for the committee to rank finalists, and then have the *appointing authority* choose candidate number three despite the committee's preference. The *appointing authority*'s prerogative not to follow the committee's recommendation should not be held in reserve, but should be noted in advance. This way, no one is surprised or made to feel as if his or her work, efforts, and opinion were not important. This unhealthy situation can be prevented easily (see *Why Ranking Candidates Is Not in Your Best Interest*, p. 125).

How does the final committee decision manifest? Does the committee recommend a single finalist, a slate of finalists, or ranked finalists? Prevailing wisdom suggests that the best method for recommendations is for the committee to present the *appointing authority* with a slate, accompanied by a description of strengths and weaknesses. The *appointing authority* makes the final hiring decision based upon the committee's advice and other organizational factors, some of which may be private to the *appointing authority*.

Search committees should always receive their *charge* before they begin. The *appointing authority* should keep in mind that a poor hiring recommendation is often the result of a poorly conceived or written *charge*. The *charge* should indicate without any ambiguity the committee's task, deadline, and budget and the characteristics and qualities of the desired candidate. See Exhibit #5: *Charge Checklist* for a comprehensive list of subjects that should be considered.

Experience discourages having the salary or hiring range as a part of the *charge* or search committee's discussions. This should be a discussion between the *appointing authority* and HR. Such discussions can be fraught with jealousy, misinformation, and inappropriate comments when shared with committee members. What is necessary to recruit a candidate may change over time due to labor market fluctuations, negotiations may necessitate nontraditional offers and incentives, and many personnel considerations often affect salary decisions. For these reasons and more, when a committee discusses and wrangles with salary

EXHIBIT #5
Charge Checklist

The *appointing authority* should draft a written *charge* and present it at the first committee meeting (when possible). The *charge* should include:

- Clarify the title(s) for the position (e.g., official title, working/honorific title, advertised title, rank, etc.).
- Provide members with a position description (e.g., position profile, job description, position specification, etc.).
- Provide members with a copy of the advertisement or *position announcement*.
- Discuss the *appointing authority*'s vision for the position. The vision should include scope, short- and long-term challenges and opportunities, and criteria that are important to the department and the institution.
- Discuss criteria for selection (e.g., essential, preferred, minimum, specialties, disciplines, etc.).
- Discuss the expected time frame for the search and anticipated start date for the new hire, emphasizing that the committee should formulate and distribute a projected timetable to appropriate constituencies (e.g., vice president/provost, dean/department head, HR or EEO/AA/diversity officer, stakeholder committees, etc.).
- Discuss institutional policy and goals on diversity and/or AA.
- Describe the scope of authority of the committee and chair. What decisions and tasks will be the responsibility of the committee (e.g., recruiting, screening, interviewing, travel arrangements, room reservations, references, recommendations, etc.)?
- Establish the *appointing authority*'s involvement during the search process (e.g., authorize budget expenditures, approve interviewees in advance, etc.).
- Discuss the preferred number of finalist candidates to visit campus and a general idea of the conduct of the campus visit.
- Discuss final recommendations: How is it to be brought forward (e.g., strengths and weaknesses of candidates, single candidate, ranked candidates, narrative description of finalists, etc.)?
- Discuss any ex officio members and *staff assistant* support during the search.
- Discuss/clarify where and how the committee will receive administrative and logistical support (e.g., from gaining department, chair's department, HR, ex officio members, staff assistant, other, etc.).
- Identify and discuss how HR or the EEO/AA/diversity office will support and monitor the process.
- Discuss the financial resources available for the search, including travel, meals, refreshments, entertainment, advertising budgets, and search support.
- Discuss documentation or reports required of the search.
- Discuss any special requirements of the search.
- Emphasize the importance of committee work.
- Thank members for their service.

EXHIBIT #6
Search Committee Chair Duties

The is a list of the chair's typical expected duties:

- Serve as the liaison among the *appointing authority*, HR department, and any other ex officio members of the search committee.
- Convene the search committee and ensure that each committee member has completed search committee training/orientation.
- Coordinate the efforts of all committee members.
- Perform all duties of a regular committee member.
- Establish ground rules for the committee.
- Ensure that the intent of the *charge* is carried out.
- Assign duties to committee members, such as note taker, host, diversity advocate, etc.
- Coordinate administrative and logistical support of the search process.
- Help to recruit, identify, and contact potential applicants, to include diverse candidates.
- Work with the search committee to develop a screening evaluation tool according to job-related criteria (i.e., position description, advertisement, *charge*, and organizational analysis), and without regard to stereotypes or presumptions regarding ability or disability.
- Review all applicant materials.
- Coordinate with other constituent groups to ensure their involvement, as appropriate, in the interview or selection process.
- Serve as lead host for candidates on campus.
- Identify internal candidates and serve as a liaison to them.
- Correspond with semifinalists/finalists.
- With the assistance of an ex officio member/staff assistant, arrange travel and accommodations for the interviews and schedule interviews.
- Ensure that proper records and minutes are kept of the selection process.
- Review late applications and bring them to the committee if they meet certain standards.
- Check references, when appropriate.
- Maintain the confidentiality of applicants, search proceedings, and committee deliberations.
- Treat all candidates fairly and equitably throughout the entire recruiting and hiring process.
- Advise the *appointing authority* of the person(s) the search committee recommends for the position.
- Perform other duties as requested by the *appointing authority*.

---

matters while deliberating, it is presumptuous and problematic for all.

Exhibits #6 and #7 provide comprehensive lists of the typical duties expected of a committee chairperson and committee members, respectively. The committee chair is responsible for the conduct of the search and ensures that the process occurs according to plan. Though that search committee members are

volunteers—in addition to their regular duties—their obligations and responsibilities are noteworthy due to their impact on the decisions made. Therefore, it is wise to provide clearly delineated duties, responsibilities, expectations, and the time frame within which their service is needed. A written list of expectations should be provided to inform members fully of the obligations to which they have agreed.

EXHIBIT #7
Search Committee Member Duties

Typical requirements for members of search committees are as follows:

- Attend all scheduled meetings (and come prepared).
- Participate fully in the committee's work.
- Help to recruit, identify, and contact potential applicants, including diverse candidates.
- Familiarize oneself with all job-related criteria relevant to this position.
- Review all applicant materials.
- Screen applicants and adhere to the evaluation criteria stated in the position description, advertisements, and *charge*.
- Host candidates.
- Participate in the interview process
- Check references, as necessary.
- Ensure EEO and treat all applicants equitably.
- Maintain appropriate confidentiality about the search committee process before, during, and after the search.
- Assist with welcoming the new employee.
- Perform other duties as assigned by the chairperson.

PART TWO

Cultivating a Rich and Diverse Pool of Candidates

CHAPTER 7

Recruiting

THREE PRIMARY TECHNIQUES are used to cultivate a rich, diverse pool of applicants. The quality of the hire is dependent upon the quality of the pool generated from committee and institution activities. This is the second most important part of the process after accurately defining the position. *Recruiting, networking,* and *advertising* are three parts of a whole. Each ensures that any vacancy receives the widest possible exposure to potential applicants.

Sourcing

HR professionals and others who work in the employment field collectively call these three terms *sourcing*.

Though many simply refer to *sourcing* as recruiting, this layman's description inadvertently causes confusion. Recruitment and advertising are fundamentally two different processes, and the general label of recruiting to refer to all *sourcing* activities exacerbates the problem (see Table 7.1, *Recruiting, Advertising, and Networking: Advantages, Disadvantages, Characteristics, and Comparisons,* and Exhibit #8 *Advertising and Recruitment Sourcing Options*). As Table 7.1 details, recruiting is an active, organizational process; advertising tends to be more passive; and networking is largely an individualized activity.

Additional confusion occurs because there is overlap among recruiting, advertising, and networking. Some activities are classified as both recruiting and

TABLE 7.1
Recruiting, Advertising, and Networking:
Advantages, Disadvantages, Characteristics, and Comparisons

Recruitment	Advertising	Networking
Active	Passive	Active
Gainfully employed individuals	Job seekers	Employed, job seekers, influencers
Market-driven	Open market	Open and market-driven
Specific to position	General & specific	General & specific
Lots of networking	Small amount of networking	Networking
Targeted	General & targeted*	Limited individual targeting
Most diversity-sensitive	Can be diversity-sensitive	Can be diversity-sensitive
Narrow focus	Wider focus*	Limited focus
Competitive offers unlikely	Competitive offers likely	Competitive offers unlikely
Outreach-focused	Passive	Active
Before & during search	During search	Before, during, & after search
By individual & organization	By organization	By individuals

*An example of targeted advertising occurs when advertising in minority media.

advertising, depending on their intent and how they are used. Posting a *position announcement* on a bulletin board at a professional conference is a recruiting activity targeting specific professionals who may or may not be in the market for employment at that particular time, yet it is also similar in purpose to advertising. Similarly, posting an announcement on the listserv of a minority group's website or newsletter is a form of both advertising and recruitment since a specific group is being targeted.

While networking is technically a recruiting technique, we define it separately as a *sourcing* methodology and address it separately in Vignette G: *Networking and Successful Diversity Recruitment* because it is a unique and specific type of recruiting. It is an individual activity that usually occurs with the encouragement, support, and endorsement of the institution. While organizations can reasonably expect their faculty and staff to announce a position vacancy to their professional network, it would not be reasonable to expect individuals to do so with their personal network as well. Nonetheless, many employees do so willingly when they are pleased with their employer, and this can be an organizational boon since personal and professional networks overlap considerably. For these and other reasons, networking is treated as a separate component of *sourcing*. Using social media is a networking activity that contains elements of recruiting

VIGNETTE G
Networking and Successful Diversity Recruitment

Networking is an ongoing recruiting technique that aims to cultivate a pool of applicants before, during, and after a search. Making professional contact with colleagues when a search is under way is an essential search activity. Networking produces specific, qualified candidates who are uncovered as a part of the referral process that evolves from outreach. Committee members, colleagues, and the *appointing authority* should contact their colleagues, friends, and associates and share the *position vacancy announcement.*

Specifically, committee members and administrators should ask their colleagues to refer one or more candidates, or to direct them to other individuals or recruiting sources that are likely to produce potential candidates. Use the age-old phrase, "Are you interested or do you know of anyone who might be interested in such a position?" When networking, committee members should specifically ask their colleagues to nominate diverse candidates, or assist them in identifying diverse recruiting resources (see Vignette: K: *Minority Recruiting: The Wrong Bait, the Wrong Technique, and the Wrong Pond*). This is a mandatory standard if one's contacts are similar to their own background or perspective.

Networking is an ongoing activity. It should be conducted prior to a position vacancy with the anticipation that when an opening occurs, targeted individuals will be predisposed to apply. They will already know of the institution and the type of positions it usually offers due to proactive information sharing. Meeting a promising young scholar and staying in contact with him or her, suggesting that a minority professional come to campus to meet key officials who may have future vacancies, or hosting the quarterly meeting of a professional affinity group are all activities that will extend the reach and influence of the institution and highlight its interest in talented professionals. An appropriate metaphor for networking is that the goal is to build the biggest web of contacts possible, in hopes of luring the right candidates into the pool of applicants at the right time.

A common pitfall of networking is assuming that you, or your network, already knows the best candidates. The assumption that one's alma mater yields the best candidates or that one's judgment is supreme when it comes to identifying talent is shortsighted and flies in the face of a meritocracy. The best candidates should be judged by a committee based upon a fair assessment of their credentials and experience in comparison to objective criteria, not whether they are known to certain people. Effective networking is expansive and inclusive. It is like an octopus with tentacles that reach out in every direction and tap into as many different communities as possible. Therefore, one-dimensional or monocultural networking activities are incomplete, flawed, and potentially biased by design.

EXHIBIT #8
Advertising and Recruitment Sourcing Options

Advertising Sources	Recruitment Activities
Advertise in newspapers (i.e., local, regional, and national).	Network with colleagues, friends, neighbors, associates, etc.
List in journal and professional publications (e.g., *The Chronicle of Higher Education, Inside Higher Ed*, etc.).	Make deliberate efforts to reach out to colleagues or associates from backgrounds different from your own.
Post in minority publications (e.g., *Diverse: Issues in Higher Education, Hispanic Outlook*, etc.).	Ask for referrals from coworkers, peers, etc.
Develop an Employment Landing Page website section for your institution.	Hire a search firm/headhunter.
Use electronic job boards (e.g., HigherEdJobs.com, ccjobsnow.com, Monster.com, etc.).	Post *position announcements* at conferences, job fairs, and public bulletin boards of target populations.
Use outlets sponsored by professional associations (e.g., job boards and listservs, etc.).	Send *position announcements* to colleges/schools with programs in the area of interest.
Identify and publish in nontraditional publications (e.g., newsletters, fliers, conference programs, e-zines, etc.).	Send to local chapters of professional associations.
Post openings on internal bulletin boards.	Seek nominations from others.
Announce and advertise internally (e.g., newsletters, memos, e-mail, *position announcements*, etc.).	Search your applicant tracking system database for past applicants.
Post at conferences and other professional events.	Develop relationships with minority organizations to encourage referrals from them.
Use radio, TV, and other media.	Use temporary agencies and professional employment organizations (PEOs) to identify candidates.
	Obtain lists and mail letters to members of professional associations.
	Develop sourcing pipeline programs to cultivate future applicants (e.g., apprenticeships, AA programs, internships, etc.).
	Identify internal talent for future openings.
	Place *position announcements* on professional association listservs that are free of charge for members.
	Send *position announcements* to college/university career placement offices.
	Seek names from directors, division chairs, deans, vice presidents, and presidents, and other leaders as appropriate.
	Consult with and recruit retirees, former employees, vendors, and consultants.
	Recruit people from competitors.
	Recruit from minority organizations that serve professionals in your targeted field.
	Sponsor or attend career fairs.
	Use social media to announce openings.

and advertising, especially when media organizations charge institutions for gaining access to their member database (see Vignette H: *Social Media and Your Sourcing Strategy*). Effective *sourcing* uses all three components, but recognizes what is separate to ensure that the advantages of each are present in cumulative activities (see Vignette I: *Sourcing Strategy*).

Diversity Tip: No effective *sourcing* strategy is complete unless it also targets diverse populations. In the same way institutions make special efforts to target faculty members with certain discipline-specific expertise, computer programmers with particular coding skills, or administrators with skills working with certain funding models, good recruitment techniques target candidates with specific backgrounds. If we have a multicultural student body, we should look for applicants who have experience living, studying, and working in, or who otherwise are familiar with, multicultural perspectives, environments, and methods of teaching and learning. Applicants who speak different languages can be targeted, as can populations similar in backgrounds to those of students. However, the focus is on the cultural competencies that are assumed, not what a person looks like. A person from a majority background who speaks a foreign language and researches ethnic populations is as valid a recruitment target as individuals of a particular demographic group presumed to have multicultural experiences and perspectives that benefit the institution. To say one has effectively advertised, recruited, or networked is not possible unless the spirit of the process is manifested by advertisements in media that target minorities, where recruitment activities are specific to under-represented populations, and when personal and professional networks are populated with people of different backgrounds.

Recruiting

Recruiting involves actively identifying and seeking qualified professionals, and calling their attention to an organization and its position openings. Recruiting

---

VIGNETTE H
Social Media and Your Sourcing Strategy

The importance of an institution having a protocol for assisting employees with recruiting, networking, and sharing information about position vacancies cannot be underscored enough in the era of social media. With the rapid expansion of various media being used to communicate with people across the street and across the world almost immediately, it is imperative that organizations craft their own message. Otherwise, it leaves to chance individual employees' publishing information that is not polished or vetted. The technologies will certainly evolve from e-mail, blogs, mass text messages, personal Web pages, and contemporary social media sites. Nonetheless, the idea of a well-crafted and deliberate message is timeless, and its impact can be lasting, regardless of the medium. It is a fundamental necessity that organizations consider the advantages and disadvantages of establishing policies and practices that permit, prohibit, or shape how social media is used in recruiting faculty and staff.

The advantages of recruiting with social media can quickly turn into a disadvantage, or even worse, a media nightmare. In the past, a lackluster or disgruntled former employee could harm an institution's reputation only so much because of his or her limited network and lack of resources to share a destructive message. Now with the ability to communicate so rapidly and widely, organizations must understand the gravity of this potential and position themselves appropriately to take advantage of the potential and defend themselves from misuse of these technologies.

Institutions should develop a social media policy to promulgate under what conditions their employees should recruit and network for vacancies. As noted previously, and as an example, a professionally prepared *position announcement* template is a small but prudent step toward controlling the look, feel, image, and message around the employment experience at an organization.

VIGNETTE I
Sourcing Strategy

Sourcing is the collection of activities, including recruitment, advertising, networking, and branding, that helps an organization attract qualified applicants for vacancies. *Sourcing* identifies applicants from a variety of places by using different techniques to cultivate a rich pool of talent. There are a number of sources available to find applicants and those sources used depend upon the particular job and the time frame for the search. Some typical *sourcing* strategies include recruiting and advertising, employee referrals, attending career fairs, using search firms, or developing an apprenticeship program with the local community college. Training, developing, and promoting internal applicants is also an often-overlooked *sourcing* strategy.

In almost every situation, HR professionals can assist with ideas about the right mix of *sourcing* activities. Building a good employment brand that will attract candidates whether or not there is a vacancy is one of the goals of *image advertising*. A good reputation regarding pay, benefits, treatment of employees, and being a welcoming place by accepting diverse people is invaluable and can determine whether the right applicants apply for an opening. The institution should be aware of its public image—whether it is considered a good place to work.

A *sourcing* strategy should be developed and an infrastructure should be built to support this strategy. As an example, having a protocol that says you advertise in three locations (i.e., print, online, and a diversity publication) for each search and then adding to this when necessary for challenging searches is one part of a *sourcing* strategy. The three locations might be *The Chronicle of Higher Education*, an online source such as HigherEdJobs.com, and a diverse media source such as *Diverse: Issues in Higher Education*. An advertising protocol is necessary to choose the right kinds of media and to control costs by spending resources where your ads will have the greatest impact (see *Yield Ratio*, p. 137).

A recruiting strategy might include HR's printing 100 *position announcements* for each vacancy and mailing 50 to a predefined list of organizations, while expecting the hiring department to share the remaining announcements with various individuals and organizations in its professional network. Last, a networking protocol that can be subsumed under the overall *sourcing* strategy would be requiring departments to develop a minority advisory committee for each major program area, and then asking its members to assist the institution in sharing information with their networks when vacancies occur.

The *sourcing* method used and when it is used depends largely upon the type of position being filled. The key element of a *sourcing* strategy is forethought. Institutions should first understand that they must take an active role in identifying the best possible talent. Then they should develop strategies and tactics that support this goal. In summary, this strategy should be institutionalized and built into the way business is conducted, not presented as an add-on to what is done under normal circumstances.

targets candidates who are not actively seeking work as well as those in the job market. Recruiting has the advantage of allowing organizations to define the candidate type, and then pursue that ideal.

Recruiting involves outreach, networking, and solicitation (see Vignette J: *The Business Case for Recruiting: The Admissions Office*). It requires building professional relationships and contacts, then at some future time informing them of the advantages of working at an institution and notifying them of position openings when they occur. Recruiting complements advertising, which announces openings to would-be job seekers through various media.

Nearly every stakeholder in the search committee process has a role in and responsibility for assisting the institution with identifying promising candidates. Every member of a department, every peer or customer of a position, every committee member, the HR

VIGNETTE J
The Business Case for Recruiting
The Admissions Office

There is no better justification for practicing the fine art of recruiting than observing the admissions offices of colleges and universities. HR professionals should be green with envy. If the college expects to have 1,000 freshmen coming to campus in September, the office starts years in advance by building the reputation of the institution in many different ways (i.e., branding). It places ads in newspapers and periodicals (image advertising), participates in or hosts admissions fairs (career fairs), and sends out mailings (*position announcements*). It also sends recruiters on the road to visit counselors and individual applicants, hosts events, purchases mailing lists, and then analyzes this information, and uses an assortment of other techniques to identify and woo potential students.

If the admissions office were like the HR department, it would simply place ads in high school newspapers and wait until spring to see who applied. Admissions officers know that recruiting is indispensable for fielding a high-quality freshman class. Without aggressive recruiting tactics, admissions professionals know they are left to the whims of 17-year-olds who will decide whether to apply, whether to accept an offer of admission, and whether to actually enroll in the fall. Good students have choices about where they go to school, and great professionals have choices of where they work. HR professionals would be wise to follow the lead of admissions officers, or at least to use the good HR practices that we know all too well, but do not use all too often.

---

department, and, of course, the *appointing authority* should recruit for vacant positions. Each stakeholder should actively reach out to share with colleagues, associates, friends, neighbors, and any other well-placed individuals and organizations the good news that his or her institution is looking for an X. Word of mouth is often the best way to find candidates and is generally called networking (see Vignette G: *Networking and Successful Diversity Recruitment*).

All *sourcing* activities should also include minority recruitment activities; otherwise they ignore many available labor markets. Such oversights do not reflect the tenets of a meritocracy. A fair and meritocratic search seeks to find the best possible candidates wherever they are. Looking in familiar places fails to embrace the full possibilities of the available talent in the entire labor marketplace. Vignette K: *Minority Recruiting: The Wrong Bait, the Wrong Technique, and the Wrong Pond* makes a compelling argument that institutions must learn to recruit differently to identify the best talent. Vignette L: *A Call to a Profession to Give Me Three Good Candidates or Why Equal Opportunity Officers Should Be Minority Headhunters* argues for each institution building an infrastructure to help hiring managers with the challenging effort to recruit minority professionals.

True recruiting identifies candidates who otherwise would not have heard about the position vacancy. These applicants are often better qualified than general applicants who responded to an advertisement because the networking individuals closest to the search are targeting individuals who have a background that matches what the organization is looking for. They have probably prescreened potential applicants for professionalism and good character before inviting them to apply, since recruiters risk their own reputation by making the referral. It is essentially a reference offered in advance of a potential interview.

In recruitment, search committee members serve as ambassadors of their institution, presenting a positive face to external audiences. Most notable, they endorse the organization as a good place to work. Implicit in this is the assumption that the institution helps committee members, team members, and others prepare to recruit to ensure that they are carrying the right message(s) and an accurate description of the position. An excellent way of doing this is to have the HR department prepare *position announcement* templates that can be tailored to each search for use by anyone involved in the recruitment process (see Appendix D). While traditional *position announcements* were attractive fliers or brochures designed for

VIGNETTE K
Minority Recruiting
The Wrong Bait, the Wrong Technique, and the Wrong Pond

A fisherman leaves his home bright and early one morning with the palatable taste of dinner on his lips. There is nothing like a Friday fish fry, he thinks to himself. On the way to his favorite watering hole, he stops by the local bait and tackle shop to pick up the usual supplies and chat with the regulars. "What are you fishing for today?" shouts one of his friends.

"I'm hoping to catch some trout today; we're going to have a fish fry tonight," he replies.

"Well, make sure you cast your line in the shallow areas of the lake since it's going to be windy out there today," advises his colleague.

It was a long, hot day out on the lake and it ended in disappointment. While the fisherman caught some small bass and perch, he didn't catch the big fish he was hoping to. As he thought about it, he had never really been able to catch trout. He wondered what he was doing wrong, so, as he approached the bait and tackle shop on his way home, he stopped in to speak with the owner for some advice.

"Well now," the seasoned and experienced owner said as he paused for a moment. He spoke slowly and told the story. "Many folks come here to find trout, but most never catch them. As a matter of fact, there aren't that many trout in this lake. However, the ones that are here are really big because they aren't caught that often."

"Why is that?" asked the fisherman.

"Well, there are three reasons." He smiles and waits a moment to deliver his sage advice. "If you want to catch trout, you have to use a different kind of bait. The bait I sell here is really good for bass and other fish, but not that effective for trout."

"Why don't you sell bait for trout?" asked the fisherman.

"Like I said, there aren't that many in this lake," laughed the owner. "The second reason is that many fishermen don't use the right technique when fishing for trout. They use the same technique for other fish and expect the same results. That's unwise," he said. "If you want to catch a different kind of fish, you have to use different bait and a different technique. The third reason is that you're fishing in the wrong lake. There are plenty of fish in the sea, the river across the state, and the pond across the way. In each of these you'll find different kinds of fish. So I would fish in the one where there are more of the type of fish I'm interested in. It sounds simple, but it's true." He added, "You won't find marlin, tuna, salmon, or trout around here."

On his way home, the fisherman thought that next week, in addition to fishing in a different pond, he'd seek advice only from those who had caught trout, not from his friends who were bass fishermen. He also decided to stop for trout bait at a different shop and to buy a book about trout fishing.

Minority recruiting is a lot like fishing. Many organizations use the same bait and the same technique, recruit in the same places they have traditionally tapped, and then expect to be successful in attracting minority applicants. To be successful at minority recruiting, institutions should use different ads, recruiting, and networking protocols; should advertise in different media; should perform outreach activities in different communities; and certainly should seek advice from experts in the field.

VIGNETTE L
A Call to a Profession to Give Me Three Good Candidates
or Why Equal Opportunity Officers Should Be Minority Headhunters

Every hiring manager on the planet seeks the same result—making a hiring decision from among good candidates. The entire recruiting, advertising, networking, and selection process will likely culminate with interviews of three candidates. The selection is usually based upon idealized criteria with the hope that the chosen candidate will be somewhat of a superhero or at least the "best thing since sliced bread." However, before we get to make this lofty decision, we have to have a pool of great candidates from which to draw. This is the major challenge in all recruiting efforts.

Most hiring managers are content experts who know their profession. Every hiring manager has a professional network, be it large, small, inclusive, exclusive, good, bad, or green. It is likely not complete, however, as this is impossible. This is why hiring managers must reach beyond their existing personal and professional networks to identify candidates who are different in background from themselves. This is easier said than done since most hiring managers have limited recruiting and networking resources because this is not their primary responsibility. Nonetheless, some professionals have the right knowledge, expertise, and resources to recruit effectively, and their experience and expertise far exceed what the average manager could ever attain.

My recommendation is that those professionals who know the most about recruiting minority professionals should be charged with recruiting minority professionals on behalf of the organization. Why should laypersons without the knowledge, expertise, or experience be responsible for performing such a sophisticated, important, and time-consuming activity? Should they attempt to learn to do so while a search is being conducted? How much success should be expected from hiring managers under these circumstances? Should the primary work responsibilities of equal opportunity professionals be helping their organizations achieve the goals of equal opportunity—which include hiring diverse candidates?

My charge to the entire equal opportunity profession is to change its focus and its purpose from advocating for diverse workplaces to enabling diverse workplaces. Advocacy, training, and enrichment programming are great to have, but they are secondary in importance to achieving results. Equal opportunity professionals should be charged with finding three good candidates through their own networking efforts on behalf of every search committee.

As a hiring manager, I dream of having three excellent finalists from which to choose for my next hire. I would be ecstatic if they were all minority candidates. This would achieve many institutional goals, enhance the educational mission of the organization, enhance the richness of internal decision making, help to mirror the community of students we serve, and help to create a more welcoming work environment. Unfortunately, the reverse is more often true—three majority candidates.

A balanced pool of candidates and a balanced pool of finalists are possible if the right efforts are made. This requires aggressive, targeted, and adroit recruiting from trained professionals. Incidentally, this is why search firms are more successful at producing minority candidates—they know how and where to look because they do it for a living. The proposal here is for equal opportunity professionals to use their professional expertise to help their organizations recruit and select diverse candidates.

A compliance orientation that trains and admonishes the organization to do the right thing, to be fair, and to follow the process is not likely to produce any noteworthy results if experience is any indicator of success. What will work is a results orientation that focuses on building and using an extensive network that includes every recruiting pool available in the marketplace. Every morning when *headhunters* get to work, they pick up the phone, reach out, and dig into every possible network they can access to find good candidates one at a time. They do not stop until they find three good candidates.

Hiring managers need equal opportunity representatives, or AA officers, diversity directors, assistant provosts for academic equity and inclusion, chief diversity officers, and anyone else who serves in a capacity that is related to diversity and inclusion to support them in finding three good candidates. Hiring managers can learn to do the right thing in many different ways and at many different times, but while conducting a search, what they need most is help finding three good candidates—and little else.

mailing or posting on bulletin boards, many of today's *position announcements* are attachments sent via e-mail. A professionally prepared electronic template designed by an advertising agency or an internal public relations office presents the institution in the best possible light.

Employment Branding, Reputation, and Minority Recruiting

Some organizations seldom recruit or advertise because they get more qualified applications than they would ever need from the right communities. This happens when the organization has a positive *employment brand* and applicants seek out the institution as a good place to work. This reputation precedes vacancy announcements, and many applicants reverse the pattern and even attempt to network inside the organization. The benefits of a positive employment brand are powerful.

Nowhere is *employment branding* more important than in minority recruiting. If different communities do not have a connection or experience with an organization, minorities will not take a leap of faith and apply for a given position. This is particularly true if few minority members are employed on a campus. Does the institution have a positive reputation in the communities where it would like to recruit? If not, outreach efforts, image advertising, networking, and other tactics should be used to cultivate target population relationships.

CHAPTER 8

Advertising

ADVERTISING INVOLVES ANNOUNCING A VACANCY in various media, such as newspapers, journals, websites, and similar outlets, to gain the interest of potentially qualified applicants. It is indispensable because of its ability to reach thousands of potential applicants in the employment market. Advertising is necessary but not sufficient to cultivate the best candidate pool because it does not target passive candidates not currently in the market for employment.

While advertising is required and has intuitive appeal, it does not guarantee finding the right job candidates, since applicants determine who gets into the pool for consideration. Therefore, the best option is targeted media outlets specializing in the groups you wish to attract. *Diversity advocates* also recommend that advertising in minority and nontraditional media is a necessity. Such advertisements complement the active recruiting and pursuit of diverse candidates.

HR departments, *appointing authorities*, and committee members should collaborate in finding the right media in which to announce position vacancies. Advertising agencies can be valuable for this reason alone, as the typical agency specializing in a particular industry will have a listing of the major and minor media outlets for their clients (Vignette M: *Advantages of Using an Advertising Agency*). These must include minority media as well. A best practice *sourcing* strategy starts with knowing one's discipline, its recruiting patterns, where good candidates are produced and found, and how competitors source candidates, then developing protocols to take advantage of this knowledge.

Online Advertising

Online advertising has become as important as print because of the ubiquitous nature of job boards, online recruiting, social media, and applicant tracking systems. The importance of having an online presence is likely only to increase. Online advertising has some advantages over printed media in that ads are generally cheaper and can be placed in a short time (see Vignette N: *Intelligent Online Advertising*).

There are at least two primary forms of online advertising—an institution's website and job boards. Do not underestimate the importance of the institution's website. Nearly every applicant who applies for a position online—whether through the institution's website or through a job board—is likely to go first to the institution's home page to learn more about the organization. Organizations would be wise to dedicate a section to future employees, just as it does to future students (see the following section, *Employment Landing Page*).

Another advantage of online advertising is that many online job boards—such as the jobs section of *The Chronicle of Higher Education* and HigherEdJobs .com—have tools that notify applicants via e-mail each week about new openings in their specific field. This is a great benefit for both employers and applicants. This "push technology" blurs the lines between recruiting and advertising. Potential candidates who are not actively looking for a new position will still become aware of job openings in their discipline, so advertisers get access to passive applicants without much additional cost or effort. Many job boards also have databases of applicants who have applied for certain positions over time (see *Labor Market Analysis*, p. 150). The information can be used to target active and passive candidates.

Employment Landing Page

An employment landing page section of an institution's website is a central repository of information that gives would-be applicants all the information they need to become interested in and apply for a

VIGNETTE M
Advantages of Using an Advertising Agency

An advertising agency operates as an agent on your behalf to place advertisements in various media, though its primary service may be the advice and expertise it offers you in this process. Such agencies' advertising and marketing services assist you with selecting the right media, the right messages, and the right presentation of images and information. Some agencies specialize in the needs of specific categories, such as medical, academic, or technical services, which require knowledge and expertise in certain industries. Such expertise is not ordinarily found in a general advertising agency that provides a broad array of services such as direct mail marketing, product advertising (think laundry detergent or soft drinks), and radio advertising. Therefore, expertise in your industry is as vital as experience with the media you are likely to want to use for recruitment purposes.

Agencies also differ in the services they offer and their pricing policy. The best recruitment advertising agencies will assign you an account representative who understands your institution and its needs. Your representative should provide you with personalized attention, whether this is assistance with redesigning an ad template, identifying minority media outlets for your discipline, determining how best to tell your story in ads, or determining the right mix of print and online advertising. This person's knowledge, availability, and responsiveness to your unique needs are service quality differentiators among agencies.

Not all agencies charge the same amount for the same services. A good agency is transparent in how it presents its costs. While many of the services for placing advertising are provided at no cost to the institution due to the commissions offered, some agencies may include add-on charges for some services. A good way to find out about pricing is to provide sample ads you have placed in the past and find out what charges would apply if the agency had created the ad for you. Ask for a sample invoice based on the past ad. Do not disclose what you paid; find out what the agency would charge. Find out whether a contract is required or what type of commitment you have to make, and who will manage your account. These questions will help you evaluate agencies. Finally, be sure to get references from institutions similar to yours.

The advantages of using an advertising agency generally include (a) expert advice, (b) access to a database of media outlets in nearly every venue in your industry—including minority media, (c) professionally designed ads that help to tell your story and build your employment brand, and (d) placement of ads on your behalf at no extra cost. Finding an agency that specializes in recruitment can greatly improve the process and add continuity to all your recruitment efforts. A generic ad placed in general media that does not highlight the best aspects of your institution will not help you compete for the best academic and professional talent.

Doug Geiling
Graystone Group Advertising
www.graystoneadv.com

VIGNETTE N
Intelligent Online Advertising

In 2007 the Conference Board first reported that more job-seekers were using online sources than print sources in their searches (73% online versus 65% in print). The trend has continued and become more pronounced. In fact, in April 2008, the Conference Board made this announcement:

> The Conference Board will no longer publish the Help-Wanted Advertising Index of print advertising after July 1, 2008. . . . Because print advertising no longer comprehensively captures changes in labor-market demand, The Conference Board will focus its efforts on . . . measuring changes in online job postings including newspapers' web-based ads.*

And it's not just candidates. According to one of the longest-running polls in the industry, WEDDLE's online survey of job seekers and recruiters, 94% of employers are using the Internet to publicize their job openings.

Academic job searches have migrated online along with the rest of the job market. While these searches present unique challenges, it's no longer a question of whether to recruit online, but of how to do so most effectively. Keep in mind *Inside Higher Ed*'s tips for successful online recruiting to build a diverse pool of great talent efficiently and cost effectively.

Advertise your institution, not just your jobs. Your marketing department is always promoting your institution to students, and some of the same marketing messages can ensure that when you have job openings, great candidates will be interested. Online advertising generally doesn't limit word counts (or charge incrementally for more). Take advantage of the opportunity to "sell" your school to prospective faculty.

Advertise beyond the job boards. When it's time to publicize a specific opening, jobs-only job boards are efficient and economical, but they're designed to reach active job hunters. Look for websites that provide a reason for professionals who aren't on the hunt to visit and that are well designed to push job content to them. (Examples might include H-Net, AACRAO.org or *Inside Higher Ed*.)

Put your job announcements to work. Print advertising sits in one place and waits to be found. The same might be said for jobs entered in an online database if you rely solely on candidates' searches to put your opening in the spotlight. Instead, take advantage of tools like Google AdSense, banner advertising, and e-mail advertising to get messages in front of great hires even when they're not actively searching.

Don't start the application process too quickly. It's typical for an online job posting to provide a link to your institutional website as the primary application method. Nevertheless, it's important not to assume that a candidate has arrived at your site to apply for a job. Always provide candidates with a quick link to your job application, but also organize the kinds of links that a person who wants to explore your institution will find useful.

(continues)

(*continued*)

Keep your application process as simple as possible to start. It's easy to get caught up in how easy your applicant tracking system can make your data collection and processing (and how willing academic applicants are to jump through hoops) and lose sight of the candidate's experience. Keep your requirements focused on what you really need at each point in the process, not on what your database can collect.

Treat *all* candidates politely. Acknowledge applications, respond to inquiries, and let people know the status of the search and their application. The person who's not quite right for the job you have open today could be a perfect fit for one that opens up tomorrow.

Finally, and perhaps most important, **write your online job postings with candidates in mind.** Too often institutions use an internal job description, or the sketchy information from an applicant tracking database as an ad—with woeful results. The thing to remember above all is that you're not just writing for people who are actively job hunting (and therefore won't be put off by jargon or a wearying experience), but for terrific hires who are *not* looking. Your ad needs to grab readers' attention with a strong statement about why a great hire should be interested. An effective way to think about it is as though you're writing a letter to the person you most want to hire.

Start by selling the job. Academics may be jarred by the idea of selling, but it's really a question of humanizing what can be a dehumanizing experience. Use a compelling job title rather than an internal designation larded with position numbers and employment levels. State strongly why your great hire should want the job. Use candidate-focused language:

"To succeed in this role, you'll need . . ." not "Qualifications."

"You'll have the opportunity to . . ." not "Responsibilities."

"If this sounds like the job for you . . ." not "Application Procedures."

Remember, once your job announcements are on public view, they're advertising. Don't be afraid to show a little personality—your model should be online dating, not online tax filing. For more about successful online recruiting, visit insidehighered.com/recruiting/tips.

Kathlene Collins
Publisher
Inside Higher Ed
www.insidehighered.com

*www.prnewswire.com/news-releases/the-conference-board-to-discontinue-help-wanted-print-advertising-index-57104497.html. Retrieved June 15, 2009.

job. Such sites are now commonplace in the digital age. A professionally built site might contain a brief overview of the history, mission, and organization of the institution; its strategic plans and initiatives (especially as they relate to personnel); and recruitment and employment policies. Videos featuring a welcome by the president, provost, or chief HR officer are becoming standard components of landing pages.

Sample site content could be dual-career, relocation, and promotion policies; compensation practices, recruitment incentives, benefits, and *perquisites*; and memberships, discounts, and services offered to employees. Links to local attractions, community information, and quality-of-life information for the surrounding area help to provide a comprehensive listing of what would be of most interest to a prospective employee. All of this information is meant either to entice applicants to consider joining the organization or to assist them in their transition from new hire to employee.

> **Diversity Tip**: Having a page or two of the *employment landing page* section of a website to attract minority candidates in particular is a wise investment. The content should speak to campus demographics, the organization's work climate, and its desire to increase diversity (if applicable), and the pages should provide examples of successful minority faculty and staff on campus. Such pages are designed to encourage minority applicants to apply for open positions, just as general *employment landing pages* encourage all applicants to consider the institution or student landing pages encourage students to apply for admission.

Advertisements (Ads) and Position Announcements

Advertisements vary in type, use, and length depending upon their overall purpose. The industry is changing rapidly as recruitment advertising on the Internet matures. Initially, online advertising mirrored print advertising in that a general announcement was placed in media to be read by the target group. However, ads have evolved over time. During this transition period, there is a blend of the old and the new. Traditional print advertisements include column, block, and image ads. New Web-based ad types include banner and social media ads.

Print Ads

Traditional print ads include in-column *help wanted*–type ads that briefly describe how to apply for particular positions. Display ads or block ads are more detailed because the additional space allows for information, such as to whom the position reports and the characteristics of an ideal candidate. They are often graphics-based and include the organization's logo, slogans, and other information that is not specific to the position, such as telling a bit about the organization itself. Telling one's story in a display ad is an effective way of luring candidates into applying (see Vignette O: *Telling Your Story or Tell Me Again Why I Should Work for You*).

Image Ads

Image ads are an indirect form of advertising because they do not explicitly announce a position vacancy. Instead, they build the institution's *employment brand*—its reputation as a great place to work. Therefore, when a vacancy actually occurs, candidates are predisposed to apply to that organization because of the earlier positive images they have of the institution. This is similar to television commercials that one sees over and over again whether or not we need a washing machine at the time. However, when ours breaks, we may think that Maytags are reliable based on the ads we have seen. A good example of image advertising in higher education is a series of ads by CUNY—the City University of New York—that exclaimed, "Look Who's Working at CUNY!" The ads featured faces of a diverse group of distinguished and award-winning faculty members. The implication is that these notable scholars would be your colleagues if you worked at or attended a CUNY institution.

> **Diversity Tip**: For institutions that do not have a recruiting presence in minority communities, image advertising can cultivate a relationship with potential applicants. Such advertisements might contain welcoming statements about the institution. The *Diversity in Academe* issue of *The Chronicle of Higher Education* published each fall provides numerous examples of well-designed image advertisements that target diverse candidates. Image advertisements placed in minority media can be particularly valuable. They should drive applicants to your website for additional information about your institution. Having a diversity *employment landing page* designed to receive this targeted traffic is a smart recruiting technique.

Web-Based Ads

Printed image advertisements have a parallel in banner ads that are placed online. Banner ads are graphic images that appear online and usually contain a slogan or message. While users may click on them and be taken to another website, they usually do not "sell" a product or ask the viewer to do anything in particular—such as apply for a job. Nonetheless, they do as they are designed—call attention to the institution. Many organizations also have online profiles located on job boards. These are a few pages that highlight—or

---

VIGNETTE O
Telling Your Story
or Tell Me Again Why I Should Work for You

Why would I apply to work for your institution? A quick look at the ads placed in *The Chronicle of Higher Education* will yield a dozen openings for professors of _____ or directors of _____. What is so good about your college, university, or community? What is it like working on your campus? Who else works there? Will I fit in? What are your institution's values, initiatives, and goals? The unfortunate thing about most advertisements is that they do not answer any of these questions. Instead, they present a generic job description disguised as an advertisement.

Most advertisements tell you the obvious. They indicate that there is a vacancy for a professorship and the professor will be expected to teach, perform service, and be involved in some mix of research, scholarship, and publications. Advertisements for directors of student services will undoubtedly list the fact that the person in the position works with students, is concerned about student development, will support various student activities, and will work for a vice president of student affairs. While these factors are essential, they are obvious and do not provide much qualitative information to entice an applicant to apply at *your* institution compared to others.

More effective advertisements might mention that professors are expected to mentor students, and an active undergraduate research program supports this ideal. An ad might describe the college's bucolic setting; indicate that it has an arboretum, museum, and a day care center on campus; promote the trailing spouse employment program; brag about the thriving service-learning program due to the founder's belief in community service; or mention that the provost is an international scholar on the first-year college student experience. Some or all of these factors might encourage would-be applicants to consider your college or university. The key is to tell your story so that like-minded professionals can picture themselves as part of your community. Most important is that when you tell your story in the ad, it starts the process of selecting for *organizational fit*. For as you describe your institution, this will naturally attract or repel the right applicants organically (see *Evaluating Organizational Fit: Why You Should and Must*, p. 107).

---

even brag about—an institution to build the institution's *employment brand.*

Regular Web ads parallel print ads, with similar in-column and display ads as they exist in print. They follow the same pattern but usually contain links that take people directly to an online employment application or applicant tracking system. Web ads do differ in a number of key ways, notably their length, which can be unlimited and contain any information an organization wants to share. A good use of Web-based ads is to have shorter print ads that direct candidates to detailed information online. This common practice continues to grow in importance, particularly as organizations develop *employment branding*–type websites designed specifically for applicants. Web ads can also include moving images, widgets, and applications; have embedded video; or contain links to other dynamic content—all with the purpose of soliciting positive viewer response.

Social Media
Social media continues to redefine how people and organizations communicate. Many experts have observed new positions within HR departments described as social media recruiters. These professionals blend traditional recruiting, advertising, and

networking by circulating position images, information, and vacancy announcements among a circle of friends, colleagues, applicants, target audiences, and other communities of interest. They might blog, write articles for e-zines, network by sending out *position announcements*, or simply be available online to answer questions from potential applicants. While their uses are evolving, the fact remains that organizations must adapt advertisements to the media used to announce their position vacancies (see Vignette H: *Social Media and Your Sourcing Strategy*, p. 42). Where possible, these announcements should contain official messages, regardless of how and where they are published.

> **Diversity Tip**: Social media is useful in getting information about the organization into the hands of minority candidates. This is particularly important if the organization uses social media to target communities for which it currently does not have a presence. Instead of building a diverse network from scratch, an institution might be able to tap into existing diverse networks through the contacts it has with members of that community (i.e., its faculty, staff, students, vendors, or associates).

Position Announcements

Position announcements have traditionally been printed brochurelike documents presented in the form of fliers that were lengthier than a display ad, often contained images, and always provided more detailed information about openings (see the *Position Announcement Template* in Appendix D). They have always been designed to be shared, whether by being posted on bulletin boards, handed to colleagues when networking, or mailed through regular postal mail. With the advent of the Internet, they are now attached to e-mails, placed on listservs, and posted on electronic bulletin boards. They are a particularly effective means of sharing information about a vacancy and have always been a basic ingredient of effective networking.

Institutions should provide downloadable electronic templates for appointing authorities and committees. This gives committees a means of cultivating applicants. The *position announcement* usually is small enough to be handled easily (i.e., a single page with information on one or both sides, or a short brochure) or used as a small attachment to an e-mail; yet should also be long enough to contain enough information

about the position, the organization, its requirements, and its story—with marketing or branding information designed to attract candidates.

Writing Ads

One of the causes of a poor hiring recommendation or failed search is a poorly conceived position description and poorly written advertisement. If the ad does not reflect the position accurately, it is analogous to fishing with the wrong bait. We might attract many fish, but they won't be the kind we seek (see Vignette K: *Minority Recruiting: The Wrong Bait, the Wrong Technique, and the Wrong Pond*, p. 45). Therefore, the *hiring authority* should draft an ad that is specific to the needs of the position and department. Expert assistance can be provided by an HR or equal opportunity officer. As noted earlier, a not-so-perfect ad is likely to attract not-so-perfect candidates.

A critical task in the drafting process is making the connection between job requirements and the type of person who is best able to perform the job. This connection must be made on the basis of the duties, tasks, and responsibilities outlined in the *job analysis* (defining a position) process and the knowledge, skills, and abilities that were identified as necessary to perform the job. Spending the needed time and attention to gain clarity will make successive decisions—like where to recruit and which selection criteria to use—much easier. A checklist of information to include in position advertisements is presented in Exhibit #9: *How to Write an Ad: Job Advertisement Checklist*.

Equal Opportunity Statements

Nearly every organization places an equal opportunity statement at the bottom of its ads. The typical phrase is simple, short, and factual, such as "The University of Williamsburg is an Equal Opportunity/Affirmative Action Employer." Other statements list a plethora of *protected classes*, including race, gender, national origin, disability, and marital and veteran status, as a way of documenting the institution's compliance with the law. The utility and effectiveness of this obligatory statement is not documented in the hiring and employment literature, but such statements are widely seen as a necessary requirement to symbolize the institution's commitment to equal opportunity and the laws that govern this doctrine.

A best practice approach to conveying the organization's position regarding diversity and inclusion is to

EXHIBIT #9
How to Write an Ad
Job Advertisement Checklist

Job Description
- Tell the story about your institution and why it is special.
- Describe the position and why it is unique and other attractive elements.
- Include position title(s) (i.e., descriptive, working, or official).
- Include essential functions/major duties and responsibilities.
- Include reporting relationships.
- Include information about the organization that would attract candidates.
- Discuss salary or hiring range (as appropriate).

Job Requirements
- Knowledge, skills, abilities required for the job
- Education, degree level and field(s)
- Licensure, if required or preferred
- Experience (type of experience and desired field[s]/discipline[s])
- Technical expertise or other special requirements
- Performance requirements (e.g., competencies, abilities, knowledge, demonstrated experience, etc.)
- Unique requirements of the department or organization

Preferred Criteria
- Special abilities or experience
- Membership or leadership in professional associations
- Certifications or unique training
- *Organizational fit* criteria (if appropriate); see *Evaluating Organizational Fit: Why You Should and Must*, p. 107, and Exhibit #29: *Organizational Selection Criteria Examples*, p. 110.

Information Sought
- Letter of interest/cover letter
- Résumé or curriculum vitae
- Statement of teaching or leadership philosophy
- Samples of publications
- Portfolio of materials or other work, if appropriate
- References with full contact information
- Letters of recommendation
- Copies of transcripts, official or unofficial
- Other information or documents that are needed to complete an initial evaluation of the applicant's credentials and experience.

Information Provided to Applicant
- Closing date or application review date
- Position availability or start date (see *Application Deadlines and Preferential Filing Dates*, p. 146)
- Where and how to apply (e.g., application address, Web address, etc.)
- Equal opportunity statements (i.e., EEO/AA, Americans with Disabilities Act statement)
- Point of contact for information (e.g., receptionist, *hiring authority*, search committee chair, HR representative, etc.)

(continues)

(continued)

Ad Placement
- Place ad in places most likely to attract appropriate applicants.
- Place ad in minority media.
- Consider ad in targeted media such as journal for that profession.
- Determine where in the printed media the ad will appear and under what heading.
- Size the ad to reflect the type of position in question, the relative availability of applicants (e.g., tight job market = bigger ad, etc.), and advertising budget.
- Determine the mix and type of ads (e.g., online, print, targeted media, etc.).
- Place a code in ads to determine which ad yielded the best applicants.
- Seek advice and assistance from the staff of the publications in which ads were placed.
- Seek advice and assistance of the HR department, equal opportunity officer, or ad agency representative (if appropriate) about drafting and placing ads.

state its values and principles rather than emphasizing its desire to comply with equal opportunity laws. Here are examples of statements that appear more earnest:

- The college has a history and strong commitment to the principles and practices of diversity throughout its community and welcomes candidates who would enhance its diversity.
- The university is committed to increasing the diversity of its faculty and therefore welcomes applications from anyone who would bring additional dimensions to the university's teaching and research mission.
- The college welcomes nominations and applications from women and members of minority groups and others who share our passion for building a diverse community that looks like our student population.
- The university has committed itself to expanding the employment opportunities of women, minorities, and persons with disabilities in its own activities and in society.
- We are committed to attracting and supporting a staff of women and men that fully represents the racial, ethnic, and cultural diversity of the nation and that actively seeks applications from underrepresented groups.
- Our university is committed to being an inclusive community and seeks to be diverse in people and programs consistent with its mission.

With a little imagination and creativity, the standard equal opportunity statement can be transformed into a recruitment tool that attracts like-minded professionals. However, the words should not contain false advertisements or indicate institutional commitment where it does not exist.

Minority Recruiting Sources
Graystone Group Advertising Agency boasts having a list of nearly 500 minority recruiting sources specific to higher education. While this number might appear surprising, mainstream media are more ubiquitous and widely known by design. This means that institutions must make the effort to identify minority recruiting sources related to their mission, curriculum, and positions they have available. There should never be the excuse, "We do not know where to look to find minority candidates"—there are at least 500 known places.

There are a number of ways an institution can build lists of minority recruiting resources. First, use an advertising agency like Graystone Group Advertising or one of its competitors (see Vignette M: *Advantages of Using an Advertising Agency*). Second, poll campus hiring managers and ask them to share sources from their discipline with which they are familiar, making this combined list a starting point. These hiring professionals may ask colleagues or professional associations for assistance if they do not have any names. This may explain why their area lacks diversity. Starting the process of identifying sources before there is a vacancy is a key to networking's future success.

Third, asking HR and equal opportunity professionals to do some research for the organization is essential. Fourth, ask members of various minority communities who are stakeholders of the institution (e.g., minority faculty, staff, students, vendors, advisory committee members, trustees, guest speakers, etc.) to provide points of contact. Everyone has a professional network, and a wise organization taps into every network available to seek the best possible talent. Finally, targeted social media techniques may provide easier entrée into communities lacking university presence by engaging that community's members with the hope that they will share positive institutional messages and vacancy announcements. The best part is the effort need be undertaken only once. Once sources are identified, they can be reused.

———————

Note: SearchCommittees.com also lists hundreds of minority recruiting sources for members of the website.

PART THREE

Screening and Evaluating Candidates

CHAPTER 9

Screening and Evaluating Candidates

THE MOST IMPORTANT AND CHALLENGING RESPONSIBIL-ITY of the search committee is screening applicants. The committee evaluates qualifications and capabilities through ever more intense scrutiny. A rigorous evaluation involves clear, relevant criteria and multiple screening methods. The more thorough this process is, the greater the likelihood that the chosen candidate will fit the position. The number and type of screening methods used should be in proportion to the importance of the position. Screening and evaluating candidates starts with a review of written application materials and ends with reference and background checks, with an assortment of other reviews being completed between these two bookends.

Search committees, hiring authorities, and HR officers should jointly determine the methods used to screen candidates for each position opening. These techniques may include various types of interviews, presentations, and tests. A comprehensive list of typical screening methods appears in chapter 13.

A Jury of Peers

The beauty of the search committee process is that two heads are better than one, and a diverse and capable committee makes sounder judgments. Upon reflection, one will notice that the most important decisions made in a democratic society are entrusted to selected groups—not individuals acting alone. Boards of directors or trustees, not chief executive officers; legislatures, not presidents or governors; juries, not judges—even more groups of judges are used in the case of appellate courts; and the best example might be that when life-or-death decisions are made, they are made by groups of doctors and surgeons. We often trust that the decision making of groups will be superior to that of the most able individuals. Thus, the argument, "The most important decision any organization ever makes is

determining who will join the organization," opens this book. The search committee process is superior to any other form of hiring due to its deliberate approach of having a well-informed group of stakeholders make these crucial decisions.

Additionally, the shared governance and group process models inherent in the search committee approach reduce bias by including multiple perspectives in the evaluation of candidate materials (see Vignette P: *Eliminating Bias From Selection*). One evaluator might misunderstand an applicant's credentials or fail to appreciate an applicant's potential contributions to the organization. Moreover, any bias (intentional or unintentional) a screener might bring to the process will be mitigated by that screener's participation in a larger group. To increase the fairness of the screening process, a group of committee members should handle each stage.

A Common Standard

In all cases, the method and criteria used to evaluate candidates must be agreed upon objectively in advance by the committee. First, evaluate applicants against a common standard to determine whether they are qualified; then evaluate them again to determine how competitive they are among other applicants. Individual committee members complete the first evaluation of written materials. The second is made by tabulating the evaluation results recorded from the full search committee. Some organizations find it helpful to have members of the HR department cull the pool of applicants and weed out individuals who are not qualified for the position, thereby making the initial screening by committee members easier and more productive (see Vignette Q: *HR Prescreen or Minimal Qualifications Screening*).

This process continues through multiple screening rounds. With consistent standards, the process is

VIGNETTE P
Eliminating Bias From Selection

All decisions regarding the qualifications, capabilities, and characteristics of candidates should be made with an objective filter derived from the organizational analysis, position description, job advertisement, and *charge*. Using these four objective standards will go far toward ensuring a fair and rigorous evaluation. Because humans filter reality through the lens of individual experience, we all carry some unintentional bias. A simple preference for graduates of one's alma mater rather than other institutions' is an example.

More destructive examples include the fact that some research has shown that men and women tend to stereotype women in their description of women's scholarly work experience (Madera, Hebl, & Martin, 2009; Steinpreis, Anders, & Ritzke, 1999). Another poignant example is a study that has been repeated numerous times with similar results that showed minority candidates with ethnic-sounding names who sent résumés received up to 50% fewer invitations to interviews than the exact same résumés sent with more common names (Bertrand & Mullainathan, 2003). To overcome the human tendency to discriminate (in a swift sorting of the world into categories to process information), and categorize people and things into groups that may or may not reflect truth, people need assistance and training.

While a seemingly difficult task, it is possible to eliminate most bias from the selection process by taking certain steps that help search committees make objective and accurate decisions:

- Learn about bias and assumptions (see *Training the Committee*, p. 29).
- Make a conscious effort to overcome bias.
- Avoid common pitfalls by learning about typical challenges.
- Use diverse groups to make selection decisions.
- Charge the group with policing itself.
- Develop and use objective criteria.
- Use total criteria instead of overvaluing a single factor.
- Use catchphrases and other cues to provide committee members with less intimidating methods of opening discussions about possible issues.
- Rely on the support and expertise of a *diversity advocate*.

During initial training, many elements can be covered and training offered to equip the committee with search techniques and antibias skills. The best defense against bias is group decision making because the multiple perspectives, experiences, and backgrounds of the group's members provide for a greater knowledge base, deeper understanding, and broader awareness of all candidates and their assets and differences. *Diversity advocates* and ex officio members—so trained—are instrumental in supporting the committee in this area.

The section *Avoiding Bias in Interviews*, p. 95, offers standard phrases for committee members to use in awkward circumstances, such as when a committee member makes a statement that reflects a uniformed or biased position. These catchphrases are invaluable in "breaking the ice" and allowing committee members to collectively discuss the ideas behind an inappropriate statement. The key is creating a safe environment for the committee to be candid. Training to acknowledge that bias naturally exists, techniques to help address bias when it occurs, and the freedom and empowerment to police bias as a group, combined with group decision making, is the best approach to eliminating bias from selection decisions.

VIGNETTE Q
HR Prescreen or Minimal Qualifications Screening

Culling unqualified applicants can be a great service for HR to offer search committees, especially considering that committee members volunteer their time to serve. This practice of reviewing all and forwarding only those who measure up against a common standard profoundly affects each candidate's chances. Best practice approaches build in safeguards to ensure with great accuracy that the right candidates move on to the next round and the wrong candidates do not.

First, HR representatives or other staff who might be asked to perform such services require training, which should include the art of reviewing résumés and some orientation to the profession for which they are receiving materials. Second, the screening should be completed using a previously approved screening instrument. Third, regardless of whether a candidate is qualified, the candidate's materials should be forwarded to the search committee with the screening results indicated. This allows the committee chair or others to double-check the initial screening, if they so desire. Fourth, the committee chair, or at least one committee person who is an expert, should also review the entire candidate field to see if any candidates were overlooked inadvertently. These quality assurance techniques are advisable because HR representatives will never be subject matter experts and might miss the nuances of a given profession.

Another approach to the HR screen is for an HR representative to prepopulate a screening matrix (see Exhibit #12: *Screening Matrix*, p. 70) or other screening instrument with the results of each candidate's background already reviewed and documented. This detailed and intensive review will save a considerable amount of the committee's time. Instead of spending time reviewing and documenting the names and activities of candidates, the committee can concentrate on evaluating the richness of each individual's background. This sort of analysis and documentation is performed because committee members are volunteers and their time is best spent in actual decision making, not in documenting the particulars. Few HR departments will have the staff to support this sort of screening, but it is a valuable service for certain key or senior positions, or when the committee needs special handling.

thorough and fair. The biggest stumbling block occurs when committee members use different criteria. Different ideas about what defines a good candidate are fodder for disagreement and will ultimately undermine success. If evaluators do not agree upon the criteria they use, they will not agree upon what a good candidate looks like when they see him or her. This point cannot be underscored enough.

The screening criteria used will determine who is deemed most qualified. (Vignette W: *Since When Is Roger Federer Not Good Enough?* p. 126, provides an interesting exposé on this concept.) It is imperative

that the committee agree upon the criteria before its members evaluate candidates. Otherwise they will be comparing apples and oranges. If the number of peer-reviewed articles is less important than the type of journal, or if the best indicator of ability is a professional certification instead of a master's degree, decide this in advance. Can candidates demonstrate the needed competencies for success even though they have not held a specific position? For example, does work as a corporate trainer count as teaching experience? While there can be considerable debate surrounding which criteria are best, the only requirement is that they be agreed upon in advance. Without clarity, trouble lies ahead.

Determining Screening Criteria and Methods

A rigorous evaluation consists of multiple methods of screening candidates. For the initial review of written materials to be good, the committee must solicit the right materials. Therefore, the information needed should be determined in advance, and then asked for in the advertisement, if appropriate. For example, in faculty searches where candidates can be appointed at the full professor rank with tenure, it may be necessary to assess candidates' impact on the profession or their reputation as a part of the evaluation process. In these circumstances, letters of recommendation, editorial reviews of their publications, or an analysis of how many times their publications have been cited by others is valuable. Ask candidates to submit this and related information in their application.

Likewise, a director of student activities candidate may be asked to submit a portfolio of items used to promote student events or an annual plan of activities. For positions requiring both leadership and managerial ability, one must consider how and when to evaluate these criteria in the selection. One may evaluate managerial ability by positions held, accomplishments in those positions, and responses to interview questions. Leadership ability is more difficult to ascertain. Statements of leadership philosophy, interview questions, letters or recommendation, awards and honors, and reference checks are all potential ways of evaluating this ability, since it is less perceptible in written form. Subsequent evaluation methods may be included as well. Nonetheless, to evaluate candidates properly, one must largely determine the number and type of methods that will be used before advertising for the position.

Here again, we use the four primary sources of position information to determine how to evaluate candidates: the organizational analysis, position description, job advertisement, and committee *charge*. Each of these provides useful information to give a 360-degree view and the full context of the position within the organization. Determining selection criteria by using these sources to develop screening instruments starts off the screening and evaluation process in an expert fashion.

Screening Instruments

Using screening instruments is fundamental because they document the position's requirements and articulate the vision and expectations of the *appointing authority* and all others who have a stake in the position's success. Such instruments communicate the relative importance of each selection criterion to the search committee and drive the entire selection process. This prevents the interjection of personal preferences, prejudices, and petty biases—whether they are intentional or unintentional. Therefore, every search must include a written screening instrument used by all committee members.

Screening instruments ensure that everyone uses the same criteria in the same way each time. Other factors may be considered later, but initial screening of candidates should be totally objective. One can accomplish this by using previously identified and agreed-upon standards based upon position requirements and the needs of the organization. These principles should be applied in at least four stages of the selection process:

1. evaluate candidates' written application materials;
2. evaluate interviews (i.e., telephone, video, and in person);
3. use with other screening methods (e.g., presentations, *work samples*, portfolios, etc.); and
4. conduct reference checks.

The quality of a search rests with good criteria and methods, making screening instruments essential for fairness purposes. They help ensure that all candidates are compared to an agreed-upon standard instead of being judged capriciously.

Selection Criteria

Carefully chosen selection criteria give the committee an objective basis on which to judge applicants' qualitative differences. Here are some generic examples:

- Degree(s) (e.g., AA, BA, MA, PhD, JD, MSW, etc.)
- Degree major (e.g., business, finance, sociology, English, civil engineering, etc.)
- Institution and its reputation

- Institution type (e.g., research university, liberal arts college, community college, etc.)
- Academic program (e.g., curriculum, emphasis, reputation and ranking of the program, etc.)
- Years of experience
- Type of experience (e.g., generalist, specialist, etc.)
- Competencies
- Experience with _____
- Knowledge of _____
- Commitment to _____ (e.g., inter-disciplinary studies, Christian education, our mission, etc.)
- Ability to _____
- Familiarity with _____
- Demonstrated expertise in _____
- Ability to use particular tools (e.g., machines, hardware, software, etc.)
- Skill with particular methods (e.g., research methods, techniques, protocols, etc.)
- Training, internships, or other learning experiences
- Certifications, licensures, etc.
- Honors and awards
- Number of publications
- Type of publications (e.g., articles, books, online, etc.)
- Type of publisher (e.g., academic, trade, commercial, practitioner publication, etc.)
- Discipline, industry, field, profession, etc.
- Institution-specific criteria (e.g., service-learning, online teaching, assessment, etc.)
- Departmental criteria (e.g., willingness to work overtime, fund-raising or grant writing, advising and tutoring, etc.)
- Accreditation requirements (e.g., number of graduate credit hours, clinical experience, etc.)
- Personal characteristics
- Interpersonal skills
- Ability to communicate
- *Work samples* (e.g., writing samples, artwork, recordings, evaluations, etc.)
- Review of results of testing
- Other . . .

The potential selection criteria are almost endless. This is why only those specifically based upon the requirements of the position and organization—those that are derived from the four sources identified earlier (organizational analysis, position description, advertisement, and committee *charge*) should be used. Committees must not invent new criteria along the way that redefine a position, usurp the authority of the *appointing authority*, or interject bias and personal preference into the decision-making process. Such actions send the committee down a different path from the one intended.

Diversity Tip: As noted in chapter 1, it would not be unreasonable to use cultural competence or another selection criterion that includes experience with multicultural populations or familiarity with teaching, service, or counseling techniques that serve diverse populations if your students, customers, or clientele include diverse populations. Such criteria are inherent to the educational process and support many institutions' missions.

Screening and Selection Methods

Each screening technique has its advantages and disadvantages. Therefore, it is prudent to use multiple screening methods to make a sound hiring decision. One should use different techniques at different stages of the process with an increasingly smaller group of applicants. For example, the written material of all applicants is screened; however, only a small number of candidates may be offered a *telephone interview*, a smaller number is asked to complete a *work sample*, and an even smaller number may be invited to an on-site interview. Last, most often references and background checks are conducted only on the preferred candidate. Chapter 13, *Additional Screening Methods*, offers a plethora of options—not all typically used, but what should be considered for higher education.

CHAPTER 10

Evaluating Written Materials

EVALUATING WRITTEN APPLICATION MATERIALS often includes reviewing a cover letter and a résumé or curriculum vitae. As noted earlier, smart searches ensure that candidates submit materials with their initial application in which the committee is most interested, such as letters of recommendation, statements of teaching philosophy, transcripts, and portfolios. A well-crafted advertisement solicits from candidates the complete materials necessary to conduct a thorough screening and evaluation of the applicant pool. This is vital, because committee members will have to make initial judgments with only the information they have on hand at the review—each candidate's written application materials.

Rarely do faculty and staff who serve on search committees receive training on how to screen and evaluate written materials (see Exhibit #10: *How to Evaluate Résumés and CVs*); their knowledge and skill are assumed. But using a screening instrument at least guides committee members through the process. A best practice approach would be to ensure that at their initial meeting committee members discuss selection criteria and how they should be evaluated. As mentioned in the *Orienting and Training* section, p. 28, the ex officio member of the committee, an HR professional, an EEO/diversity officer, or a committee member who has professional expertise in this area can provide this instruction. Regardless of how the search is designed, the hiring decision is largely predetermined within the boundaries of this initial process stage. Here individuals graduate from names on paper—applicants—to potential candidates.

Each committee member makes private determinations of whom he or she wants to consider further while scouring through piles of paper, often at home or in the office during the wee hours of the evening. Members also may review applicant materials online on a computer screen, one by one. An applicant's chance of getting the job is usually determined at this time. If enough committee members do not favor the candidate, the committee as a whole is unlikely to discuss this person.

Rating and Ranking Candidates

It is more effective to rate candidates than to rank them; however, there is a place for both in the search process. Rating involves evaluating candidates against a defined standard. Ideally, each candidate is evaluated against criteria that are based on the position description, job advertisement, and *charge* to the committee. Rating candidates objectively ensures a degree of rigor and fairness in the selection process. Committee members rate each candidate's written application materials and interview(s), and they may also rate each in presentations or on other related measures. When the ratings of individual committee members are tabulated, a natural distribution usually occurs. This gives a relative comparison of candidates to one another in terms of their background against the factors that are considered most relevant to the position and institution.

A best practice approach to evaluating the written materials by individual committee members is assigning each applicant a nominal rating of Yes, No, or Maybe (i.e., 1, 2, or 3; Competitive, Qualified, Not Qualified; Consider Further, Hold, Do Not Consider). This three-tier approach allows the committee chair to tabulate members' responses and share a matrix of scores with the committee. It is not necessary for committee members to rank candidates at this point, as ranking is conducted more effectively by the committee as a whole when deliberating over the pool of applicants.

Ranking involves putting candidates in an order based upon their objective ratings or the previously agreed-upon standards. An organic ranking occurs by simply aggregating the ratings of individual committee members. This summary of ratings represents a natural

EXHIBIT #10
How to Evaluate Résumés and CVs

Allot sufficient time to screen all or a sizable portion of the résumés at once. Compare the credentials of applicants with the context of other applicants in mind.

- Create a rating standard that you will use throughout the résumé review.
- Avoid ranking candidates from best to least, 1 to "n."
- Review the position description before reviewing applicant materials.
- Review the advertisement for the vacant position.
- Review the *charge*.
- Use a predetermined screening instrument to evaluate candidates against objective criteria.
- Make comments, notes, or other observations on the screening instrument about each candidate. This will be a useful reminder when you start to discuss candidates with the committee as a whole.
- Use an agreed-upon rating scheme: Yes = consider further, Maybe = hold, No = do not consider further; 1 = very qualified, 2 = qualified, 3 = not qualified; 1 = poor, 10 = best.
- Avoid the applicant's name, address, gender, or other personal information to limit subconscious biases.
- On your first evaluation of résumés, do not overemphasize the format or writing style of the résumé; look instead for the quality of the content.
- Compare stated education and experience requirements with those listed on the résumé.
- Ensure that colleges attended also indicate that a degree was awarded.
- Ensure that the candidates are still employed in the most recent position—check dates.
- Compare employment history and its applicability to the position for which the candidates are applying (e.g., positions in similar industry, similar responsibilities, etc.); length of time in each position; promotions or awards received; and reason for leaving each position; check dates.
- Note gaps in employment but do not assume they were due to negative reasons (i.e., note whether this is addressed in the cover letter).
- Look for an excessive number of jobs in a short time.
- Note whether changes in position appear to be promotional, progressive, lateral moves, or simply changes.
- Notice whether there is a career pattern, an industry pattern, or a random collection of past jobs.
- Note special skills or intangible characteristics or experiences not required for the position and add these to comments (e.g., familiarity with certain computer software, alumna of your school, different degree, etc.); however, do not use such preferential criteria to qualify candidates.
- Make a list of questions about applicants that arise from reviewing their résumés.
- If necessary, screen the top group again to narrow down the candidates further.
- Group résumés into piles of yes, no, and maybe candidates. (If you have too many "yes" candidates, you might review the "yes" pile to narrow it down to a more manageable number. In addition, if you do not have sufficient "yes" candidates, re-review the "maybe" pile to see if you can increase the size of the pool of those considered.)
- Share your grouping with the committee chair.

One can use these considerations and others to guide a thorough evaluation of the competitiveness of applicants.

Used with permission from www.SearchCommittees.com.

starting point for committee deliberations. Committees can then scrutinize qualifications of only the top candidates based upon the strength of their combined rating. A new standard—often higher—is established once the group combines its collective insight to gain a greater understanding of the background and characteristics of each candidate, and compares and contrasts individual evaluations.

During the next round of evaluations, the top candidates are now evaluated against the additional considerations presented in the *committee's charge* and against any additional institutional or departmental criteria that were identified in the organizational analysis. After these evaluations are complete, the committee can rank the candidates to determine who will be interviewed.

Informed decisions and a solid ranking are not possible until after completely reviewing each candidate's written materials, and after a series of comparisons are made against agreed-upon criteria. Using an objective screening instrument is a prerequisite to all other forms of evaluation. Examples of screening devices commonly used by search committees appear in the following sections.

Selecting Candidates to Interview

Selecting candidates for on-campus interviews involves objective screening to evaluate written application materials and culling candidates down to a manageable number. Then, one or more additional screening methods are applied before proceeding further. It is tempting to simply talk over a group of candidates all of whom received high marks from committee members, and then choose from among the group through intense debate. While this might be easy if only a handful of candidates stand out, it is far more likely that some committee members voted yes to two dozen candidates whereas others said yes to only one or two. An effort must be made to come to group consensus about what factors within each selection criteria are deemed good, better, and best. A recommended approach would be to use another screening method to help deliberations (see chapter 13, *Additional Screening Methods*).

Since not every selection criterion can be listed in an advertisement or is easily articulated, other criteria

from the *committee charge*, organizational analysis, advertisement, and job description can weigh in at this stage of the process. Preferred criteria also start to gain importance after committee members have made their initial objective evaluations. These criteria can be evaluated by using an additional screening method such as a questionnaire sent to candidates still under consideration (see chapter 13, *Additional Screening Methods*). Similar questions can be posed in *telephone or video interviews* as well. Interviewing four to eight candidates this way can pinpoint the pool of candidates who present better on paper than they do in real life.

After identifying competitive candidates for further consideration, the committee must determine how many should be invited to campus. Most organizations interview the top three in person. If a committee considers interviewing more than three or four candidates in person, an additional, alternative screening method should be considered. This decreases the potential indecision that adds time, effort, and cost to a search without adding much value because, at the end of the process, only one person will be hired. Additional screening is time well spent to manage the number of finalists interviewed in person, not to mention the added rigor gained by the use of an additional screening method.

Regardless of how the committee proceeds, dozens of details are involved in preparing for interviews. Chapter 11 provides expert advice on this process. Advice to the committee includes getting help from ex officio members with the many administrative and logistical details that often prove cumbersome to the volunteers conducting the search.

Screening Instrument Examples

At least four different categories of screening devices can be used to evaluate candidates' written application materials. Examples of typical screening instruments are qualitative, quantitative, checklists, and matrix-type screening devices as shown in Exhibits #11–14. (*Note*: The different methods discussed in the following exhibits and the techniques included in the interview evaluation instruments section can be combined or adapted creatively to produce a variety of screening tools.)

EXHIBIT #11
Screening Checklist

A screening checklist can help search committee members quickly verify whether each candidate has the required qualifications. A checklist is often a simple delineation of the required and preferred criteria listed in the advertisement or *position announcement*. A more complete evaluation includes the major position requirements documented in the position description, *charge*, and organizational analysis, notwithstanding the fact that not all of the requirements of a position can be determined or evaluated from written materials. The checklist nonetheless ensures that applicants are compared against the essential selection criteria.

The following checklist is an example of a review created from an ad for a career placement counselor:

A bachelor's degree and demonstrated experience with career counseling and job placement are required. The ideal candidate will also possess the following characteristics: experience with individual and group counseling as well as case management techniques. The ability to develop and deliver training materials and a proficiency with the technologies used in the profession are also necessary for success in this position. Knowledge of employment trends and alumni affairs is a desirable qualification. A master's degree, counseling licensure or certification, and experience in higher education are preferred criteria.

Screening Checklist

Candidate's Name _____

Rated by _____   **Date:** _____

Required Qualifications:	Yes	No
Bachelor's degree	_____	_____
Demonstrated experience in the field	_____	_____
Individual counseling experience	_____	_____
Group counseling experience	_____	_____
Multicultural counseling techniques experience	_____	_____
Training knowledge and skill	_____	_____
Technology proficiency	_____	_____
Proficiency with written communication	_____	_____
Preferred Qualifications:	_____	_____
Master's degree	_____	_____
Professional licensure or certification	_____	_____
Higher education experience	_____	_____
Knowledge of employment trends	_____	_____
Alumni experience	_____	_____
Experience with internships and cooperative education	_____	_____

List Candidate's Other Characteristics (e.g., degree field[s], special skills, etc.):

Comments/Notes:

Consider Further?   Yes _____ No _____ Maybe _____

EXHIBIT #12
Screening Matrix

A screening matrix provides an objective method of comparing candidates both against a standard and to other candidates. This relative evaluation can simplify the process of selecting which candidates to consider further. It also provides a convenient means of spotting trends among applicants, such as the average number of years' experience among applicants. Having a spreadsheet that allows committee members to enter comments of an appropriate length, or using legal-size paper for the same purpose allows matrices to strike a balance between brevity and completeness with just enough information to discern better-qualified candidates. Again, the best matrices include criteria garnered from the position description, advertisement, *committee charge*, and organizational analysis, as appropriate.

The following advertisement and matrix demonstrates the use of selection criteria for a career center director:

Master's degree in related field required, doctoral degree preferred. Minimum five years' experience in career development and employer relations required. Budget and staff management experience as well as a command of business and industry employment trends are also required. Past success cultivating relationships with a diverse mix of student employers is also desirable.

Candidate's Name	Degree	Applicable Experience in Field	Budget & Supervision Management Experience	Industry, Connections, & Placement Experience	Engagement in Profession	Comments	Advance Candidate to Next Round of Screening
	Type & Field	Number of Years	Yes/No	Yes/No	Describe		Yes/No/ Maybe
Sophia Holeman	MBA	2	Yes	Some	No		No
Gracie Hill	PhD Psychology	4	None indicated	Yes	Student club advisor	Rising star, limited experience	Maybe
Hector Gonzalez	MA Counseling	16	Yes	Yes	Yes, writes articles	Former journal editor	Yes
Alexander Jones	MA Student Personnel	12	Yes	Yes	Various memberships		Yes

EXHIBIT #13
Narrative or Qualitative Screening Instrument

Using a qualitative screening instrument allows a more meticulous and nuanced evaluation of candidates. This multidimensional approach provides individual details, a summary of candidates on each criterion, and an overview of individual candidates as a whole—that is, including the complementariness of the candidate's qualifications and characteristics with required and preferred criteria. Typically, this method analyzes the strengths and weaknesses of candidates by acknowledging that few, if any, candidates are ever perfect in every way.

The sample screening device is for an assistant professor position.

Candidate's Name: _____

Title: _____ **Institution:** _____

Teaching effectiveness/potential:

Research and publication record/potential:

Service-learning knowledge or experience:

Is the candidate's teaching philosophy consistent with the mission of this institution?

Which courses has the candidate taught at the undergraduate level?

What is the degree to which the candidate has experience with our type of students (e.g., commuter, graduate, underrepresented, veteran, or older students)?

What are the candidate's strengths as a scholar?

What are the candidate's weaknesses?

Other considerations:

Consider further _____

Maybe _____

Do not consider further _____

Reviewer's Name: _____ **Date:** _____

EXHIBIT #14
Quantitative Screening Device

For those who are more comfortable using numbers to assess different phenomena, the quantitative screening method is a suitable tool. An advantage of this approach is that it provides an intuitive method of describing the relative degree to which a candidate measures up against agreed-upon criteria. Each committee member will have a slightly different definition of what is "average," "good," or "great," so each one's assessment of candidates will vary—despite the use of the same numerical scale. Nonetheless, a quantitative screening instrument can speed up deliberations by using a common framework and vocabulary to compare candidates.

If and how selection criteria will be weighted and tabulated should be determined when the screening instrument is designed. Having a doctoral degree is not necessarily worth twice the "points" as a master's degree in a numbering scheme, having six years' experience is not necessarily twice as good as having three years of experience, and there is no way of objectively valuing the difference in having served in four different positions compared to having served in two positions for longer periods. Agreement on descriptions and weightings is essential. As long as quantitative devices are used as a general guide and not a definitive assessment, they can be very effective selection techniques.

The following is a sample quantitative screening device for a director of financial aid position

Quantitative Screening Device

Candidate's Name: _____

Rating Scale: 0 = None; 1 = Low; 2 = Average; 3 = High

1. Managerial Skills & Experience   _____

     Written communication
     Organizational skills
     Planning experience
     Budgeting experience
     Supervisory experience
     Conflict management experience

2. Financial Aid Knowledge & Experience   _____

     Knowledge of federal financial aid rules
     Loan experience
     Scholarships
     Fellowships
     Endowment/foundation experience
     State financial programs

3. Professional Activities   _____

     Professional development activities
     Membership/leadership in professional associations
     Publications/presentations/research
     Knowledge of industry trends
     Awards or honors

4. Evidence of Ability to Work With Others   _____

     Work with students & families
     Work with faculty
     Work with staff/administrators
     Multicultural student experience

                                   TOTAL SCORE _____

Committee Member's Name: _____   **Date**: _____

CHAPTER 11

Preparing for Interviews

AFTER ON-CAMPUS INTERVIEW FINALISTS have been selected, the committee must decide how the candidates will be evaluated, who will evaluate them, and how the overall interview will be conducted. A recommended approach is for an HR professional to advise the committee chair and members about how to structure and manage the interview process and help the group determine how many interviews and interview types will be used. Moreover, an HR professional, an ex officio committee member, or a *staff assistant* assigned to the committee can also assist the committee chair in arranging all of the administrative and logistical details. This is difficult if one does not do this sort of thing often and is not as familiar with campus policies and procedures. This is one of the instances where HR advice and assistance is priceless.

Interview or Interviews?

The on-campus interview process consists of an interview with the search committee at a minimum, but will also likely include many other opportunities to screen and evaluate candidates. A deliberate approach to this process establishes each activity's purpose in advance, determines the participants, and clarifies the role of each participant in the selection decision. It is a good idea to invite department members to a teaching demonstration or town hall gathering if they are a part of the interview process. It is never wise to forget to include their input in the selection process. Worse yet, if the committee selects a candidate other than a popular front-runner from such events, its credibility is undermined. Determining who will be involved in the interview and how and when their input will be gathered and incorporated into the decision-making process must be determined in advance. Continuing the shared governance framework as a guiding principle in the search process, committees should be as inclusive as possible by finding ways of involving all stakeholders for the position in the selection process.

Types of Interviews

While a search committee might consist of only five members, dozens can be involved in the campus interview process. Therefore, the interview is more than likely a series of interview events. Here is a sample of the many potential types of interviews used in higher education:

Basic Interview (one-on-one): a hiring manager or other campus representative sits with an interviewee and holds a structured conversation about the candidate's qualifications and abilities and his or her relative match to the institution's needs.

Panel Interviews (classic search committee format): consists of a group of several faculty or staff members evaluating a candidate using a common screening instrument.

Telephone Interviews: are typically short interviews held via conference calls to determine who will be invited to campus for a regular on-site interview.

Video Interviews: are held via video technology and are valuable in determining who will be invited to campus for a regular on-site interview. Candidates participate through the use of a personal video camera using Internet technology, or they are asked to go to a predetermined facility at a designated time to interact and converse with the search committee.

Open Forums or Town Hall Meetings: are meet-and-greet-type sessions wherein any campus community member or invitee can drop in to interact with the candidate. These can be structured or unstructured, free-flowing events to give the candidate and the campus community a general impression of one another. Often these question-and-answer sessions are preceded by a short presentation to the audience about the candidate's background or approach to work, or on another topic of interest to the group.

Group Interviews: are interviews held in a variety of formats by constituent group members who are not a part of the search committee (e.g., faculty senate leaders, honors program committee, entire department, etc.) and can be structured interviews to further screen a candidate for his or her competence and *organizational fit.*

Meals and Receptions: are social occasions to introduce the finalist to the community and give the community a chance to interact with or screen the candidate.

Presentations: are teaching demonstrations, speeches, or training events where candidates present on either a predetermined or self-selected topic, which gives the search committee and community the opportunity to further evaluate the candidate.

Interviewing With Governing Boards: Governing boards alone have the responsibility and authority to select chief executives. Typically, they use a search consultant or committee to make a recommendation, and then they interview one or more finalists. They may also simply interview a sole finalist at their discretion after a search committee has recommended a candidate.

Vice presidents and other senior executives are often introduced to and sometimes interviewed by governing board members after the chief executive has already made a preliminary selection decision. This courtesy type of interview is not usually used to select candidates; however, at the peril of the candidate who does not present well, governing boards almost always have veto authority.

Equal Opportunity Interviews: many institutions practice having some applicants interview with the AA/equal opportunity/chief diversity officer, *diversity advocate,* or other institutional representative charged with matters related to diversity and inclusion. While the practice varies according to which positions are interviewed (e.g., faculty, senior administrators, certain key staff, etc.) and who interviews the candidates, the purpose of such interviews is not always clear. As with all interviews, these meetings' importance should be made transparent and how the information gleaned from these interviewees will be used in the selection process must be clarified and agreed upon.

Screening Calls (conversations with consultants, search committee chairs, or HR staff): someone is charged with contacting candidates to gather more information when a semifinalist is identified, but important additional information about the candidate is needed to determine whether he or she will be invited to an interview. Though these are not formal interviews, they might as well be since information gleaned from them is used to evaluate candidates.

Airport Interviews: are usually held away from campus for executive positions and are designed to evaluate 6–12 candidates quickly. These are held in airports or similar locations convenient for getting a large number of busy people in and out for a prescreening interview. This preserves the privacy of candidates, maintains the integrity of the selection process, and keeps the identity of candidates confidential to avoid arousing unnecessary curiosity on campus.

Special Interviewing Occasions: any of an assortment of meetings or conversations with candidates are held to further evaluate their qualifications and *organizational fit* for employment. These may include occasions such as second interviews, coffee, follow-up conversations in person or over the phone, visits to the candidate's home campus, and numerous other interactions. While they may be viewed as social or informal occasions, they are used to either select or disqualify a candidate from consideration.

The various types of interviews vary in their degree or rigor, formality, and structure. Some appear to be unstructured and informal; however, information from these events is almost always used in the selection process to select candidates or disqualify others from further consideration. A word to the wise for candidates is to assume that every interaction with a potential employer can and will be used to determine the candidate's suitability for employment.

Stakeholder Involvement in Interviews

Most candidates for faculty, administrative, and professional positions meet with the search committee and with others with whom they will interact once hired. Stakeholders may include prospective peers, those who report directly, subordinates, customers, faculty, students, alumni, and others. Faculty senate leaders might meet with faculty candidates, professors might meet with librarian candidates, students might meet with counselor and student activity candidates, budget managers might meet with comptroller candidates, various employee groups should meet with HR director candidates, and so on. Depending upon the position, candidates might meet with the chief academic officer, deans, department chairs, vice presidents, provosts, the president, or even community officials. As a result, the interview often takes a half- to a full day, depending on the position in question. For senior academic and administrative positions, a day and a half or two days may be needed. Exhibit #15: *Typical Interview Day Schedule* presents the activities of a typical interview day.

The type and number of interviews are correlated with the level of the position, who will be involved in the selection process, and how candidates will be evaluated. Determining the number and type to be held is a circular process as each depends upon the other. Yet the more involvement with the candidate, the more information that is gathered, which is likely an advantage for the organization. The only limitation is in time and resources balanced by the fact that the organization is potentially making a multimillion-dollar decision. The type and number of interviews is similar to the conundrum of "which came first, the chicken or the egg?"

A wise approach to this dilemma is to err on the side of more when possible. Nonetheless, each person who has an opportunity to interact with a candidate must have the opportunity to share his or her informed opinion with the search committee. A recommended approach is to develop a feedback instrument that allows stakeholders to share their opinions or assessments with the search committee. Experience tells us that this feedback should follow these guidelines: (a) it should be in written form only, (b) it should be based upon predetermined criteria defined by the search committee, and (c) it should be provided immediately after each candidate interviews.

Committee members will never have enough time to talk to every stakeholder to get their feedback individually—nor would they want to do so. It would also be prudent to avoid numerous hallway conversations between different individuals and committee members. Furthermore, having a feedback tool helps to avoid politics and reduce unnecessary advocacy for certain candidates by different factions of the community. This is precisely why search committees should not ask stakeholders to rank or rate candidates. They should ask for their feedback only on a *few* predetermined criteria established in advance by the

committee. (See Exhibit #26: *Group Feedback Instrument for Town Hall Meetings or Open Forums,* p. 93, along with other instruments to evaluate the interview process.) It is the role of the search committee to assimilate this feedback and determine the competitiveness of candidates.

Web-Based Screening Instruments

Another recommendation is for the group feedback instrument to be delivered online instead of in paper form. A simple Web survey can gather feedback about candidates. This expedites the process of gathering information and allows for quick tabulation and analysis of the feedback about candidates. A reiteration of one tip offered earlier is to make the survey available immediately after each candidate has interviewed. Campus community members should provide their feedback while their impressions are fresh and should not wait until after all candidates have been interviewed. This approach avoids community members' either forgetting key information or attempting to rank candidates.

Those Pesky Senior Leaders and Their Role in the Process

When candidates meet with leaders—presidents, vice presidents, provosts, deans, and so on—the committee should agree with these leaders in advance on the role and purpose of their interviews. The leaders should be advised that their role is to evaluate *organizational fit*, vision, potential, or some other conceptual idea. It is unwise to have a professional difference of opinion with leaders about whether a candidate is qualified, competent, or competitive, especially since their determination will be based upon limited information gathered in a short period compared with the committee, which has much more information compiled over a longer time and more interactions. Nonetheless, the appointing authority's, or other official's, professional opinions and judgments are sound, and they are honed from years of experience and success.

Leaders will ultimately sign off on the committee's recommendation, so a strong difference of opinion with the committee undermines the entire search process and discounts the role, function, time, effort,

EXHIBIT #15
Typical Interview Day Schedule

8:30–9:00 a.m.

Meet With Host

(e.g., search committee chair, staff member, HR, other host, etc.)

9:00–9:30 a.m.

Campus Tour

9:30–10:30 a.m.

Meet With *Appointing Authority*

10:30–10:45 a.m.

Break

10:45 a.m.–12:15 p.m.

Interview With Search Committee

12:15–1:15 p.m.

Lunch

(e.g., with *appointing authority*, department, peers, other stakeholders, etc.)

1:15–1:30 p.m.

Break and Preparation for Presentation

1:30–2:30 p.m.

Presentation

2:30–3:00 p.m.

Meet With Other Stakeholders

3:00–4:00

Participate in Town Hall Meeting

4:00–4:15 p.m.

Benefits Brief

4:15–4:30 p.m.

Exit Interview With HR Representative

usefulness, and judgment of the committee. This situation can be avoided by simply agreeing in advance that leaders are evaluating candidates for a specific purpose that is noted and agreed upon. A friendly and professional way of shaping this process is to offer the leader a screening instrument that is tailor made for his or her role in the process.

Here is a clever example that might have the intended effect. If diversity, service-learning, research orientation, community involvement, or a similar concept is a part of the institution's strategic plan, a part of the bully pulpit of the leader, or part of an institution or college/school initiative, then ask the leader to emphasize this in his or her meeting with candidates. A screening instrument with three to five questions in one or two of these areas will channel leaders in the right direction. It will enhance the rigor of the search, help to determine *organizational fit*, and help to clarify the role and function of all involved in the search process. (See Exhibit #27: *Leader's Assessment of Candidates Based Upon Institutional Priorities*, p. 94, along with other instruments to evaluate the interview process.)

Keeping Notes and Keeping Track of the Process

Keeping track of the many interviews, events, and stakeholders can be a daunting task. The search committee chair should assign at least one search committee member to attend all interview activities (e.g., open forums, presentations, stakeholder group interviews, etc.) where possible and appropriate. This person's attendance provides some continuity of activity and oversight over the process. Where possible and appropriate, basic notes should be recorded. Note taking should be simple and procedural and should capture only essential information (see Exhibit #16: *Minutes of the Meetings: Keeping Track of Proceedings*). General notes can be compiled into one master document that summarizes an entire interview day.

Coordinating the Campus Visit

There are a lot of moving parts in the process of communicating with candidates and inviting them to

an interview. Some are informing stakeholders and various other constituent groups, coordinating their involvement in the process, handling candidate travel, scheduling meeting rooms, and arranging catering and other logistics. As noted earlier, many of these activities should be coordinated, or at least facilitated, by HR, an ex officio member, or a staff assistant so the committee can concentrate on evaluating candidates. If the staffing, policies, and practices of your campus do not support this approach, then the committee chair should assign different committee members with responsibility for handling such arrangements. The committee chair may also ask the hiring department to assist with the many administrative and logistical requirements of arranging and holding on-site interviews.

Exhibit #17: *Interview Preparation Checklist* suggests a few considerations when inviting candidates to campus. Since on-campus interviews will likely involve multiple meetings, events, meals, functions, and many different people, the committee chair should send candidates a schedule of events in advance. The schedule should note the names and titles of the individuals with whom the candidate will interact. Copies of the schedule should be given to these individuals and should identify those responsible for escorting the candidate to and from meetings. This information can accompany a welcome package that should be sent to all interviewees (see Exhibit #18: *Welcome Package for Interviewees*).

Making Travel Arrangements and Accommodations

The search committee should notify each candidate in writing of the institution's travel and accommodation policies. Candidates should know before they visit the campus which expenses the institution will reimburse them for. Depending upon the distance traveled, lodging may or may not be reimbursable, just as airfare to one area airport may be reimbursable, whereas airfare to another area airport may not be. For instance, one of these notifications should indicate whether to rent a car at area airports or train stations or to hire a taxi (or whether a host will pick up the candidate). The search committee should ask the HR department or business office to advise candidates about such matters or provide user-friendly written descriptions of

EXHIBIT #16
Minutes of the Meetings
Keeping Track of Proceedings

The record of the proceedings of a search committee need not be extensive or involved; however, there must be records documenting how the committee progressed through its work. Such documentation is necessary for regulatory purposes—in case the search is challenged—but is also a quality assurance measure. A practical technique is to keep a simple bulleted list or a simple narrative of major activities.

Dean of Natural Sciences Search

Bulleted List

September 15, 2014

- Committee met for its first meeting.
- Dr. Hernandez, committee chair, welcomed everyone and thanked us for our service.
- The committee received its *charge* from the provost.
- Committee established a meeting schedule.
- Received training and orientation from HR manager.
- There have been 64 applicants so far.
- Discussed the screening matrix.
- Made assignments to complete before the next meeting.

September 29, 2014

- Committee reviewed the top 21 candidates based upon the voting of candidate résumés sent by the chair between meetings.
- Preferred criteria and *committee charge* used to narrow list of candidates.
- Committee agreed to set up telephone interviews with seven candidates after deliberations.
- Dale Jones agreed to arrange for a meeting room, teleconference equipment, and refreshments.
- Everyone was asked to draft one question and send it to the committee chair.

Search Committee Minutes

(Narrative Version)

September 15, 2014

"The committee met for the first time, even though the committee had received several pieces of correspondence from the chair over recent weeks. By the time of the first meeting, we had already had a chance to review the search committee materials, including a written version of the *charge*, the committee's timetable, the job description, advertisement, and screening matrix. The committee spent the majority of the time receiving training from the HR department and its *charge* from the provost. After the training we planned what we would do over the coming weeks."

"Specifically, we were asked to review the application materials for all 64 applicants within the next 10 days using the screening matrix that was provided. At the next meeting we plan to talk about the best candidates. Before the meeting we have to send a list to the committee chair of the candidates whom we rate highly. He will tabulate the votes and have the staff assistant make copies of the materials of the candidates who receive the most votes."

The committee chair should either take notes or assign a note taker to keep track of the activities of the committee. These records help construct or deconstruct the committee's activities after the search is over.

EXHIBIT #17

Interview Preparation Checklist

Here is a typical list of activities that are necessary to plan a successful campus visit:

- Prepare and send *welcome package* to interviewee.
- Confirm travel and lodging arrangements.
- Arrange transportation from airport or other location (arrange parking, if necessary).
- Arrange tour of local community (if appropriate).
- Arrange campus tour.
- Schedule meeting with search committee.
- Schedule meeting with *hiring authority*.
- Schedule meeting with chief executive, provost, vice president, as appropriate.
- Schedule meeting with any appropriate standing committee or group.
- Schedule meeting with EEO/chief diversity officer/diversity and equity representative, as appropriate.
- Schedule meeting with an HR representative who will discuss benefits (see *Benefits Briefs: Recruiting With Total Compensation*, p. 148).
- Schedule candidate's presentation.
- Obtain meeting and presentation rooms.
- Arrange for audiovisual support, if necessary.
- Plan for meals and breaks, as appropriate.
- Send communication and confirm schedule and arrangements with all involved (including candidate).
- Assign hosts to escort candidates from place to place on campus.

---

the same. Similarly, candidates should be notified of any special arrangements with travel agencies, rental car companies, hotels, and restaurants. Furthermore, all candidates should be informed that they will be assisted by the HR department or another department with any special accommodations they may require due to a disability or other consideration.

Welcoming and Hosting Candidates

The committee chair is usually the chief host who will often seek volunteers or assign committee members to host candidates. Committee members may be responsible for picking a candidate up from the airport, taking him or her on a tour of the campus, having dinner with him or her, and answering questions about the position in question or about the selection process. At this stage, the committee is both evaluating and

recruiting the candidate. To prepare the candidate for his or her big day, the individual should receive a package of information from the institution. Exhibit #18: *Welcome Package for Interviewees* provides a sample list of information to orient the candidate, prepare him or her for the interview, and recruit the candidate— that is, create a favorable impression of the college or university.

Many of the intangibles, such as how candidates are treated, can make the difference between who accepts or declines an offer of employment. During committee orientation members should be advised to be on their best professional behavior when communicating or interacting with candidates. Colleagues who make offhand or disparaging comments about the campus, the community, or the institution's leadership will give candidates reasons to seek employment elsewhere. Committees should police themselves and ensure that they are professional in every interaction with the

EXHIBIT #18
Welcome Package for Interviewees

Here is a sample list of information that could be mailed, shared electronically, or handed to candidates who are invited to campus for an interview:

- Employee/faculty handbook
- Benefits synopsis
- College or university catalog
- Departmental brochure
- Organizational chart (e.g., department, institution, etc.)
- History of institution
- Annual reports
- Statement of mission, goals, objectives, and initiatives
- Links to pertinent websites
- Travel policies related to the cost and reimbursement expenses for the interview
- Directions to the campus
- Information on parking or ground transportation related to the campus visit
- Information from the local chamber of commerce or area tourism authority (e.g., about housing, schools, or other relocation information, etc.)
- Favorable articles about the department, institution, or community
- Promotional materials
- Student admission brochures
- A welcome letter from the committee chair

VIGNETTE R
Dating Game

Regardless of who invited whom to the dance, interviewing is an important recruiting activity as well as a traditional screening and evaluation process. While the college or university has the upper hand, the candidate is also deciding whether to accept an offer and commit to the institution. In a bit of a tango—it takes two—the candidate is also watching your every move. He or she is trying to determine whether your campus is a nice place to work, if the colleagues (family members) are nice, and whether he or she will like the place.

Just like people on a first date, candidates may be thinking,

I am not going to divulge any negative information about myself until after you have fallen in love with me (i.e., made me an offer, and maybe until after I have started work). Therefore, your due diligence is necessary to find my flaws through observation, direct questioning, or deep evaluation because after we both have committed we are stuck with one another—unless, of course, we go through a drawn-out, painful, and expensive divorce (i.e., termination process). So, let's just take our time and get it right up front. You should treat me nicely and be fair, but hold me accountable. I will try not to take offense when you ask me difficult questions, pry into my background and relationships (i.e., past employers), and verify my history and determine whether I am who I say I am (i.e., background check).

candidate, whether in the interview, during dinner, or walking between meetings. After all, each member of the search committee is expected to be an effective ambassador for the institution, a role that is essential in the recruitment and selection process (See Vignette R: *Dating Game*).

Diversity Tip: Some institutions follow the practice of having candidates interview with the chief diversity officer, a *diversity advocate*, or others who represent that institution's interests related to diversity as a way of communicating the institution's commitment to diversity. The presumption is often that such *equal opportunity interviews* can be a way of making minority candidates feel welcome, particularly when there aren't many minority members participating in the interview process (i.e., in cases where the campus, search committee, and/or other stakeholders are not visually very diverse). However, this practice should be examined to ensure that candidates are not provided with additional interviews based upon their demographic profile. If such interviews are afforded to one candidate, all candidates should be given the same opportunity or scrutiny. This is the only way to signal the institution's commitment to diversity to all candidates.

CHAPTER 12

Interviewing

THE MOST IMPORTANT PART of the selection process is the interview, and the most important part of the interview is asking questions. The interview, where key decisions are made, is a meeting between a person seeking employment and one or more employer representatives who ask questions about the interviewee's background and experiences to determine the degree to which his or her qualifications and personal characteristics are a match with the employer's needs. Most institutions will interview two to four candidates before making an offer of employment to the chosen finalist. A defining characteristic of the search committee process is the use of *panel* or *group interviews*. Additionally, there are numerous details and considerations to make the process unfold smoothly; Exhibit #19: *Tips for Conducting the Interview* provides a few helpful hints for conducting a good interview.

should be used in conjunction with other screening methods. Although interviews are necessary, they are not sufficient alone for a quality search.

To improve interviews, it is advisable to (a) use a structured interview format for all interviews, (b) have multiple interviews of each candidate, and (c) use additional screening methods in conjunction with interviews. An example of a rigorous selection process would include telephone interviews of semifinalists; having separate interviews with the search committee, hiring manager, and other stakeholders; and having finalists complete a work sample as a part of their on-campus interview. Having faculty and administrative candidates make another presentation is one way of conducting a thorough interview process. A collection of these activities during the interview day is a recipe for success.

Structure and Rigor in Interviews

When interviews are performed well, they are structured conversations. A structured interview consists of a slate of questions that are formulated around the predefined requirements of the position and a predefined evaluation method. Ideally, questions quiz interviewees on their experience and abilities related to criteria established in the job description, advertisement, and *committee charge*. The common slate of questions asked of all interviewees ensures a degree of fairness, consistency, and rigor in the selection process. An interview evaluation instrument ensures that the evaluation is objective and is not just a popularity or beauty contest.

Though valuable, experts indicate that interviews are among the most unreliable screening methods for selecting candidates with regard for their ability to predict the success of a candidate in a given position (Mathis & Jackson, 2003). To enhance the rigor and success of the selection process, interviews always

Multiple Stakeholders, Multiple Interviews

A word of advice regarding multiple interviews—when candidates are asked to participate in various interviews, the search committee chair must be aware of the place and purpose of each separate interview and how information gathered will be used in the selection process. If a candidate for the dean of arts and science is interviewed by the leaders of the faculty senate, does the senate provide advice, suggestions, comments, or a recommendation to the search committee, the search committee chair, or the *appointing authority*? Will this information be conveyed verbally or in writing? Will the committee be asked to take notes or complete a predetermined feedback form? When will this information be provided—as soon as possible, or before the search committee meets to deliberate? Do comments come from an appointed leader of the group or by each individual separately? If the faculty senate is vehemently opposed to the preferred candidate, how does that information weigh against

---

EXHIBIT #19
Tips for Conducting the Interview

Before the Interview
- Reserve an appropriate meeting room.
- Review the job description, advertisement, and *charge*.
- Draft and agree upon the interview questions to be asked.
- Review the candidate's résumé/CV and application materials.
- Agree on the format for the interview.
- Ensure that you know and can identify the quality indicators of candidates' ability to perform the job.

During the Interview
- Introduce committee members.
- Attempt to establish rapport with the candidate with a minute or two of small talk.
- Describe the format of the interview.
- Ask open-ended informational, situational, and behavioral questions.
- Let the applicant do most of the talking.
- Keep the interview on track.
- Observe nonverbal behavior.
- Take notes.
- Leave time for the candidate to ask questions at the end.
- Describe the remainder of the search process and the time frame.
- Ask if you can check references and pursue references not listed on the résumé.
- Give the candidate a point of contact in case he or she has future questions.
- Thank the candidate for his or her time.

After the Interview
- Review notes and complete the evaluation of the candidate on a screening instrument.
- Document any other pertinent matters related to the interview.
- As a committee, discuss the candidate and summarize his or her strengths and weaknesses.

---

the recommendation of the committee or the wishes of the *appointing authority*? The shared governance process invites input, so this input must be gathered and considered in a deliberate, systematic, and professional manner.

The central point here is that each participant in the search committee process should know what his or her role is and how it fits into the selection process. If faculty senate leaders are invited to participate, they should understand and agree to their role. Ideally, it is a structured interview, with a predefined purpose, using a feedback form that summarizes the strengths and weaknesses of a candidate on a single form, which is sent to the committee chair immediately after the interview is completed. Senate leaders should not share their views

with anyone else and should be held to the same confidentiality standards as everyone else in the process. A good predefined purpose for faculty senate leaders is to evaluate a dean candidate's understanding and support of shared governance, not to evaluate whether the candidate is qualified to lead the college—that is the role of the search committee (also see Exhibit #26: *Group Feedback Instrument for Town Hall Meetings or Open Forums*).

In summary, interviews are the most important part of the selection process and should be organized and evaluated in a structured format with selection criteria drawn from the position description, advertisement, organizational analysis, and *committee charge*. Everyone in the process should know his or her role in the process in advance. Ideally, multiple interviews should take place, along with other screening methods to increase the rigor of the selection process.

Conducting the Interview

Structured interviews imply a slate of questions deliberately developed to mirror the core requirements of the position, the use of a screening instrument to evaluate responses, and a coordinated effort by the committee to ask and follow up on key questions. The advantages of using a screening instrument to evaluate candidates apply here as well as they do for evaluating written application materials. Such instruments demonstrate due diligence, guarantee connection to the priorities for the position, reduce bias, and ensure that everyone is operating from the same assumptions. (Three examples are provided for committee use: Exhibits #21, #22, and #23.)

Conducting effective interviews is also an art. Some candidates put on a good show that masks their true capabilities. The goal is to select the best candidate for the position, not the person who is able to mask his or her inability to perform the job behind a great interview performance. Therefore, the conduct of the interview and the questions asked must be developed and executed deliberately.

In addition to a structured interview with well-crafted, job-specific questions that will elicit qualitative responses that differentiate among candidates, multiple interviews give the committee the best chance of learning the true character and capability of candidates. Therefore, using more than one type of interview is advisable (see *Types of Interviews*, p. 84). Like multiple interviews, extending the length of the typical interview adds rigor. Most search committee interviews are 60 minutes long and consist of a slate of 10 to 12 questions. While this is a prudent pattern, it may not be thorough enough to evaluate candidates and allow for sufficient follow-up questions. A 75- to 90-minute time frame allows for a more thorough search committee interview.

Scheduling extra time allows the committee to evaluate for *organizational fit* as well as competiveness (see *Evaluating Organizational Fit: Defining and Documenting Fit*, p. 108). If candidates were asked to complete a work sample or submit additional materials prior to the interview—this is recommended—the additional time can also be used to discuss their submission. An extended interview also leaves ample time

for the candidate to ask the committee questions. The degree to which the candidate is prepared and the type of questions he or she asks can be quite telling.

Follow-Up and Candidate-Specific Questions

While all candidates should be asked the same slate of questions to ensure fairness and rigor in the selection process, follow-up questions can and should vary from candidate to candidate. Additionally, at least one or two questions should be specific for each candidate based upon his or her particular background. Here are some examples:

- In your graduate education, did you learn how to apply the "xyz" technique?
- Can you tell us how many assistant or associate provosts there were in your office?
- What were the reporting relationships of each assistant provost, and how did your work responsibilities compare to his or hers?
- You have coauthored a number of publications; why have you chosen to do so in contrast to conducting research by yourself or submitting publications as an individual author?
- On your résumé you indicate that you increased your department's success despite budget cuts. How did you do that?

Clearly, the goal is to evaluate all candidates fairly, but it is negligent not to ask candidates specific questions about their past that are pertinent to the position for which they are interviewing.

Of course, equal opportunity advocates advance appropriate caution with regard to treating candidates differently. Such caution is valid if the treatment is different due to a candidate's race, gender, nationality, and so on. As long as questions are work related or centered upon the candidate's ability to perform the work, they should be within legal bounds. Committees must be frank and forthright and police themselves to ensure that they do not allow anyone within their ranks to ask difficult or follow-up questions only of minorities, or ask women questions about their ability to travel for business reasons (reinforcing the stereotype that family responsibilities preclude such activity). Candidate-specific questions should be limited to clarifying the degree to which candidates can perform the essential functions of the job and ensuring that all candidates are thoroughly vetted.

Exhibit #19: *Tips for Conducting the Interview* presents suggestions for conducting interviews. This checklist guides the committee through a protocol to plan for, properly conduct, and complete a professional interview. In addition to the proper format and approach, asking the right questions rounds out a professional interview.

Good Questions

Good interview questions will illuminate a candidate's experience well enough to indicate his or her prospects for success in the position. Bad interview questions will provide no indication of these prospects and may even expose the institution to certain legal liabilities (see Exhibit #20: *Interview Questions to Avoid*). Generally, all questions should be related to the knowledge, skills, and abilities necessary to carry out the duties and responsibilities of the job successfully. Questions about professional competencies such as work ethic, decision making, problem solving, and interpersonal relations that indicate a person's professional character are also fair game.

Certain principles apply when drafting questions. There are three rules of thumb for determining which questions are acceptable: (a) ask only for information that you intend to use to make a hiring decision, (b) know how you will use the information to make that decision, and (c) recognize that the practice of seeking information that you do not use can be difficult to defend (Ford, 1993, p. 13). These rules suggest that the best questions will emerge from a careful analysis of the position.

Asking the Right Questions
The most important part of the interview process is asking questions. Therefore, no committee's work is done well unless its members formulate and ask questions that elicit responses that help to make distinctions among the candidates. The right questions help determine the right person for the job.

There are several different types of interview questions, including informational, situational, behavioral, and case study. Each question type can be asked in an open- or closed-ended fashion. Open-ended questions allow a free-form response, while closed-ended

questions limit responses to yes, no, or similarly brief responses. Open-ended questions are usually more effective in eliciting qualitative information from candidates that allows committees to better judge which candidate is best.

Asking good questions is more difficult than it might seem. Many committees are tempted to dust off the questions used the last time a search was conducted and modify them as needed. Yet, it is more prudent to ensure that the questions truly reflect what is expected of the position today, considering changes in technology, regulatory requirements, needs of the department, and other requirements such as those that support strategic initiatives. All questions should be drafted with current needs in mind.

There is an art and a science to asking questions, and committees must understand both when drafting questions. Practicing good art involves asking questions the right way. Indeed, how a question is asked determines the type of information you receive and whether this information is valuable in making the decision about who will work best for your organization. Applying sound science is using the right type of question given the selection criteria you are evaluating.

Here is an example of putting the art and science of asking questions to a test. If you are trying to evaluate a candidate's ability to manage the financial affairs of an academic unit, you could ask the question any number of different ways:

Q: Tell us about your budgeting experience.
Q: Tell us about your experience with managing the budget of an academic department.
Q: What process would you use to establish a departmental budget for a newly formed academic division?
Q: Have you ever had to cut a budget in the middle of the year, and if so, how did you decide what to cut and what to keep?

Each of these questions will generate responses such as general factual information, detailed examples of financial prowess, problem-solving ability, or detailed knowledge about the mechanics of organizational financial management.

A response to the first question might be too general to evaluate the degree to which a candidate has experience or so specific as to bore the committee with details. The second question might be more on target

---

EXHIBIT #20
Interview Questions to Avoid

You cannot ask any question during an interview that relates to an applicant's race, color, religion, age, gender, national origin, disability, or genetic predisposition. In some states, inquiries about a candidate's sexual orientation, marital status, or veteran status are also illegal. As a rule, you may ask only work-related questions. The following questions are examples of those that should not be asked:

Questions to Avoid
* Are you a U.S. citizen?
* Where were you born?
* What is your birth date?
* How old are you?
* Do you have a disability?
* Are you married?
* What is your spouse's name?
* What is your maiden name?
* Do you have any children?
* Do you have child care arrangements?
* What is your race or ethnic origin?
* Which church do you attend?
* What is your religion?

The following questions should be asked only when there is a bona fide, job-specific reason to ask them. If you ask them of one candidate, them you should ask them of all candidates for the same position.

Acceptable Alternative Questions
* Do you have any responsibilities that conflict with the job's attendance or travel requirements?
* Are you able to work in the United States on an unrestricted basis?
* Are you able to perform the duties on the job description with or without *reasonable accommodations*?
* Have you ever been convicted of a felony?
* If hired, can you provide proof that you are at least 18 years of age?
* Do you have any conflicts that would prevent you from working the schedule discussed?
* What languages do you speak or write fluently?
* Have you worked under any other professional name or nickname?
* Do you have any relatives currently working for this institution?
* Would you have any problem working overtime, if required?
* Would anything prohibit you from making a long-term commitment to the position and the institution?

---

for evaluating a dean candidate's experience, yet it might not give you enough information without a follow-up question that asks for specific examples. The third question is excellent if you are assessing a candidate's financial competency, and a full answer is likely only to come from candidates who have knowledge and understanding of and experience with the subject. While the fourth question would be better used to evaluate a candidate's problem-solving and decision-making skills, and maybe even his or her approach to shared governance, it might fail to provide enough detailed information about the candidate's financial acumen.

Situational or Behavioral Questions

Most interview questions are either situational or behavioral. Though they differ in their purpose and intent, they can be equally effective if used properly. Behavioral questions start with the premise that the best predictor of future performance is past performance. Therefore, they ask the candidate to recall a past experience and share how he or she responded. Behavioral questions ascertain the nature of the candidate's past behavior, but they are only effective if each candidate has had similar experience and is not seeking a promotion. An example of this question might be, "Give us a situation when a student vehemently disagreed with how you graded one of his or her written assignments and how you resolved that conflict."

By contrast, a situational question attempts to determine how a candidate might respond in a given scenario. This type of question can be used to evaluate experienced candidates as well as those who are changing to a position different from their current one, such as a faculty member becoming an administrator. A typical example of a situational question is, "If you had a disagreement with colleagues over a faculty governance matter, how would you work with them to resolve the situation if you disagreed on the underlying facts of the matter at hand?" Situational questions ascertain a candidate's response to a hypothetical or real-life situation that tests his or her ability to analyze and solve problems or make decisions.

Information Questions

Information questions are direct questions that gather specific information or verify facts or data. These are sometimes called factual questions. Information questions ascertain the specifics of a person's education and career. Often information questions can be answered with a *yes* or *no* or very simply, yet they provide essential information about the candidate. Here are a few examples:

Q: Are you willing to accept a non-tenure-track position?
Q: To what position does your current job report?

Q: When you moved from Small Town College to Big State University, did you consider that to be a lateral move or a promotion, given that the duties and responsibilities were similar?
Q: Why do you feel you are the best candidate for this job?

The primary uses of information questions are to verify information provided in the résumé, follow up on a previous question, or collect factual information. These questions gather information; they do not necessarily test candidates on how they may think or might react in a professional setting. Situational, behavioral, and case study questions are better designed to assess a candidate's knowledge, skills, and abilities.

Case Study (Scenario) Questions

The case study question assesses how a candidate processes information, makes decisions, and solves problems. It also provides a glimpse into how a candidate might react to adversity, how well candidates "think on their feet," and how they speak extemporaneously. Sometimes called scenario questions, case study questions present a challenge or dilemma that is not easily solved or may not even have a solution. The committee then evaluates how the candidate processes information and might approach his or her work. The following example illuminates this sort of approach:

Q: What would you do in a dysfunctional department that was trying to balance a budget and could not agree on the priorities of the department, the curriculum of the department, or with the leadership's approach to solving this particular problem? You have three colleagues who agree that A is the best course of action, three colleagues who believe B is the best course of action, and you as the department chair think that C is the best option. Meanwhile, the university leaders think that none of the options proposed is viable. How would you handle this situation?

Clearly there is no right answer. Yet, how the candidate responds to the question gives you a lot of qualitative information about how he or she approaches work, works with others, thinks, and might work if he or she were employed by your institution. Case study questions provide an unscripted glimpse into how candidates handle difficult situations and how they might respond to the unpredictable environment of work.

Asking Questions Right

The key to asking the right questions is acknowledging that asking good questions requires forethought. Appreciating the fine art of inquiry and approaching the process deliberately will improve the selection process. Yet, a simple three-step process can virtually ensure success in selecting the best candidate. First, you must have clarity about the concept you are investigating—that is, financial acumen or decision making. Second, you must determine which type of question is best for dealing with that subject. Third, you must be careful to phrase the question to elicit the qualitative information you seek.

Bad Questions

In addition to advice that helps you to draft good questions, here are some tips for identifying and avoiding bad questions:

- Long questions: Long and wordy questions are often a telltale sign that the question was ill conceived.
- Generic questions: Generic questions are so general that they do not help evaluate the specific skills candidates need for a position. Instead of asking the overused question, "What are your strengths and weaknesses," ask, "If we were to call your references, in what areas of academic administration would they give you accolades, and in what areas would they give you critical feedback?"
- Compound questions: Be careful of compound questions that have too many parts. They can lack focus or clarity and be confusing.
- Too many questions: Preparing too many questions and then asking the candidate to provide brief responses can undermine the committee's ability to ascertain the qualitative differences among candidates' responses. Holding a 75- to 90-minute interview instead of 60 minutes might help this situation.

- Similar questions: Questions on related topics that are not complementary should be dissected or combined so that one does not answer or provide clues to the other.
- Favorite questions: Committee members who want to ask their pet question regardless of the particular position should be redirected to the position advertisement or position description for a more appropriate line of inquiry.

The importance of good interview questions is too great to be handled haphazardly, so care and attention to drafting and delivering good questions is advised.

The Final Question: A Summary

The questions you pose will determine the answers you receive. Poorly worded questions can make a less-qualified candidate appear to be a viable choice and handicap those whose experience would normally set them apart from their peers. The slate of questions asked of each candidate should be sound individually and should be complementary to provide a holistic evaluation of candidates. Ideally, questions are based upon the description of the position, the job advertisement, and the committee's *charge*. Yet, the best questions start with the notion that how you ask questions matters.

It is indispensable in the selection process to ask the right type of question to evaluate a candidate's background and experience, as well as his or her fit with your organization. Just as there are many different ways of solving a problem, there are many different ways of asking questions—some better than others. Expert advice for search committees is to use the right tool for the right job—situational, behavioral, information, or case study questions—as determined by your selection criteria. Most often, you will use some combination of all four types. Final question—"Do you have increased confidence in your ability to draft effective interview questions after having read this overview of question types?" Good luck on your search.

Evaluating Interview Responses

The search committee and all stakeholders involved in the selection process should use a screening instrument to record their observations of each candidate. The type of instrument used depends upon the purpose of the evaluation and who is involved in the process. The search committee's instrument should be based upon the requirements of the position and needs of the organization, while generic feedback instruments should be crafted for stakeholders who participate passively in town hall meetings or group gatherings. Students should be given a prescribed evaluation form to rate a candidate's teaching demonstration. Nonetheless, the evaluation criteria are determined in advance, agreed upon, and documented as a matter of course. The following exhibits (Exhibits #21–#27) provide useful tools you may adapt for your use.

EXHIBIT #21
Interview Evaluation Based on Responses to Questions

Candidate's Name: _____   **Date:** _____

Rating: 10 = Excellent Response; 5 = Good Response; 2 = Poor Response

Weighting: 1 = Low; 2 = Medium; 3 = High

	Question	Score	Weighting	Subtotal
1	Why are you interested in leaving your current assignment, and why do you feel this position is a good one for you?		3	
2	Describe how your past school and work experiences have prepared you for the job for which you are applying.		3	
3	Tell us about your preferred work environment.		1	
4	Have you ever been told you could not implement a great idea you had? How did you react? What did you do?		2	
5	Describe your level of computer proficiency and the programs with which you are familiar.		2	
6	What would you do if you accidentally hung up the telephone on a customer who had been waiting for a long time, and the customer called back and used loud and offensive language to tell you that you were incompetent?		2	
7	How do you go about organizing your work each day?		3	
8	What do you dislike most about your current job?		2	
9	Where would this position fit into your career development goals?		1	
10	Why are you the best candidate for this position?		2	
			Total	

Name of Search Committee Member: _____

EXHIBIT #22

Interview Evaluation Based on Essential Knowledge, Skills, and Abilities

Candidate's Name: _____   Date: _____

	Possible Points	Points
MASTERY OF A BODY OF KNOWLEDGE	40	
In your opinion, did the candidate demonstrate sufficient mastery of a body of knowledge in _____? Was the candidate's area of professional emphasis evident? Was his or her level of knowledge in this area sufficient to be considered an expert?		
TEACHING ABILITY	20	
Was the candidate's teaching philosophy consistent with the needs and expectations of our institution's students and faculty? How would you evaluate the candidate's presentation? What elements of the candidate's instructional materials show evidence of a grasp of pedagogy?		
SCHOLARSHIP	20	
Did the candidate have a well-thought-out and planned research agenda? To what degree are the candidate's publications of the caliber expected at _____? To what degree is the candidate's professional presentation evidence of a productive scholar? Is his or her depth and breadth of scholarly activities rich enough to be noteworthy?		
SERVICE RELATED TO THE PROFESSION	20	
What is the degree of engagement of the candidate in his or her discipline? What is the candidate's record of college/university service? How is the candidate actively engaged in his or her profession?		
General Comments		
Total		

EXHIBIT #23
Interview Evaluation Based on General Observations

Position and Organizational Requirements: Managerial and Financial Acumen, Vision for Future and Leadership, Accreditation Experience, Research Ability, and Interpersonal Skills

	Yes, No, Some
1. Was the candidate professional in appearance, demeanor, and interaction with everyone involved in the interview process?	
2. Did the candidate communicate clearly and effectively?	
3. Did the candidate answer all questions to your satisfaction? If not, which questions were left unanswered?	
4. Does this candidate appear to be able to perform the job?	
5. Did it appear that the candidate had sought information about the college before arriving on campus?	
6. Did the candidate seem genuinely interested in the position?	
7. Do you have any reservations about this candidate's ability to succeed at this institution?	
8. Other comments or information:	
9. Candidate's strengths (compared to position and organizational requirements):	
10. Candidate's weaknesses (compared to position and organizational requirements):	
11. How would you compare this candidate to the other candidates we have interviewed?	

Candidate's Name:_____ **Date:** _____

(Circle one)

Consider Further, Maybe, Do Not Consider Further

EXHIBIT #24
Presentation Evaluation Checklist Instrument

Questions for Evaluating Presentations
Was the presenter's bearing professional?

— Was the presenter well prepared?
— Were the learning objectives clear?
— Did the presenter attempt to establish rapport with the audience?
— Did he or she demonstrate mastery of the subject?
— Did he or she present the subject matter in an effective manner?
— Were his or her handouts or other learning aids useful?

(continues)

(*continued*)

  — Did he or she use learning aids effectively?
  — Did he or she handle questions well?
  — Did he or she engage the audience and hold its attention?
  — Did the presentation start and end on time?
  — Did you learn something worthwhile from the presentation?

General Comments:

Rating: Excellent, Very Good, Good, Poor (circle one)

EXHIBIT #25
Teaching/Presentation Evaluation Questionnaire

Candidate's Name: _____ **Date:** _____

Observer: _____

Question	Strongly Disagree	Disagree	Neutral	Agree	Strongly Agree
1. The presentation appeared to be designed and planned well.					
2. The learning objectives were clearly stated or obvious.					
3. The approach to teaching helped me to learn the material.					
4. The learning environment was positive or helped me to learn.					
5. The communication style of the presenter was good.					
6. The information was presented in a logical or orderly manner.					
7. The presenter attempted to teach in such a way as to support different types of learners.					
8. The presenter used visuals, training aids, or technology appropriately to help convey the information.					
9. The presenter appeared to be knowledgeable about the subject matter.					
10. The presenter provided a challenging learning experience.					

(*continues*)

(continued)

Question	Strongly Disagree	Disagree	Neutral	Agree	Strongly Agree
11. The presenter appeared to be enthusiastic about, interested in, or excited or intrigued by the subject matter and his or her instructional delivery conveyed passion for the subject.					
12. The presenter effectively engaged with or involved the audience.					
13. The presenter appeared to care whether the audience learned the material.					
14. I would rate the overall effectiveness of the presenter highly.					
15. I would rate the overall learning experience highly.					
Total					

(Circle one)

Consider Further, Maybe, Do Not Consider Further

EXHIBIT #26

Group Feedback Instrument for Town Hall Meetings or Open Forums

Chair, Department of Business

The requirements for this position were determined according to the duties of the position, the advertisement, and the factors considered most important for State University. Please provide your feedback of the candidate based upon the following criteria.

Indicate the degree to which the candidate possesses the characteristics or ability to perform the duties and/or be successful in this position:

	Strongly Disagree	Disagree	Neutral	Agree	Strongly Agree
1. Establish a vision for the department					
2. Manage departmental affairs					
3. Lead reaccreditation efforts					
4. Develop curricula					
5. Serve as a role model for students					

(continues)

(*continued*)

	Strongly Disagree	Disagree	Neutral	Agree	Strongly Agree
6. Be a productive scholar					
7. Succeed at fund-raising					
8. Develop relationships and partnerships outside of the university					
Comments:					

(Circle one)

Rating: 1   2   3   4   5   6   7   8   9   10

EXHIBIT #27

Leader's Assessment of Candidates Based Upon Institutional Priorities

Please note the degree to which the candidate displays the competencies that are needed for the position and the degree to which the candidate's approach to work mirrors the requirements of the University of North Yarmouth.

The candidate:

Is committed to student assessment and continuous improvement of instruction.

      1   2   3   4   5   6   7   8   9   10

Has a well-developed research agenda/potential that reflects the university's strategic directions.

      1   2   3   4   5   6   7   8   9   10

Has experience, values, and/or perspectives that support the university's commitment to diversity.

      1   2   3   4   5   6   7   8   9   10

Supports the use of service-learning as a valued methodology.

      1   2   3   4   5   6   7   8   9   10

Has interest or demonstrated success in interdisciplinary studies.

      1   2   3   4   5   6   7   8   9   10

Comments:

Overall Candidate Rating

     1   2   3   4   5   6   7   8   9   10

Avoiding Bias in Interviews

Since we all have blind spots, we are all biased in some way, and we all have conscious and unconscious preferences. The best defense against bias in interviews is training to point out typical challenges in an attempt to sensitize committee members to the dynamics of bias and help them avoid common pitfalls. It is more likely that any bias that exists in the search committee process is covert or unintentional rather than overt and intentional. If that is the case, these subtle forms of bias might not be obvious or easy to detect. As noted earlier in this chaper, an example would be asking more difficult follow-up questions only of women and minorities. Another might be the display of body language and other nonverbal cues that show one's displeasure with a candidate or his or her responses during the interview. This is a subtle way of subconsciously swaying the opinion of other committee members. Experts Edna Chun and Alvin Evans (2007) discuss the awkward use of silence as a means of undermining the evaluation of minority candidates.

Expert JoAnn Moody outlines over a dozen subtle forms of bias in her booklet, "Rising Above Cognitive Errors: Guidelines to Improve Faculty Searches, Evaluations, and Decision-Making" (2010). They include the following: simple favoritism or positive and negative stereotypes that either unnecessarily favor or disqualify minorities; distorting or ignoring the evidence when minorities are involved; seizing the pretext—waiting and looking for an opportune moment to introduce withheld information that attempts to prove one's favor or disfavor of a candidate with or without good evidence; using stereotypes; and elitism. The section of this book titled *Evaluating Organizational Fit: Defining and Documenting Fit*, p. 108, tells of someone who exclaims that a candidate is "not like us" or "would not be happy here." This is another subtle form of bias that undermines the candidacy of individuals who are different from the person raising a false objection.

Stereotyping, unintentional bias, and other conscious and unconscious acts can sometimes derail good intentions. Committees must be empowered to police themselves and work toward reducing or eliminating bias from their decision making. A frank discussion about the need to do so should take place during the first committee meeting when the training and orientation session occurs. The goal is creating an environment in which all committee members feel safe in speaking their minds. A helpful technique is using cues, phrases, or debate icebreakers that make it easier to introduce an objection or call attention to a concern. Three examples of such phrases are, "Can we pause and discuss that point before we use that information to make a decision?" "Is that an opinion, a preference, or a known fact?" and "Wait! Are we now using _____ as a selection criterion?" Committees whose members are trained to be consciously aware of the need to be open and up front about their deliberations have a better chance of making objective decisions (see Vignette P: *Eliminating Bias From Selection*, p. 62). *Diversity advocates* are search committee assets in this regard as they are trained to support committees when addressing these exact sort of issues.

Interview Questions

General Interview Questions

In the spirit of ecology and sustainability, here is a series of 119 interview questions that have been recycled for your use. The beauty of these questions is that they have been used before and have proven to be effective at eliciting the desired responses from candidates. Please use them freely and share them with others to further prove that good questions are a renewable energy source. However, use and adapt only those that are related to your specific position.

1. Tell us a little more about your professional experiences, particularly those not mentioned on your résumé.
2. Why are you interested in leaving your current assignment, and why do you feel this assignment would be better for you?
3. How is our institution similar to or different from other organizations or institutions where you have worked?
4. Do you feel this position is a promotion, a lateral move, a broadening of your professional experience, or just a change? Why do you think so?
5. How does this position fit into your overall career goals?
6. Describe the duties of your current job and your current reporting relationship to others.

7. What do you dislike most about your current job?

8. What is your favorite part of your current job, and why is it your favorite part?

9. What are the three college courses that best prepared you for your current job?

10. What is the best method of creating a _____ [i.e., a relevant product or service]?

11. What qualities or experiences make you the best candidate for this position?

12. Describe two or three major trends in your profession today.

13. On the basis of the information you have received so far, what do you see as the major challenges of this position, and how would you address them?

14. Describe a situation in which you did "all the right things" and were still unsuccessful. What did you learn from the experience?

15. Discuss the committees on which you have served and the impact of these committees on the organization where you currently work.

16. Why did you choose this profession/field?

17. What new skills have you learned over the past year?

18. Think about an instance when you were given an assignment that you thought you would be unable to complete. How did you accomplish the assignment?

19. Have you ever had a great idea but been told that you could not implement it? How did you react? What did you do?

20. Describe the best supervisor and the worse supervisor you have ever had.

21. Describe your ideal job.

22. How would you describe your ideal work environment?

23. If we were to check your references on you, what would your past supervisors say about you? How about past coworkers?

24. If you had one big idea that would significantly improve your work environment, what would it be?

25. Can you describe how you go about solving problems? Please give us some examples.

26. What is the biggest conflict you have ever been involved in at work? How did you handle it?

27. What new programs or services would you start if offered the position?

28. Please share with us your philosophy about customer service in an academic environment and give us some examples of service that illustrate your views.

29. Tell us how you would learn your new job in the absence of a formal training program.

30. How would you characterize your level of computer literacy? What are some of the non-traditional applications you use that would illustrate your competency?

31. Think about a coworker from the present or past whom you admire. Why do you admire him or her?

32. What characteristics do you prize most in an employee/coworker? What behaviors or characteristics do you find intolerable?

33. Can you share with us your ideas about professional development?

34. Describe some basic steps you would take in implementing a new program.

35. Describe one or two of your proudest professional accomplishments.

36. What is your understanding of the unique role of a _____ [i.e., two-year college/liberal arts college/research university]?

37. How do you feel about diversity in the workplace? Give us some examples of your efforts to promote diversity.

38. Tell us how you go about organizing your work.

39. Describe how you have used computers or other technology to improve your work.

40. Please tell us what you think are the most important elements of a good _____ [e.g., service, activity, product, class, etc.].

41. Describe your volunteer experiences in community-based organizations.

42. What professional associations do you belong to, and how involved in them are you?

43. Tell us about your preferred work environment.

44. What experiences or skills will help you manage major projects?

45. In what professional development activities have you been involved over the past few years, and why did you choose those activities?

46. What volunteer, civic, or social activities have helped you develop professional skills?

47. What things have you done on your own initiative to help you prepare for your next job?

48. Do you have any concerns that would make you have reservations about accepting this position if it is offered to you?

49. What do you think most uniquely qualifies you for this position?

50. What unique skill set(s) would you bring to this position?

51. How have you prepared yourself over the past few years for your next opportunity?

52. What have you learned over the past six months to a year that is new?

53. In what areas do you feel you need further professional development?

54. What are your professional development or continuous learning plans?

55. Do your assignments normally come from your boss, or do you go to your boss with suggestions?

56. What professional development activities have you completed recently that help to qualify you for this position?

57. What professional development activities have you completed in the past two years?

58. Have you ever spent your own money on your professional development? When, how, and why?

59. What social, civic, or community organizations do you belong to that have helped you grow professionally?

60. Tell us what you know or have heard about the culture of higher education and why this environment might interest you.

61. Have you ever worked in a nonprofit organization, and how do you think such an organization is run compared to for-profit companies?

62. What were some of the things your supervisor said about you during your last performance appraisal?

63. How are your job duties different from what they would be for similar jobs in other organizations?

64. Describe your activities during a typical day on your current job.

65. What subjects did you like least and best in school? Why?

66. Are your grades from college a good reflection of your ability? Why or why not?

67. If you had it to do over again, would you have chosen the same course of study? Why or why not?

68. What were your major duties and responsibilities in your last job?

69. Describe the largest project you were involved with and your role in its success.

70. How would you describe your work ethic? Give us two examples that demonstrate it.

71. How has your current job helped you grow as a person and as a professional?

72. What could your past employers count on you for without fail?

73. What is the most disappointing aspect of your current job?

74. What part of your current job would you describe as fun?

75. What excites you most in your current job?

76. Do you feel that your workload in your current job is too great, too light, just right, or other? Why?

77. What did you do in your last job that made you more effective?

78. Has your present job changed while you have held it? If so, how?

79. Tell us about a time when you and a supervisor disagreed and how the issue was resolved.

80. Would you return to work for any or all of your previous employers? Why or why not?

81. Do you think you are fairly compensated for the work you currently do? Why or why not?

82. What suggestions have you made in your current job to improve how work is performed?

83. What polices or procedures of your current company do you disagree with?

84. How would you describe your relationship with your current supervisor?

85. Have you ever asked for new responsibilities or assignments? What happened?

86. What motivates you?

87. Tell us what about our mission resonates with you most.

88. Would you rather take initiative and some risk or play it safe and steady? Why? Give an example.

89. If hired, what would you do in the first 30 days?

90. Describe some specific contributions you would make during the first six months in this position.

91. In your opinion, what does it take to be a "success"?

92. What are the most challenging parts of your current job?
93. What have you done at work to make your job easier?
94. What tools or methods do you use to keep your supervisor informed of what you are doing?
95. In what kind of environment are you most comfortable?
96. How is your education related to your career?
97. Tell us about three professional skills you have developed, and how that knowledge makes you qualified for this position.
98. Tell us about the last time you lost your temper at work.
99. Tell us of a time when you had to handle a highly emotional employee or customer.
100. What do you do to encourage others to do their best?
101. What expertise do you have that coworkers come to you for assistance in?
102. How do you attempt to persuade others to your way of thinking?
103. Tell us about a time when a supervisor criticized your work.
104. How do you assert yourself to get what you need?
105. What do you know about our college/university?
106. What are three keys to successful _____ [i.e., important aspect of position]?
107. What should a _____ know about students [i.e., name of position in question]?
108. Tell us about a personal or career goal you have accomplished, and why it was important to you.
109. How do you go about solving problems?
110. Tell us about a specific time when you eliminated or avoided a potential problem before it happened.
111. Think about an instance when you were given an assignment that you were not sure of or thought you would not be able to complete. What did you decide, and how did you eventually accomplish the assignment?
112. What professional associations do you belong to and at what level are you involved with them?

113. If someone told you that you had made an error, describe how you would react and what you would say in your defense.
114. You are a committee member and disagree with a point or decision. How will you respond?
115. Describe what you would classify as a crisis.
116. What strengths did you rely on in your last position to make you successful in your work?
117. Tell us about your present or last job. Why did you choose it? Why do you want to leave?
118. Do you have any additional information you would like to share?
119. Do you have any questions for us?

Faculty Interview Questions

Here are 78 interview questions for personnel involved in teaching, research, scholarship, publications, service, and associated instructional and faculty-related activities:

1. Describe your philosophy about teaching and learning.
2. What specific applications of technology have you used in the classroom?
3. How do you engage students to learn and explore even in an introductory or survey course for nonmajors?
4. What are the most important elements of a good instructor?
5. Why are you interested in teaching in a two-year college/liberal arts college/research university instead of a four-year college/liberal arts college/research university?
6. Why do you feel your teaching style will work to best serve our student population?
7. What experiences have you had working with students outside the classroom [e.g., advising, tutoring, sponsoring student groups, etc.]?
8. What professional development activities have you been involved in over the past few years?
9. What pedagogical trends or changes do you see on the horizon in your discipline?
10. Can you describe the value of your research to a layperson?
11. What are the limitations of your research? Use this as an opportunity to discuss where your research may be headed.
12. What are your plans for securing funding to support your research?

13. Which do your prefer most: teaching, research, or writing? Why?

14. Who are the major scholars in your field, and how does your work compare to theirs?

15. What do you think of _____ 's work [pick a leading scholar]?

16. What is your research plan for the next three years?

17. How do you see your research fitting in with the department's?

18. How do you incorporate contemporary ideas into your courses that are not necessarily specific to your discipline [e.g., diversity, globalism, sustainability, etc.]?

19. What elements do you incorporate into your teaching that address different learning styles or diverse ways of learning?

20. How do you adjust your style to the less-motivated or underprepared student versus the strongly motivated, well-prepared student?

21. Give us examples of your ability to work effectively with a variety of students.

22. What are some of the things you have done particularly well in your teaching career or in which you have achieved the greatest success?

23. Starting with your last position, tell us about any of your student-related achievements that were recognized by your superiors, coworkers, students, or others.

24. What has been your greatest frustration or disappointment in teaching, and why do you feel this way?

25. What do you particularly enjoy about teaching?

26. Describe a successful experience in dealing with different students and what you learned from it.

27. In your academic career, what subjects challenged you the most and why?

28. What motivates you, and how would you motivate students?

29. What do you think are the most important characteristics and abilities a person must have to become a successful faculty member?

30. What is your greatest teaching achievement? Why?

31. What is the main point of your dissertation, and why did you choose your topic?

32. What specific research agenda will you pursue if you are selected?

33. How has your experience and training prepared you to teach the courses required?

34. What courses would you prefer to teach if you were given complete latitude in designing them?

35. What experiences or interests do you have in college-wide activities and service?

36. How do you feel about mentoring, advising, and sponsoring student activities?

37. How would you encourage students to major in _____?

38. What role(s) should faculty play in the lives of students outside the classroom?

39. What is the greatest intellectual idea you have ever had, and what have you done with it?

40. Where do you see your work going in the next 10–20 years?

41. With whom in the department do you envision interacting the most and why? Outside the department/university?

42. To what degree do you see integrating undergraduate and graduate students into your research program?

43. Is your students' work usually closely related to your research focus, or is it fairly independent?

44. How do you help graduate students get started on a research project?

45. How would you respond to a student who is foundering?

46. Of the courses you have taught, which are your favorites?

47. What is your impression of our institutional mission statement? How is this statement related to your views, values, goals, or interests?

48. What is the most useful constructive feedback you have received about your research, and how did you respond to it?

49. Tell us about an unsuccessful research project you have been involved in.

50. What is your experience with underprepared students?

51. Tell us how your research has influenced your teaching.

52. In what ways have you been able to bring the insights of your research to your courses at the undergraduate level?

53. What do you think of service-learning, and have you ever used it in your classes?

54. Do you believe you should build rapport with students? If so, how?

55. What experience have you had with team-teaching? What is your opinion of it?
56. What are your views of assessment, and how do you incorporate it into your teaching plan?
57. Which professors have most influenced your teaching style, and why?
58. Tell us about one of your former students whom you think modeled the kind of outcome you seek in students.
59. How do you teach students to use higher-order thinking skills in your classroom?
60. What important trends do you see in our discipline?
61. What is the value of your work to an educated person outside the field?
62. What theoretical approaches have had the most influence on you?
63. What journals best suit your work?
64. How would you as a faculty member balance academic integrity with our open door admission policy or concerns about retention?
65. Tell us your opinion of how the workload of a faculty member should be split and into what areas [e.g., percentage teaching, scholarship, advising, etc.].
66. What changes have you brought to the traditional teaching of _____?
67. How would you go about being an advocate and resource person on our campus for _____ [e.g., interdisciplinary studies, service-learning, information literacy, etc.]?
68. What courses have you created or proposed in the past five years?
69. Describe your experiences working with non-academic populations, community service, or other extension activities.
70. Describe any experiences you might have had to support grant writing as a faculty member?
71. Have you participated in any sponsored research?
72. Do you aspire to be a full professor? Why or why not?
73. How do you define *good teaching*?
74. What do you think of interdisciplinary studies?
75. What are your greatest strengths as an instructor?
76. As a faculty member, in what areas do you feel you can use some further development or would you like to diversify into?
77. How do you structure your courses?

78. What textbook would you use in a particular course, and why this particular resource?

Interview Questions for Administrators, Executives, or Supervisors

Here are 57 interview questions for those who are involved in management and leadership activities, such as having responsibility for personnel, budgets, programs, or other administrative activities:

Personnel management

1. Tell us about your best and worst hiring decisions.
2. What type of employee do you find the most difficult to manage?
3. Have you ever terminated an employee? Why?
4. How do you reprimand people who work for you?
5. What was the most challenging personnel issue you've had to deal with, and how did you handle it?
6. How would you build a team from scratch?
7. How do you handle performance appraisals?
8. How would you train a new staff member?
9. What has your experience been in supervising others?
10. How do you determine what to delegate and what to do yourself?
11. How do you give feedback to your staff members?
12. How do you manage, monitor, and direct the performance of your staff?
13. What do you want your staff to do when they encounter problems?

Decision making

14. Tell us about any unconventional methods you have used to solve problems.
15. What criteria, factors, or methods do you use to make decisions?
16. How long does it typically take you to make a decision?
17. What is the last major decision you had to make?
18. What kinds of decisions are the most difficult for you to make and why?
19. What kinds of problems are you best at solving?
20. What is the biggest error in judgment you have made in a previous job? Why did you make it? How did you correct the problem?

21. To whom did you turn for help the last time you had a major problem, and why did you choose that person?
22. Tell us about a time when you had to make an unpopular decision.
23. What do you do when you need to make a decision and there are no procedures in place to do so?
24. Describe a recent decision you made that would normally have been made by your supervisor. What was the outcome?

General administration

25. How do you "sell" or persuade others to accept and support necessary change?
26. How do you make your opinion known when you disagree with your boss?
27. What do you do when you know you are right and your boss disagrees with you? Give us an example of when this happened in your career.
28. What did you do for a past employer that made a difference and for which you believe you will be remembered?
29. Tell us about your experience in leading and managing an organization similar to ours.
30. Tell us about your fiscal management experience: budgeting, reporting, cutting costs, building and maintaining reserves.
31. What is the largest budget you have ever managed?
32. How do manage meetings?
33. Have you ever had a great idea and were told that you could not implement it? How did you react? What did you do?
34. Describe for us a time when you came across questionable business practices. How did you handle the situation?
35. A new policy is to be implemented organization-wide. You do not agree with this new policy. How do you discuss this with your staff?

36. How do you communicate priority projects to your staff when you are concerned that they already feel overloaded?

Leadership

37. How would your subordinates describe your leadership style?
38. On a scale from 1 to 10, how well would your employees say you listen?
39. What do you find most difficult when managing others?
40. What characteristics help you to be effective as a leader?
41. What would it be like working for you?
42. What does it mean to be a leader?
43. How do you reward the people who work with you?
44. What do you do with your staff to develop teamwork?
45. What is the most important job of a leader?
46. What sort of criticism have you received from your staff?
47. Before you fire someone, what factors would you take into consideration?
48. How many women and minorities have you hired?
49. What have you learned from your mistakes as a manager?
50. Tell us about your current boss or supervisor. What is his or her leadership style?
51. What has been your most significant leadership responsibility?
52. If you were promoted and had to hire someone to replace you in your current job, what kind of person would you look for?
53. Describe your communication style.
54. Tell us about a new project you initiated.
55. What would you like to have done more of in your last job? What held you back?
56. If your supervisor got sick and you had to step into his or her job for six months, what would you do first?
57. How do you and your staff celebrate success?

CHAPTER 13

Additional Screening Methods

Reviewing résumés and conducting interviews are necessary but are not sufficient for a thorough evaluation of candidates. Prudent search committees use multiple screening methods to increase the rigor of the search. The more fastidious the examination of candidates, the greater the likelihood that the selected candidate will be a good match for the position.

Using multiple screening methods in the right combination is a matter of search committee art. Nonetheless, at a minimum, a four-part model is recommended for every search. Evaluating written materials, conducting interviews, administering a work sample, and selecting with *organizational fit* in mind together create a complete and thorough review of candidates. In either case, the requirements of the position to be filled should dictate any additional screening methods. Choosing additional methods from the following list is advisable:

- Review of application materials
- Additional interviews (see *Types of Interviews*, p. 73)
- Telephone or video interviews
- Work samples
- Presentations or lecture demonstrations
- Portfolios
- Written questionnaires
- Statements of philosophy or approach to work (e.g., teaching, leadership, diversity, service, etc.)
- Standardized tests (e.g., cognitive ability tests, personality inventories, honesty tests, etc.)
- Medical examinations
- Drug tests
- Verification of credentials (e.g., degrees, licenses, etc.)
- Reference checks
- Background checks

Used in the right combination, additional screening methods virtually ensure a wise selection decision.

Interviews: Why You Must Do a Face-to-Face Interview

Aside from a systematic review of written application materials, interviews are the second most commonly used screening technique. There is no substitute for seeing, talking to, and interacting with a candidate to ensure that the person who appears on paper resembles the person in real life. Institutions expose themselves to extreme liability if they consider hiring individuals whom they have never met in person. In today's world of identity theft, impersonations, and online teaching, an extra bit of prudence is advised to ensure that the identity of every candidate is verified before he or she is hired, even professors who only teach online via the Internet.

Interviews are an indispensable part of the hiring process, so care must be taken to ensure that they are conducted in a professional manner. However, experts note that interviews have low reliability; thus, they should not be used as the only selection method. Additional screening methods are necessary in every selection process. The best additional screening method is to administer a work sample (see the *Work Samples* section later in this chapter).

Telephone or Video Interviews

The use of technology for conducting interviews is increasing in frequency. A little more than a decade ago, telephone interviews were not very common. Today, video interviews are in vogue due to the availability of inexpensive cameras and Internet connections. While there is no substitute for a face-to-face interview, a video interview might be a close second, and a telephone interview third. Aside from the many complications and pitfalls of technology failures, these interviews are an excellent addition to the search process because they allow committees to complete multiple evaluations of candidates.

Two significant advantages of telephone and video interviews are that they can reduce costs and save time. Such interviews are essentially cost-free, especially compared to campus interviews and travel costs. A half-dozen candidates can be interviewed in a day, accounting for much less time and fewer logistics than on-site interviews necessitate.

The structure and conduct of telephone or video interviews should be similar to that of a regular interview, except that they are shorter in length and focus on a few critical elements of a position (see Exhibit #28: *Tips on Conducting Telephone or Video Interviews*). Multiple committee members should ask candidates questions about the core requirements of the position from a prepared slate of questions developed from the position description, advertisement, and *charge*. If the individual in the position will have to travel, teach online, raise funds, or perform some other critical function, it is wise to get answers to these essential work-related questions as early in the process as

---

EXHIBIT #28
Tips on Conducting Telephone or Video Interviews

Planning and Arranging the Interview
- Schedule a call for 30–45 minutes with the interviewee and interviewers.
- Review the interviewee's application materials.
- Prepare questions related to the core requirements of the job and those specific to the candidate's background.
- Develop a screening instrument.
- Determine who will ask questions and the order in which questions will be asked (e.g., only one person, all committee members, etc.).
- Test speakerphone, teleconferencing, or Internet video equipment and procedures.

Conducting the Interview
- Introduce the individuals participating in the interview.
- Describe how the interview will be conducted.
- Ask questions pertaining to the résumé (e.g., questions about gaps in employment, special training, a change of professions, etc.).
- Ask why the person is interested in leaving his or her current position.
- Ask one or two technical questions about the job.
- Ask one or two questions that will help you determine the interviewee's interest in your institution's ways of doing business.
- Ensure you ask gatekeeper-type questions (e.g., Are you willing to teach online, seek grants and external funding, or advise student groups?) that would otherwise disqualify candidates from further consideration.
- Ask follow-up questions as appropriate.
- Ask the interviewee if he or she has any questions.
- Explain to the interviewee the next step in the selection process.
- Thank the candidate for his or her time.

After the Interview
- After reviewing notes, assess the candidate against screening criteria.
- Share observations with the committee chair.

Note: Do not call a candidate on the spur of the moment and request an interview at that time. No one wants to be torn between talking to a potential employer and dealing with other important business or personal matters. Allow the candidate to set aside time for the interview by scheduling it in advance. Experience shows that the use of cellular phones by any candidate should be discouraged, if not disallowed.

possible. The telephone or video interview provides an opportunity to do so. Asking such gatekeeper-type questions early is important to prevent the institution from considering candidates who are unsuitable for a position or who might refuse an offer if they were aware of certain duties or responsibilities (e.g., "Are you willing to teach online?" "Will you serve as advisor to student groups?" etc.).

Another good use of telephone interviews is to ask questions specific to the candidate, particularly those that clarify facts and information about his or her résumé or professional experience. Such questions leave no doubt that the candidate is as capable and experienced as is needed for the position before he or she is invited to campus. Telephone and video interviews serve a gatekeeping function—they prevent the institution from investing too much time and money in bringing a dud to campus. The questions posed should be as important as, or more important than, questions that are asked during an in-person interview.

Work Samples

Work samples are the "mother of all tests." They are the best method for screening applicants, regardless of the position. A work sample is the only true evaluation of whether a candidate has the ability to perform the job. Therefore, every committee should design a work sample as a part of the selection process. Having faculty candidates deliver a lecture—preferably to actual students—is a great example of a work sample. A financial aid applicant might be asked to analyze a sample Free Application for Federal Student Aid (FAFSA) for mistakes. A computer programmer could be asked to debug some computer code. A benefits manager might be asked to review a statement of benefits coverage and distill its legalese into a summary document for employees.

The best work samples involve taking actual work to be completed and giving it to candidates to complete. The committee can assign samples to use in determining who should be invited for an on-campus interview. They can be sent in advance of interviews for the committee's review, brought to the interview, or completed while the candidate is physically on-site during the interview day. The nature and type of the work sample helps to determine when and how this exercise is provided, reviewed, and evaluated. In all cases, a work sample should be considered a mandatory part of every search since it is the only surefire way of knowing whether a candidate is able to perform the job.

Presentations

The purpose of a presentation or lecture demonstration is to determine how well the candidate conveys information, communicates or expresses his or her ideas, interacts with other people, and demonstrates mastery of a particular body of knowledge. The search committee might ask each candidate to give a presentation on the same topic or allow each candidate to choose his or her own topic. Candidates for faculty positions should present lectures to students, when possible, for it is far easier to teach a lecture on organic chemistry to chemists than it is to 19-year-olds. Regardless of whom the audience is, its members should evaluate candidates using an agreed-upon screening instrument. Exhibit #24 (p. 91) offers a checklist of questions for evaluating candidates' presentations, and Exhibit #25 (p. 92) presents a sample evaluation instrument for presentations.

Portfolios

Portfolios are a useful screening method to ascertain the degree to which a candidate is qualified for a position. Since the portfolio is a collection of past work, it is one of the best indicators of the quality of work a candidate can produce as well as an indicator of his or her potential contributions. Portfolios can be solicited as a part of the application process, requested of semifinalists as a screening tool before an on-campus interview is extended, or as a product for finalists to bring to the interview.

This collection of evidence provided can be the choice of either the candidate or the committee. A committee might say, for example, "In advance of your visit to campus, please send the following materials to the committee for review: a past syllabus, past student evaluations, a writing sample, a statement of your teaching philosophy, and any taped or recorded presentations that you may possess." In contrast to this approach, a committee may simply ask the candidate to bring to the interview any samples of past work. Today, many portfolios are electronic as well. Personal and professional websites may also serve as parts of a portfolio.

Here is a list of sample contents for a typical portfolio:

- Copies of documents
- Photographs
- Websites
- Publications
- Writing samples
- Instructional support materials
- CD/DVD recordings
- Student evaluations
- Awards
- Research monographs
- Lab materials
- Drawings
- Miscellaneous samples
- Computer files
- Software

In short, any artifact that can be documented or viewed can be part of a professional portfolio. Some sophisticated candidates are known for bringing bound copies of their professional portfolios to their interview, whether or not they are asked to do so. They know that a great portfolio is the best way of sharing their expertise with the committee.

Written Questionnaires

Questionnaires serve the same purpose as statements of work philosophy, yet their format is different. Instead of a documented global statement about which a candidate is asked to respond in prose, questionnaires pose a handful of questions that direct a reaction to particular areas of focus. A questionnaire might ask the following: (a) What are the advantages of a liberal arts education? (b) Other than cost, what are the threats to a liberal arts education? (c) How should technology be incorporated into a liberal arts education? and (d) Is interdisciplinary education simply a modern reinterpretation of a liberal arts education?

Questionnaires can also be used as knowledge tests. Asking a candidate to explain how the financial aid process works or how he or she would go about generating research proposals are examples of the use of questionnaires. Questionnaires sought in advance—either with written application materials or before an invitation to interview—provide an opportunity to ask more detailed questions than are possible in the brief interview setting. Questionnaires are not used as widely in academe as they are in many other industries. Finally, like statements of work philosophy, questionnaires discourage frivolous applications because the time and effort required to respond discourages those who are not truly interested in the position from applying.

Statements of Work Philosophy

A standard practice for many institutions is to request that applicants draft a letter outlining their philosophy, approach, or method of working in a particular area, such as teaching, leadership, or service, or an expression of their commitment to diversity or service-learning. A teaching philosophy statement might outline one's pedagogical experiences, techniques, and methods. A leadership philosophy statement might provide a search committee with some insight into how a candidate would respond to managerial challenges. Such statements also provide the committee with a preview of a candidate's written communication skills.

Most often such statements are solicited as a part of application materials, along with a résumé and cover letter. They are a useful way of having candidates take a stand on an issue that is a determining criterion for selection. It is best that such criteria be well established, such as things related to an institution's mission, culture, or strategic goals. They should be highlighted and documented as a part of the organizational analysis mentioned earlier. Examples include ascertaining the candidate's perspective on the value of a liberal arts or Christian education, information literacy, teaching for knowledge or skill building, or the place of technology in teaching and learning. A best practice approach is to ask candidates to respond to questions about their statement during the interview process, should the applicant be invited.

Standardized Testing

A number of different types of standardized tests can be used to screen applicants, including cognitive ability, honesty and drug tests, interest and values batteries, personality inventories, other psychometric-based tests, and medical examinations. A caution here is that standardized tests should be administered only by trained professionals using tests that meet stringent validity, reliability, and norming standards. Typically organizations purchase such tests or use testing services from reputable and established vendor firms. One must consider a number of legal factors when using tests, so it is best that hiring mangers only use these screening techniques after the institution's HR department or legal counsel has approved them.

Notwithstanding the many cautions about using standardized tests, the information they provide can be critical to certain successful searches. Using standardized tests can provide valuable data to evaluate candidates.

Employment tests must be proven to be job related, and their use must not have an adverse impact on *protected classes* (Mathis & Jackson, 2003). Before asking candidates to take one of these tests, the search committee should consult with the HR department to ensure that the test is necessary to determine candidates' qualification for the position. In some cases, information obtainable through an employment test can be gleaned from other sources, such as a work sample or reference.

Cognitive ability tests come in many varieties, and experts suggest that they can be invaluable in ensuring that candidates can meet the standards for certain jobs—such as spatial aptitude for would-be pilots or artists. Yet an intelligence test, like many cognitive tests, is difficult to justify as job related. How much intelligence do you need to do the job in question? How do you know that a given amount of intelligence is needed? How do you define *intelligence*? There are easier, less risky, and more job-related ways of evaluating so-called intelligence. One way is to ascertain a candidate's professional credentials, such as degrees, certificates, and licenses. Another is to gather evidence of success, such as grade point average, awards, and accolades from former supervisors (references). Like intelligence tests, personality tests can give rise to legal challenges. Yet, personality traits can be gleaned from multiple interviews and reference checks without the same legal risks.

Standardized selection tests often represent a legal minefield. Nonetheless, if the search committee wishes to use such tests, it should:

- consult with the HR unit and legal counsel before deciding which test to use;

- be able to argue that the test is essential to the hiring process (i.e., that no effective hire can be made without the test);
- ensure that the test has proven to be valid and reliable according to research involving its use in the same or similar positions;
- ensure that the test is relevant to the skills needed to perform the job;
- have no other way to obtain information similar to that provided by the test; and
- administer the test to all candidates.

Many employment tests can be avoided if candidates are asked to present samples of their work. Faculty members might be asked to present copies of syllabi, published articles, student evaluations, and audiotapes of conference presentations. Department heads might be asked to present policies or procedures they developed, descriptions of products from programs they administered, copies of evaluations of their staff they completed, or other indicators of managerial prowess.

Medical Examinations

For positions that require significant physical exertion, an organization would be negligent in hiring someone who could not physically perform the essential functions of the job. As with all screening devices, medical examinations must be related to the work being performed. If one candidate is asked to take a physical examination, then all candidates for the job must do so, not just candidates who are perceived to have a disability. The Americans with Disabilities Act requires that physical examinations be administered after all other steps of the hiring process have been completed and an offer of employment has been extended (albeit contingent upon successfully passing the examination).

Pre-Employment Drug and Alcohol Testing

Pre-employment drug and alcohol testing may be appropriate for highly sensitive or responsible positions, such as those in which large sums of cash are handled. Law requires employers to have such policies for law enforcement personnel and individuals holding a commercial driver's license. Drug tests are also commonplace for positions requiring a high degree of public trust—such as pharmacy professionals, military personnel, airline pilots, or persons handling dangerous chemicals or sensitive research materials.

Drug and alcohol screening for new employees should be consistent with the drug and alcohol policies applicable to current employees and with the Drug-Free Workplace Act of 1988 for institutions bound by this requirement. The *hiring authority* must seek the advice of legal counsel and the HR department before requiring pre-employment drug and alcohol testing.

Credential Verifications

Verification of degrees, licenses, certification, and related credentials is often conducted as a part of the background check. Therefore, while it is a de facto screening method, verifications are often used as a selection procedure since the employee is likely to have been chosen as the final candidate. These checks only matter if the employee does not actually hold the credential he or she claims. In this case, the offer of employment would be revoked. Such verifications can be completed by HR, the *appointing authority*, or a third-party vendor who completes other background checks. This process consists of contacting the granting organization to ensure that a credential was awarded, or purchasing access to commercial databases designed for such purposes. This process is often taken for granted; however, it is the most basic requirement for evaluating candidate ability.

Additional Screening Methods Summary

Additional screening methods are essential for ensuring sufficient rigor in every search. The insight provided with each added method helps committees make better decisions from among a smaller number of competitive candidates. There is undoubtedly a positive correlation between the effectiveness of screening methods and a successful search. The best methods for the position in question, used adroitly,

will virtually ensure that committees select the right person.

Reference and background checks are both screening and selection techniques that can be more involved and time-consuming than other methods due to their importance and potential liability exposure. For this reason, they are covered in greater depth in chapter 14.

Evaluating Organizational Fit: Why You Should and Must

While the primary purpose of interviews is to determine how competitive candidates compare to one another, the secondary, and almost as important purpose, is to determine *organizational fit*. How do a candidate's abilities and attributes best match the job's duties and align with the organization's mission, culture, and values? The most-qualified person is rarely offered the job. The well-qualified candidate who will work best and be successful in the particular environment should be the preferred candidate. This screening criterion must be incorporated into the selection process to achieve an optimal outcome, but it must be completed in a professional and nondiscriminatory manner (see the following section, *Evaluating Organizational Fit: Defining and Documenting Fit*).

Here are a few generic examples that illustrate the importance of selecting for fit in addition to qualifications. A person whose primary interest is research is unlikely to do well in a teaching-oriented institution. A person who is not respectful of diversity is unlikely to do well in an HR office. Likewise, a faculty member who believes in a classical education and knowledge for the sake of knowledge is unlikely to do well in an institution that emphasizes cooperative education. Last, some professors would never consider teaching online, while some institutions see tremendous value in making this option available to students.

These generic examples highlight professional differences, yet individual differences are also fair game in selecting *organizational fit*. However, this area is fraught with potential bias and complication. If used properly, this screening method ensures that you are selecting for retention as well. While tigers and lions are similarly fast, fearless, and ferocious, not every cat will be successful in every environment. Mountain lions, arctic tigers, and lions found on safaris are fundamentally different. Getting a well-qualified and capable "king of the jungle" requires you to select for fit also.

The metaphor of a natural habitat where animals live and thrive in certain climates and conditions that are conducive to their survival seems to apply to humans and retention in organizations that complement their characteristics, preferences, and work style. Part of the art of selecting well is selecting individuals who are already predisposed to or who already exhibit the personal characteristics that are consistent with the mission, values, goals, and initiatives of your institution. You do not have to worry whether a person who graduated from a community college believes in the community college mission when selecting faculty for a teaching position at a community college.

A person—regardless of race—is likely to support your organization's diversity goals if the individual has several references on his or her résumé to working in environments, advising student groups, or volunteering in communities that are different from his or her own. A similar conclusion could be made for individuals who have served in the Peace Corps. In *Hiring Right: Conducting Successful Searches in Higher Education*, Hochel and Wilson (2007) argue that just as it is necessary to recruit minorities, we must also recruit those who value diversity. This is a good example of a requirement for *organizational fit* that supports retention and equal opportunity for success. Support for diversity could be an *organizational fit* criterion that is easily substantiated and evaluated.

Similarly, candidates who say they are committed to research but cannot provide a half-dozen abstracts of research ideas they are considering probably do not have the curiosity, drive, or commitment to research to be successful in a research institution. A degree from a so-called "good" school does not provide enough evidence of fit for a research university professorship. However, if fit is defined well, in a nondiscriminatory manner, and evaluated by the use of evidence, these factors can virtually ensure the success of a new hire for years to come as he or she will naturally flower in an environment that complements their personal philosophy.

Evaluating Organizational Fit: Defining and Documenting Fit

Organizational fit is a commonly used term, but it is also as commonly misunderstood as it is misapplied. Often, fit is described as a displeasing characteristic of a candidate that disqualifies him or her from employment. Yet just as often, it is displeasing only because it is different from a committee member's personal preferences. An interviewee is said to be capable, but he or she does not seem to "fit" here. Some typical examples are: "He would be happier at a place that has more resources"; "She seems too quiet to want to work with a bunch of loud extroverts like us"; or "His background is too prestigious. I'm not sure if he would eventually stay at our institution." When a member of the search committee makes these statements, others may consider these new criteria, even though they were not applied to other candidates.

When additional criteria are included in an ad hoc fashion during deliberations, and then used to eliminate otherwise well-qualified candidates, this is a classic case of conscious or subconscious subterfuge. Suddenly, "nice to have" or esoteric preferences appear as important as primary criteria (see *Red Flags*, p. 154). Such tactics are often veiled attempts to call inappropriate attention to minority and women candidates. The goal in these circumstances is to undermine someone's candidacy by discrediting the candidate's differences. According to diversity expert JoAnn Moody (2010), it is a common search committee tactic that differences are defined as good as long as they are not different from "me."

To prevent such misuse of *organizational fit*, the selection criteria upon which *organizational fit* is applied should be either observable or measureable, and either stated or documented. And like all other selection criteria, *organizational fit* must be agreed upon in advance, and the fit criteria must appear in the organizational analysis, position description, job advertisement, or *committee charge*. Good fit criteria are found in the organization's bylaws, mission, strategic plan, initiatives, or goals. Leaders at all levels commonly hold these widely used ideas or beliefs. Good fit elements are often practiced as well.

Documented Examples of Organizational Fit

Examples of *organizational fit* that meet the criteria of observable or measureable and either stated or documented are factors such as belief in cooperative education, service-learning, egalitarianism, student-centeredness, globalism, or a sense of humor (see Exhibit #29: *Organizational Selection Criteria Examples*). Cooperative education can be found in the curriculum; service-learning is a major funding initiative; egalitarianism is noted in our bylaws; student-centeredness can be found in our cocurricular programming as well as in the fact that faculty participation in student activities is a factor in tenure evaluation; globalism is illustrated by our study abroad and international programs; and a sense of humor is evident from the president's speeches, the annual faculty and staff talent contest, and the traditional lampoon edition of the student newspaper. These factors can and should be used, but the committee must agree in advance on which factors to use when considering fit.

Just as vital as agreeing upon which criteria to use, committee members must also agree how to evaluate the presence of the fit criteria. A *sense of humor* can be defined as the "attempted" use of humor on multiple occasions such as in written materials and during interviews. Evaluating who is funny is impossible. A commitment to interdisciplinary studies can be evaluated by course syllabi, coauthorships with others outside of one's discipline, and the examples used in responses to interview questions.

As noted previously, the proper use of *organizational fit* as a screening criteria and selection method can be an invaluable tool. It affords a multidimensional evaluation of a candidate's potential for success in a particular institution. Not only is fit a preferable requirement, it is an indispensable one. When selecting for fit, you are also selecting for retention.

Organizational Fit Criteria

To determine which candidates will best fit a particular department and the institution as a whole, the *hiring authority* can develop a list of organizational characteristics to inform the process of selecting for *organizational fit*. Extreme care must be taken in including and evaluating such attributes to make sure they do not reflect one person's personality or preferences. As noted, they should be observable or measureable and either stated or documented (see Exhibit #29: *Organizational Selection Criteria Examples*). Such factors can be used as a tool for screening candidates who have been identified as semifinalists. The attributes could be listed in *position announcements* and advertisements to describe the ideal candidate, but they should not be described as required. Instead, they should be used as a tertiary screening criterion, considered only *after* all other objective measures have been exhausted.

The best advice is to use *organizational fit* criteria only when considering the final two or three candidates. This should occur at the conclusion of interviews to evaluate candidates in light of their interview performance and the complete strengths and weaknesses they would bring to the position. Including notes about organizational fit in the committee's recommendation by listing each candidate's strengths and weaknesses is a good approach to incorporating fit into a final evaluation.

Summary: Final Selection

Every screening method has its advantages and disadvantages as well as its appropriate uses. Each additional screening method that is used adds rigor to the selection process. Planning which screening methods to use at which stage of the process to evaluate the essential and preferred requirements of a position and the needs of the organization is a building block to a successful search and a great hire. Due to the multiple criteria, the multiple selection methods, the input of many stakeholders, and the dynamic nature of the selection process, some organizations find it useful to create a final selection evaluation matrix to help them compile and consider all of the information collected (see Exhibit #30: *Final Evaluation Matrix Instrument*). This final evaluation matrix can also justify or explain the recommendation made to the *appointing authority*. Its visual nature is a very effective communicative tool. Finally, at the conclusion of this process, committee ratings and other objective evaluations should be preserved as official records of the search process and can prove the inherent fairness of the process should it be challenged.

EXHIBIT #29
Organizational Selection Criteria Examples

To complement the various additional screening methods, it is often prudent to have organizational screening criteria that represent overarching ideas that apply to most, if not all, positions within an institution. These criteria are usually based upon the most important values, beliefs, goals, and purposes of the organization. Wise organizations establish, publicize, and promote the practice of these ideals in many ways, including in the selection of faculty and staff.

Since all positions exist within the context of a department and an organization, these criteria have a place in the search committee process. Therefore, it is necessary to note these ideas in the organizational analysis, job descriptions, and advertisements, and/or otherwise state the essentialness of them in the *charge*. The following are some examples of requirements that reflect the character, qualities, and nature of a specific department or institution:

Institution- or Department-Specific Criteria (Examples)
- Is customer service- or teamwork-oriented
- Supports innovative teaching methods
- Understands diverse learning styles
- Believes in volunteerism
- Is committed to public service
- Is committed to continuous learning
- Has published, given presentations, done research, received grants
- Possesses sense of humor
- Supports flexible scheduling
- Supports professional development
- Has interdisciplinary interests
- Advocates the use of technology in teaching
- Is a proponent of ecology or environmental responsibility
- Shows sensitivity to and/or support of diversity and multicultural matters
- Has entrepreneurial, creative, or innovation spirit
- Supports community service and "town and gown" relationships
- Possesses cultural competence needed to work with students, clients, etc.
- Supports globalism
- Accepts people with disabilities
- Welcomes new ideas and perspectives
- Other factors outlined in the strategic plans of the institution
- Other factors stated as institutional goals or initiatives

These additional criteria are used as yardsticks for measuring the "best fit" of applicants in relation to the department and organization. To help identify the best candidate for the organization, both the college and the applicant can use these intangible, yet important requirements to determine whether there is a marriage of similar hearts and minds.

However, it should be noted that adherence to the explicit job description criteria (i.e., essential functions) is usually required in initial stages of the screening process and may assist in defending against allegations of discrimination or unequal treatment. Nonetheless, these additional criteria are helpful in ensuring that finalists fit well with the context of the job, department, and the organization's culture.

To this end, some of the language of the additional criteria is often used in *position announcements* and advertisements to describe the ideal candidate, but they are not listed as required qualifications. These additional criteria are most useful and fair to all involved if used only at the finalist stage of the screening process, *after* all other objective evaluations have been completed.

───────

Note: Bias on the basis of race, natural origin, citizenship, religion, gender, sexual orientation, disability, age, or other *protected classification* should not be allowed to enter into this evaluation (see *Evaluating Organizational Fit: Why You Should and Must*).

EXHIBIT #30
Final Evaluation Matrix Instrument

Candidate's Name _____

Committee Member's Name _____

AGREED-UPON SELECTION CRITERIA	Cover Letter	Résumé	Telephone Interview	Work Sample	Teaching Demo	Portfolio	Interview	Other	Remarks
Mastery of instructional design		X		H		M			
Competent instructional delivery					H	H			Engaging demonstration
Scholarship potential						M	H	X	
Quality of publications		M				M			Small number
Multicultural competence		M	M		H		H	X	
Support of service-learning	X	X				M	H		Conversant on subject
Interest in student research							M		
Communications ability	H	X	X		X		X	X	
Understanding of mission of a community college	H	H	M	H	H	X	H	H	
Sense of humor present	X		X		X		X		
Other									
Final Ranking	Very nice mix of competencies, good match with our agreed-upon criteria. I regard this candidate as 1 of 3.								

H = High; M = Medium; L = Low; X = Present

CHAPTER 14

Background and Reference Checks

UNTIL REFERENCE AND BACKGROUND CHECKS are conducted, all of the information about a candidate comes from the candidate. Therefore, due diligence is required to verify the identity, character, work experiences, and accomplishments of candidates as documented in their application materials. To a large degree, reference and background checks are honesty tests that are wholly warranted since, according to the Society for Human Resource Management, up to 61% of résumés contain some inaccurate information (Burke & Schramm, 2004).

Reference and background checks, usually the last screening technique to evaluate candidates for employment, are generally conducted only for a single finalist. Institutions may have a de facto legal requirement to verify and uncover these facts. Otherwise, the institution could face legal action on the grounds of *negligent hiring*, a tort doctrine recognized in many states (Burke & Schramm, 2004). This occurs if an employee with a criminal, violent, or marred history harms someone, and it is subsequently found that the injury to others could have been prevented if the company had uncovered the information in a background check. Emerging case law indicates that the same liability may apply if a candidate destroys property or brings injury to a company's reputation or ability to do business.

Due to the nature of the workplace today, it is prudent to gather as much information about potential employees as possible and to verify factual information as a basic way of doing business. College and universities, and particularly professors, hold a special place of trust in our society, so having a trustworthy faculty and staff is indispensable to preserving the reputation of institutions. Hiring the wrong person can harm a college or university's ability to recruit students, among other concerns. This is a step where shortcuts can have disastrous consequences. Exhibit #31: *Background Check Checklist* presents a checklist of considerations for conducting a thorough reference and background check. Without a deliberate policy and practice of verifying the background of potential hires, organizations invite the unscrupulous or dangerous to enter their ranks (see Vignette S: *Something to Hide? Apply Here!*).

References

It can be a challenge to obtain reference information because many individuals and organizations are reluctant to give references due to a fear of litigation. As a result, many organizations have policies that limit the information they provide for verification of employment and dates of employment. A second challenge with many references is that they may produce very little useful information because candidates provide a carefully chosen and select group of people who will always offer only a 100% positive account of their background, regardless of the facts. The most prudent advice to overcome the limitations of references is to ask the candidates for 8 to 12 references from groups that you define, such as coworkers, vendors, former supervisors, subordinates, customers, and so on; then you select a handful of them to pursue. This technique overcomes the predefined group of referees that will always say only nice things about a candidate, and it increases the likelihood that you will receive more balanced reference information (see Vignette T: *A Good Reference Is Hard to Find: A Few Cautions in the Reference-Checking Process*).

In addition, permission should be sought to pursue references from others to whom the reference checker is directed while completing references. For example, if you are asking a former colleague about whether a candidate is a good budget manager, and the colleague says he or she does not know, you might ask who would know such matters and be referred to another

---

EXHIBIT #31
Background Check Checklist

Here are a number of factors to consider and questions to ask when verifying a candidate's background:

- Are you aware of your school's policy on background checks and reference checking?
- Have you received the candidate's permission to check his or her references?
- Ask the candidate if you can seek references from individuals not listed on his or her reference list if someone is referred to you during the referencing process.
- Ask if there is anyone you should not contact and why.
- Ask the candidate to notify references to let them know you will call.
- Ensure that all references are individuals who have worked with the candidate in a professional capacity and who are not relatives or friends of the candidate.
- Ask the candidate if he or she is *professionally* acquainted with any of your employees.
- Insist that two or more references be former supervisors.
- Ask the candidate if he or she has worked under any other name than the one given to you.
- Review (or seek) written letters of recommendation.
- Verify dates of employment.
- Verify the title(s) and time in each position listed on the résumé to ensure they are the same.
- Verify salary, if applicable.
- Verify education and licenses.
- Seek to verify the candidate's character (e.g., general description of person's habits, personality, work ethic, etc.).
- Attempt to identify professional strengths and weaknesses.
- Ask for copies of past performance evaluations, where appropriate and available.
- Ask how well the candidate works with others (including diverse populations).
- Ask the reference's opinion of how the candidate would perform in the position.
- Ask if the candidate is eligible for rehire at the institution or if supervisors would rehire the person if they had the opportunity to do so.
- Ask why the candidate left or is leaving the position in question.
- Check a similar number of references for all candidates (i.e., do not check seven references for minorities and women and five for all others).
- Seek the services of a background-checking firm, where appropriate.
- Does the job application or other process state that falsification of information is cause for termination or revocation of the employment offer? If so, ensure that the application is signed.
- Ask whether the candidate was the subject of any disciplinary action or legal proceedings in his or her previous position.
- Consult with HR or legal counsel about the desirability of checking criminal records, driving records, credit reports, or other sources.
- Document all reference-checking activities.

---

person. If financial acumen is critical to the evaluation of a candidate, it would be wise to speak with the other person. Caution is provided here that for many reasons—legal and common courtesy among them—you should ask for permission in advance (see Vignette U: *Calling a Friend: Oops Goes the Reference Check*). Candidates who deny you the opportunity to speak with others not on their reference list should give you reason to pause. This in and of itself is good reference information.

Despite the common fear that many have of providing reference information, the good news about reference checks is that individuals and organizations do not have much liability for providing references if the information is known to be true and is provided by someone in a position of authority. That

VIGNETTE S
Something to Hide? Apply Here!

Is your organization one of the few in the 21st century that does not conduct background checks? Individuals who have something to hide notice whether your job advertisements have the telling statement, "Background checks are required for all positions at XYZ University." You will become a haven for well-qualified but questionable individuals who know they would not survive an adequate background check.

One technique they use is to apply for temporary employment as a way of bypassing the more stringent background checks of full-time, regular employment. Once they are inside, they apply for regular employment. By then you have fallen in love with them and many organizations fail to complete background checks on *current* employees.

Some campuses conduct background checks on staff but not faculty. Despite noble protestations from articulate faculty who warn of the misplaced intentions and folly of such actions, the simple fact remains that not checking faculty is unwise and exposes the institution to unlimited liability (see *Negligent Hiring*, p. 168). Most notable, the reputation of the institution would be irreparably harmed if someone discovered that a new faculty member had been convicted of a heinous crime and is now employed teaching our sons and daughters.

Prudence dictates and case law demands that anyone who is hired undergo a reference check and background check process. Remember, the cost of a bad hire is significant and can be avoided easily with a little time, effort, and money.

VIGNETTE T
A Good Reference Is Hard to Find
A Few Cautions in the Reference-Checking Process

Checking references is a critical part of the employment process and should be undertaken with great care. People who have something to hide, who wish to persuade you to hire them despite some facts that would make you avoid them, or who simply are not who they say they are will try to manipulate this process to impress or persuade you. Here are some serious scenarios that illustrate the point.

Best Friends, Relatives, and Sisters: Good friends and relatives can be relied upon to speak well of their friends and family in almost any circumstance. They are certainly willing to help one another get jobs. Spouses, sisters, and in-laws often have different last names. It is common to have dual academic couples in higher education, and spouses can and do offer references for one another. Therefore, it is imperative to ask references about their professional and personal relationship with the candidate and whether they are related.

Fake Reference-Checking Firm(s): In 2009, ABC News and other media outlets reported that a series of fake job reference companies had sprung up to provide references for people who

(continues)

(*continued*)

were having difficulty finding jobs during the tough economy. For a small fee, such organizations would pretend to be an employer and offer positive references for individuals. It would be prudent to verify the name, phone number, position, and other identifying information of the person who is offering you a reference.

Competitors (You Would Be Lucky to Hire Him): If a competitor is too supportive of losing a great candidate, be cautious. "I secretly wish that Bob would leave, and I know that if I give him a bad or lukewarm reference, you will not hire him away from me." So, I might exaggerate his ability in the reference process, otherwise I am stuck with him.

Half-Truths: Almost anyone who has ever held a job performs some aspects of the job well. These are precisely the facts that appear accurately in letters of recommendation; however, the rest of the story may be missing. Due diligence demands that every letter of recommendation be taken with a grain of salt. If performance appraisals are any indication of human behavior, people are naturally reluctant to put negative information in writing and tend to inflate ratings. They are more likely to divulge the truth, however, if asked pointedly. Letters of recommendation should be verified via a reference-checking conversation.

The Best Recommendation I Ever Received: It is the best because I wrote it. With a Web browser and a word processor, anyone can create a letter with a logo that appears to be from nearly any official. Letters of recommendation should be verified.

Drs. Smith and Jones: Academe is filled with professionals who have doctoral degrees and other impressive titles. Clarifying whether a reference actually worked with or supervised a candidate for employment is a fundamental part of the reference check. Colleagues, particularly in academic departments, often give one another references or write letters of recommendation for one another. Furthermore, since the department chair position in some departments is a yearly rotating position, it is possible that a candidate's peer was the "administrative" head of the department, but not one who had de facto supervisory responsibility. Since only a true supervisor can ever have a full view of one's contributions, this perspective must be included in the reference-checking process. It is critical to ensure that the reference's relationship with the candidate is crystal clear during the reference-checking process.

In addition to the tips provided, a few techniques can help to improve the quality, accuracy, and veracity of the reference-checking process: (a) when asking for references, designate from where and which type of positions you prefer to have references instead of asking for a generic slate of references (i.e., please provide a list of three former supervisors, two subordinates from X employer, a colleague at ABC institution, a representative of the association where you served on the editorial board); (b) complete 6 to 10 references instead of the traditional three to five; (c) ensure that your references include multiple former supervisors—without exception; (d) get off the standard reference list; and (e) verify the identity and position of the people who offer you references.

References

Gomstyn, A. (2009, August 26). Faking job references for a price. ABC News Business Unit. Retrieved from http://abcnews.go.com/Business/fake-job-references-real-jobs/story?id=8401993

Gurchiek, K. (2008, October 1). Staffing management: Mensa member, other resume lies. Retrieved from www.shrm.org/Publications/StaffingManagementMagazine/EditorialContent/Pages/1008gurchiek.aspx

VIGNETTE U
Calling a Friend
Oops Goes the Reference Check

The practice of "calling around" to investigate the background of applicants is a potentially unprofessional and unethical practice that should be stopped. For a number of reasons, a candidate might want to keep his or her candidacy private for a time. Calling around is discourteous to the candidate and can put the candidate into difficult situations with his or her supervisor, peers, friends, or family depending upon the circumstances. The rumor mill might start and misinformation might also derive from this misplaced practice.

Here are four stories based on real-life situations that reinforce the point that each individual's identity must be preserved and all search activities should be confidential.

Me Too: The premier academic program in a particular course of study announced a vacancy. The search committee chair decided to call the program head from the graduate school from which a young rising star graduated to inquire about the potential candidate. He was very surprised and embarrassed to learn that the program head was unwilling to give an endorsement to her former student since she had recently applied for the vacancy herself.

Do I Know Her?: A professor shared with a departmental colleague who was not on the search committee his frank opinion of one of the finalists who was coming to campus. He asked because he knew his colleague had graduated from the same program a few years earlier. Much to his chagrin, he learned later that his disparaging comments were about his colleague's fiancée, who was attempting to relocate to the area to be with her future husband. The colleague did not disclose to anyone that his fiancée was in the pool to avoid any appearance of favoritism or impropriety. Not only had the committee member violated the confidentiality of the search committee process, he was also checking references before having the authorization to do so.

Colleagues and Competitors: Two former colleagues were semifinalists for the same presidential position. A peculiar situation was avoided when the search committee member who started calling around noticed that each had listed the other as a reference. If the candidates had not listed one another, an embarrassing situation would have occurred.

Trust and Loyalty: Unfortunately, some leaders do not support the professional growth and development of their subordinates and regard someone's looking for another job as an act of disloyalty or disengagement. A particular dean was recruited into the finalist pool for the provost position at a prestigious college and reluctantly accepted the offer of an interview due to a particularly persuasive search consultant. "It would be good interviewing experience," the consultant said, "in case one day you decide you really want to be a provost." The experience turned out poorly when the candidate returned to campus, was called into her own provost's office, and heard, "I thought you said you took the day off to take care of personal business." Worse yet, the dean's supervisor called into question her loyalty, commitment, and performance numerous times in the ensuing months. She was eventually terminated under questionable circumstances.

(continues)

(*continued*)

> The act of calling around could expose an institution to libel and slander charges. Confidentiality is a matter of both principle and professionalism. Organizations must vet candidates completely, investigate their background, and scrutinize their reported capabilities. Institutions that seek unfettered access into a candidate's background can do so by asking the candidate's permission to call additional people to be diligent in their investigation. If a candidate disagrees, then this is in and of itself information. However, in all cases, candidates should be aware that someone is looking into their background, if for no other reason than common courtesy.

is, a supervisor who notes that a person's performance was below average based upon evidence and the supervisor's professional judgment does not have anything to worry about. The concerns about liability are warranted when references speak to coworkers or others who do not have a full picture of a person's performance and they say unverifiable or subjective statements about the person's work or reputation, such as, "No one liked working with her." Giving accurate statements that can be supported by evidence from a person in a position to rightfully provide the information is the best defense against liability exposure. Usually this person is the supervisor only—that is, dean, provost—not a colleague.

Similar to conducting a good interview, reference checks should be structured and should contain a slate of prepared questions to elicit pertinent information about the candidate's character, work ethic, and ability to perform the job. The best reference check asks job-related questions from factors identified in the organizational analysis, job description, job advertisement, and *charge*, including *organizational fit* criteria. Exhibits #32 and #33 present sample forms for checking references over the telephone.

Diversity Tip: References present a good opportunity to verify the experiences of candidates who claim to have experience with multicultural populations or to have diverse professional experiences. The mere presence or absence of demographically diverse references is one indicator. Also, references can be asked about the finalist's professional activities and behaviors. Questions about whether the candidate worked with, supported, volunteered, or socialized with different populations at professional events and functions are fair opportunities for verification.

Liability for Libel and Slander

Checking references can expose employers to legal liability if they are conducted in an unprofessional manner. As a general rule, the search committee should ask permission to seek references in advance and tell the candidate which individuals it plans to contact. With this permission, the committee should also ask whether it can pursue information from others if one of the references refers them to others. Committee members should know what types of information they can seek and how the information can be used. The committee should consult with HR or legal counsel if it has any questions or doubts about these matters (see Vignette U: *Calling a Friend: Oops Goes the Reference Check*). Training on reference checks can be covered in the initial committee training. Using a preapproved reference-checking form is a safe method of managing this issue.

Background Checks

There are numerous methods of obtaining background information on candidates. Here are a few of the most commonly used searches or techniques:

Reference checks	Motor vehicle records
Criminal history records	Social Security number check
Drug screening	Sexual offender record registry
Degree/licensure verification	Credit history
Bankruptcy filings	Publication review
Employment verification	Military records
Litigation records	Internet search*
Civil records (e.g., court filings, judgments, liens, etc.)	

*See Vignette V: *To Google or Not to Google, That Is the Question.*

EXHIBIT #32
General Reference-Checking Form

Candidate's Name (and/or former name): _____

Person Called: _____**Person's Position:** _____

Company Name: _____

Note: Be sure to tell the reference the position for which the candidate is applying.

1. What is/was your relationship to _____[candidate's name]?
2. How long did you work with _____? From _____[date] to _____[date].
3. Can you verify the position(s) he or she held? _____
4. Can you provide us with a general character reference of _____?
5. Did you have the opportunity to observe _____ as a _____[former position title]?
6. How would you describe his or her overall performance? Please provide examples.
7. What do you see as _____'s strengths and areas where he or she needs/needed additional development [weaknesses]?
8. How would you compare the performance of _____ to that of others who have held the same or a similar job?
9. Please describe _____'s work ethic, including any issues with tardiness, absenteeism, attitude, abuse of sick or vacation time, dependability, trustworthiness, or completion of assigned tasks.
10. What sort of environment do you think _____ would work best within?
11. Why did _____ leave your organization, or why do you think he or she is interested in leaving?
12. If you had the opportunity, would you hesitate to employ/re-employ or work with _____?
13. Is there any *additional* information you feel we should know in considering _____ for employment?

Other types of information can be considered; however, since the laws vary by state, counsel should be consulted to ensure that the checks are allowed in your state. Verifying the accuracy of a candidate's background and uncovering facts relevant to the duties of the position sought is always prudent.

Most organizations use private firms to complete background checks but may perform reference checks internally. In recent years, however, reference-checking firms are becoming more prevalent. If undertaken by a party other than the employer, any such check (including a reference check, criminal background check, and credit check) must be overseen by the HR office to ensure that it meets all the requirements of the Fair Credit Reporting Act, which governs such activities.

Due Diligence

How much of a candidate's background to check into is consistent with the principle of due diligence? The right amount depends on the position and the organization in question. The scope and depth of a check might increase with the seniority and sensitivity of the position. Verification of degrees, licenses, and skills is probably more critical in background checks of physicians than in background checks of librarians—though it is a requirement to check for both. Checking credit reports is more critical for chief financial officers and accounts payable professions but is not necessarily appropriate for groundskeepers and counselors. In either case, the institution must comply with the requirements of the Fair Credit Reporting Act.

EXHIBIT #33
Position-Specific Reference-Checking Form

Department Chair, Business Department

Candidate's Name (and/or former name): _____

Person Called: _____ Person's Position: _____

Organization Name: _____

Introduction: _____[candidate's name] has applied for the department head position in the Business Department at Williamsburg College. If you have a few minutes, I would like to ask you a series of questions about [his or her] potential for success in this position.

1. Can you provide me with a general character reference for _____?
2. Can you describe two or three examples of _____'s abilities with financial planning or budgeting-related matters?
3. This position requires management of the day-to-day affairs of an academic department. Can you describe _____'s work history with managing personnel, class schedules, student complaints, and related matters in an academic department?
4. Our department is seeking accreditation from the AACSB. Can you describe _____'s experience with related accreditation efforts?
5. We are looking to revamp our curriculum; with your experience and in your professional judgment, do you think _____ has the knowledge, experience, and leadership ability necessary to help a department successfully complete such a potentially difficult and contentious task? Why? Please give us examples to support your assessment.
6. How active is _____ in student-related matters? Please mention any mentoring-related activities and experiences if you are aware of any.
7. To the best of your knowledge, how is _____'s scholarship viewed on campus and within the discipline?
8. What fund-raising activities and successes has _____ had at your institution?
9. How would you describe _____'s ability to develop relationships and partnerships with others inside and outside the university?
10. Are you aware of any violations of policy, law, or legal or ethical issues in which _____ was involved while working with your institution?
11. Is there any *additional* information you feel we should have in considering _____ for employment?

Your Name: _____ Date: _____

HR professionals should develop a policy to guide which kind of checks will be conducted for which positions (see Vignette V: *To Google or Not to Google, That Is the Question*). This protocol should be followed in all hiring as it could be discriminatory to use it for certain candidates and not others (i.e., candidates from *protected classes*, or only for positions targeted by socioeconomic status). The policy should also address how adverse information will be handled. A good practice is to make a group decision about the net effect of negative information. Suggested candidates for this "groupthink" decision-making process are an HR professional, the *appointing authority*, and a senior professional who is not involved in the

VIGNETTE V
To Google or Not to Google, That Is the Question

In the era of the Internet and social media, the often-asked question is, "Should we or should we not Google our finalist before we invite him or her to campus?" Another way of asking the question is, "Should we conduct a public records search to obtain valuable information about candidates before we make the mistake of inviting someone to campus whom we would not hire?" There is considerable debate among experts about the ethics and legality of this practice.

First, the legal caution is that in researching a candidate, one is bound to learn whether the candidate is male, female, or has a different sexual orientation or identity. The candidate's race, marital, disability, veteran, or other status and other personal information is also likely to be available on the Internet. This information can be used in a discriminatory manner. Second, ethical arguments surround privacy, advance notice to candidates, favoritism or preferential treatment for those like us, or bias against others due to other characteristics or circumstances. Advance knowledge obtained on the Internet is ripe for misuse of information about candidates.

An argument in favor of conducting an Internet search into the background of candidates is that it would be irresponsible not to review publically available information. Additionally, according to the tort doctrine of negligent hiring, if information is available in a public place, the institution "should have known" it. If negative information is uncovered later, after a person is hired, then the institution may share some culpability for the potentially negative actions of a new hire (see *Negligent Hiring*, p. 168), albeit this occurs only in extreme cases where an employee causes harm to individuals or to an organization's property or reputation. Similarly, if the organization has a religious mission, and it is discovered at the interview or after an offer has been made that the person is agnostic, this would likely indicate a bad *organizational fit*. Advance information would prevent this embarrassing situation.

Another argument for conducting Internet searches of all semifinalists and using this information to validate whether an already selected candidate should be asked to interview is to consider the specific information candidates willfully placed on the Internet as an indicator of their character and judgment. If candidates proudly tout their membership in a sexist, racist, or separatist organization; use foul and degrading language to describe their current supervisor and workplace; post lewd pictures and drunken behavior on their social media pages; are involved in illegal activities (e.g., downloading pirated music or software); or display other questionable statements, actions, or affiliations, this information can and should be used to determine their suitability for employment. With the appropriate legal cautions, the caveat here is to take action on information the candidate deliberately placed on the Internet, such as information on social media profiles or personal and professional websites.

A final argument for Internet searching is to verify the information candidates have provided. Confirming employers, employment dates, professional memberships and affiliations, and awards, as well as verifying the names and titles of references, are among the many examples of information that can be checked with a simple Internet search.

Colleagues, students, peers, parents, and the general community will learn in seconds after the finalist for a dean of engineering position is announced that one of the candidates was

(*continues*)

(*continued*)

accused, but never tried for, trafficking in illegal or unethical material, as well as the fact that one of the other candidates is the inventor of a medical device that has saved thousands of lives. The question for search committees and institutions is, Should they use the Internet to learn about this information and, if so, when should they do so and how should they use it? Completing Internet searches of candidates is a risk-and-reward proposition. The risk of not knowing negative information early is as substantial as the risk of legal proceedings.

Colleges and universities should develop policies concerning use of the Internet in screening and evaluating candidates and completing background checks. The appropriate legal precautions should govern how such public record searches are used and should ensure that they are not used for discriminatory purposes. However, each institution, with the help of legal counsel and HR professionals, should determine whether using the Internet is acceptable to evaluate candidates.

selection process (i.e., someone who does not have anything to gain or lose by the decision). Legal counsel should be consulted as necessary.

Summary

In all cases, all finalists should be subjected to a thorough vetting process to ensure that they are who they say they are and that they have done the things they claim to have done. Absent a thorough verification process, the institution has not conducted a thorough, rigorous, and professional search. For the reasons noted in Vignette S: *Something to Hide? Apply Here!* and as described in chapter 19, internal candidates should be subject to a background check as well. No search is complete without a complete background check.

PART FOUR

Making the Selection

CHAPTER 15

Making a Recommendation

AFTER FINAL INTERVIEWS, the search committee determines which candidate(s), if any, to recommend to the *appointing authority*. Recommendations vary in style and approach—committees may recommend one candidate, rank all of the finalists, or provide a report outlining the strengths and weaknesses of each finalist. The search committee's recommendation should be presented in the manner requested by the *appointing authority* in its *charge* to the committee.

The best practice format for recommendations is for the committee to provide a narrative detailing the strengths and weaknesses of each interviewee according to standards outlined earlier in the process. This approach gives the *appointing authority* multiple options, all of which are in the best interest of the institution. Aided by the committee's recommendation, the *appointing authority*—the person who is ultimately responsible for the success of the position—will likely consider numerous other factors in determining whom to hire. Strategic plans, personnel matters, diversity considerations, short- versus long-term trade-offs for a candidate who might have an immediate impact compared to another who might be an investment for the future, and a plethora of other operational factors within the department or the institution may be considered. If the preferred candidate does not accept the position, the *appointing authority* knows the relative advantages of selecting one of the other candidates because the thorough recommendation includes each candidate's strengths and weaknesses. This recommendation format has proven effective in preventing failed searches.

Why Ranking Candidates Is Not in Your Best Interest

Committees are discouraged from ranking candidates in their final recommendations for a number of reasons. Rankings can create factions and winners and losers. When committees vote and committee members advocate for certain candidates at the expense of others, this process can spill over into the workplace. If committee members whose candidate did not succeed are unhappy, they might feel slighted and unintentionally harbor negative emotions against fellow committee members and even the new hire. There are many stories of candidates, particularly in leadership positions, whose failures started before they were hired because a faction of committee members began to undermine them before they ever arrived on campus. In these situations, the slighted committee members emphasize the weaknesses of the new hire instead of the person's strengths when speaking of him or her to others. The new hire starts work with a less than ideal reputation, instead of the normal enthusiasm that greets a new member of the community. Rankings also tend to make those in the minority feel as if their voice was not heard. Moreover, some might object so vehemently to the ranking that they draft a minority opinion (see *Dissenting Opinion*, p. 166) as a way to express their views in a collegial but direct manner to the *appointing authority*. The contentiousness of a dissenting opinion can be avoided if the committee presents a slate of candidates with an honest assessment of all of their strengths and weaknesses. Further, all recommendations are relative and represent more art than science (see Vignette W: *Since When Is Roger Federer Not Good Enough?*). Thus, a full explanation of all of the factors considered is the best recommendation method and should rely on the collective judgment of the committee, with the final analysis resting with the *appointing authority*.

Confidentiality Reemphasized

Committees should remind themselves during their deliberations that their discussions are confidential. No one other than the *appointing authority* should be privy to the content of the recommendation. The identity of applicants and the content of committee deliberations should be kept confidential before, during, and after the committee does its work—into perpetuity. In addition to confidentiality breaches with applicants, nothing can be as unnecessary and disheartening as a colleague learning that he or she was the second choice five years ago (see Vignette W: *Since When Is Roger Federer Not Good Enough?*).

Additionally, who applied for a position is a matter of privacy and principle. Some candidates would not apply or would withdraw from a search if it were known that they are candidates. Some candidates wait to tell their family that they have applied until they are a finalist so their family does not get excited about an opportunity that might not materialize, or they may want to wait to tell their current employer until an offer is nearly in hand. Unfortunately, there are many

VIGNETTE W
Since When Is Roger Federer Not Good Enough?

Any ranking system has its advantages and disadvantages. Often rankings are perceived to be absolute when, in fact, they are relative assessments of candidates' strengths and weaknesses against certain criteria. The key word in the previous sentence is "certain." The criteria chosen predetermine whether the relative advantage of a top candidate stands or disappears. This exercise is inherently more difficult if the criteria are not clear, accurate, and agreed upon in advance. The waters are muddied even further if committee members are allowed to introduce new criteria in the midst of deliberations.

Whether ranking tennis players or biologists, committees should understand that rankings are not a panacea of quality. For this reason and others, experts advise that *appointing authorities* ask for committee recommendations in the form of the strengths and weaknesses of finalists instead of rankings. This gives the *appointing authority* the full measure of information needed to make a good decision about whom to hire. Saying a candidate is number one of three does not provide any useful qualitative data. And as mentioned, it then raises the questions, "According to what criteria?" "Compared to whom/what?" and "Under what conditions?" If the organization has done a good job recruiting, every search should elicit multiple competitive candidates who would be successful in the position.

During the early to mid-2000s, before Roger Federer earned the accolade of being considered the best tennis player of all time, he struggled against his nemesis, Rafael Nadal, who is almost five years his junior. Despite the fact that Roger has won significantly more masters' titles than any other tennis star, Rafael has won more head-to-head matches against Roger by a wide margin. Furthermore, it also matters which type of surface they are playing on. At one point, Rafael had won against Roger 11-2 on clay, while the two were even on hard courts 4-4, and Roger held the advantage of 2-1 on grass. The two also shared the world's top two tennis rankings between 2005 and 2010, despite having won or lost to one another several times during those years, including at Wimbledon. Some considered their 2008 Wimbledon match the greatest tennis match ever.

Imagine you are on a search committee and you have to choose between these two great players. Which would be a better approach: ranking the two players or presenting the strengths and weaknesses of each to the *appointing authority*. It is clear that Nadal has bested Federer in one-on-one competitions, so it would be natural to assume that a search committee would rank him higher. But, wow . . . the committee would be turning away the best tennis player (or biologist) of all time. It would be even worse then to have to tell everyone that you considered Roger as second best.

The truth is, whom to hire would depend on the needs of the organization: whether it needs someone to play on clay, grass, hard courts, a combination thereof; what time of year the person would play; whether it needs immediate results or is planning for the future; and other factors. Therefore, the far better approach to making a recommendation is to provide the *appointing authority* with enough information to make a good decision. Therefore, the recommendation should reflect the strengths and weaknesses of candidates based upon previously agreed-upon standards—those documented from the position description, advertisement, *committee charge*, and organizational analysis.

verified cases of supervisors who have blackballed employees or, worse yet, attempted to terminate staff members whom they see as having changed their loyalties to other priorities when they applied for other positions. For these and countless other reasons, sharing the names of applicants for a position with individuals outside of the committee is bad form, ethics, and practice.

Some states have "sunshine laws" that require the name of any applicants for public jobs to be made available to the public. A quick Internet search will reveal many of the lists. They have unwittingly limited their supply of talent, which undoubtedly will give them a disadvantage in selecting future faculty and staff. Confidentiality is an absolute requirement for all searches.

Preventing Failure

If the preferred candidate does not accept an offer of employment, the *appointing authority* may offer the position to another candidate in consideration of their relative strengths and weaknesses. He or she may also extend or reopen a search. A failed search can be an indicator of an ill-defined position, inadequate recruiting techniques, an inadequate pool of candidates, or ineffective selection methods. The *appointing authority* should get advice from the search committee chair and the HR representative. He or she should attempt to diagnose the variables that undermined the previous effort before deciding to reopen, extend, or end the search.

In addition to approaching the search and the recommendation in the right way—focusing on candidates and their relative strengths and weaknesses against predetermined and appropriate criteria—the best defense against a failed search is *laying the groundwork* properly for an effective search, as indicated in Part One of this book. Many search committees are tripped up along the way by needless errors in how they conduct their work. A deliberate and systematic approach to searches—such as the ones outlined in this book—can prevent common pitfalls.

CHAPTER 16

Making an Offer

YOU HAVE SPENT MONTHS TRYING TO FIND the right candidate; do not fumble the ball on the goal line, fall during the final act, or forget your lines in the final scene. After the *appointing authority* has received a recommendation from the committee and selected the preferred candidate, it is time to make an offer of employment. A competitive offer package must be created (see Vignette X: *The Third-Best Candidate*). The committee should tell candidates about the institution's compensation policies and total compensation package, including benefits, bonuses, or other *perquisites*. If the candidate is not aware of the dollar value of your benefits package, he or she might accept a competitor's employment offer that includes a higher salary but lower *total compensation*.

Other factors that should be considered are the intangibles that may enrich the employment value proposition for candidates—such as flexible work schedules, more generous leave accumulations, work location, and even the amount of support for advanced education or professional development. Each organization uses different recruitment and retention programs, and managers should know what their options are before extending an offer to a potential employee (see *Recruitment Incentives*, p. 149). Since employment offers are legally binding, hiring managers should follow any verbal offer with a written letter confirming the terms and conditions of employment, but should use the standard language or form letter produced by their HR department or legal counsel (see Exhibit #34: *Offer Letter Checklist*).

How to Make an Offer

The most import advice about making an offer is not to make an offer alone if you have not made an offer successfully at least four previous times. One should get help from an HR representative or another senior manager. Do not risk losing your chosen candidate over a minor issue after you have spent months conducting a search. Your first assumption should be that your candidate is still in the job market, which means that this great candidate has (or will have) other competing offers. Your goal is to have the candidate accept your offer *and* keep your offer. That is, if an offer comes in from another institution, the candidate will turn it down.

Since your candidate is on the job market, it is wise to assume that he or she has interviewed elsewhere but has not heard back or still has other interviews scheduled. If you do not make these assumptions, you put your good offer at risk. There is an art to building rapport with the candidate and having the person feel comfortable with your offer. First, be aware that your offer is not a financial transaction. It is a "total package" consideration; experts call this the employee value proposition—meaning that the candidate will consider the overall advantages and disadvantages of your offer, including compensation, benefits, perquisites, and other tangible and intangible factors. The following list provides an overview of many typical factors a candidate takes into account when reviewing an offer of employment:

- Salary
- Total compensation (incentive and merit pay, other pay policies, promotional opportunities)
- Benefits
- Perquisites (perks): research support, spousal employment opportunities, campus events, etc.
- Institutional factors
- History
- Campus culture
- Campus leadership
- Prestige
- People (e.g., colleagues, quality and types of students, etc.)
- Location

> ## VIGNETTE X
> ### The Third-Best Candidate
>
> We had a great applicant pool and our interviewees were all outstanding. After much deliberation, we recommended our slate of finalists to the executive director for her action. The preferred candidate did not accept the offer because it was not as competitive as she would have preferred. We were not terribly disappointed since our second candidate was equally well qualified but did not have as much experience. We were surprised when he also turned down our offer because he was making more than our offer in his current position.
>
> Finally, the executive director went to her vice president and HR person and received authorization to offer a more competitive salary to the third candidate, who eventually accepted our offer. This offer faux pas could have been avoided if we had conducted research and a labor market analysis and established a competitive hiring range at the start of the hiring process (see chapter 4, *Building the Foundation*). Doing so would have allowed the organization to snag the first and chosen candidate.

- Size of institution
- Duties and responsibilities
- Challenge and opportunities
- Intangibles (e.g., the college is located close to the candidate's family, you have a museum on campus in an area of interest to the candidate, etc.)

All of these factors are important and each factor varies in importance to individual candidates.

Second, the candidate is not aware of all of the great things about your institution, so this is an opportunity to tell or remind him or her. This supports the emotional part of the job offer.

People certainly must have money to make a living, but they serve and remain with institutions that are right for them on a number of levels. This perspective articulates the idea that the salary is only one part of the offer, and we must consider their commitment, engagement, and retention. Avoid the situation where the candidate accepts an offer he or she is unhappy with because the candidate needs a job, but emotionally he or she is not settled and never fully commits to your organization. This candidate will accept employment but will make plans to leave at the first opportunity. How offers are made is vitally important.

Making the Offer

The following guidelines provide advice for delivering a good offer.

- Schedule a time to speak with the candidate, or ensure that he or she has at least 15 minutes to talk.
- Start with how excited you are about talking with the candidate and hope that at the end of the conversation he or she agrees that XYZ college/university is the right place for him or her at this time.
- Compliment the candidate. Give one of the reasons why the candidate was selected, such as: "The committee was impressed with how you work with students. . . ."
- Talk about your institution and the great place it is, your community and its highlights, and so on. You should brag about your great colleagues as well.
- Ensure that the candidate has a list of or is familiar with your institution's benefits offerings *and* their relative value in dollars. HR can assist hiring managers with presenting this information in the best possible fashion (see *Benefits Briefs: Recruiting With Total Compensation*, p.148).

EXHIBIT #34
Offer Letter Checklist

Offer letters are legally binding documents that detail the terms and conditions of employment for a new position. As such, anyone extending an offer should use templates provided only by the HR department or the provost's office. Legal counsel should preapprove these templates to avoid confusion and legal issues. Offer letters will differ by types of position.

Here are some terms and conditions that are usually negotiable or that should be included in offer letters:

- Type of appointment (e.g., tenure track, joint, regular, temporary, etc.)
- Restrictions on funding of position, if appropriate
- Start date
- Date for new-employee orientation
- Availability of specific types of equipment (e.g., laptop, lab, furniture, etc.)
- Availability of specific resources (e.g., budget, staff, professional development funds, etc.)
- Specific assignments (e.g., committee participation)
- A date in the future when the new faculty member will be required to procure part of his or her salary from outside grants
- Assignment of a mentor or mentoring experience
- What is expected for promotion and tenure
- Sabbaticals and/or professional development leave
- Availability of spousal employment, dual-career couples, trailing spouses
- Institutional support in the form of nominations for other awards and grants
- Annual performance review
- Continuing support for a specified amount of time in the event the new faculty member does not get funding, if research support is required
- Conditions for renewal of appointment or probationary period
- Support for a trip to look for housing
- Parking
- Criminal background check prior to employment
- Requirement by schools of medicine that incoming faculty members sign a confidentiality certificate for compliance with HIPAA regulations
- Disclosure of outside employment activities
- Notation that the offer is contingent upon approval by the appropriate institutional officers or board of trustees, etc.
- Reference to governing documents (e.g., you are bound by the provisions of the faculty or staff handbook, etc.)

- Discuss any perquisites. Most often candidates do not know about these. Examples include new assistant professors get training from the sponsored programs department on how to find grant opportunities, the children of employees can attend summer camps for half price, or telework opportunities are available while candidates are relocating.
- Discuss intangibles. Talk specifically about things that might be important to the candidate based upon what you know about him or her. Tell musicians about the annual jazz festival, brag about the quality of the local schools to parents, or share your views about the beauty of the lake near campus for naturalists.

This process is critical because nonprofit institutions do not compete effectively on the basis of salary; they compete with better benefits, perquisites, quality-of-life factors, and mission. If a hiring manager cannot articulate the organization's benefits and the cost advantages of them, he or she may not be properly illustrating the total value of future compensation to the candidate. Some examples are the retirement contribution rate, health insurance deductibles, lower co-pays, or a short-term disability insurance program that your competitor does not offer. In this case, a candidate may accept another position with a higher salary, but with less total compensation.

Delivering the Salary Offer

When actually delivering the salary offer, you should keep the following in mind:

- Ideally, when you notified the candidate that he or she was a finalist and invited the candidate to the interview you discussed the salary range—so now the range should not come as a surprise.
- Talk about equity. Say something like, "We have tried to establish a fair and competitive salary for you in comparison to the pay of colleagues inside the institution as well as at peer institutions."
- Give the salary amount.
- Tell the candidate that you hope that the great college, community, total salary and benefits, and excited colleagues are enough to welcome him or her to your college.
- Even if the candidate accepts the offer on the spot, say that you will put the offer in writing, fax or e-mail it, and offer to let the candidate think about it overnight and confirm the offer the following day.
- Change the subject and ask about the candidate and his or her family, or work, or the weather and so on; here you want the candidate to talk so you can detect any concerns or indifference.
- Ask if there are any lingering questions or thoughts that you can answer or research.
- Remind the candidate that you are looking forward to being colleagues with him or her soon.

There is too much at stake to take this task lightly. A candidate who is borderline may choose another institution, or, worse yet, the offer is flubbed and an otherwise excited candidate gets started in your organization feeling underappreciated.

Who Should Make the Offer

Expert advice regarding offers is that the *appointing authority* and an HR professional should make the offer together. If the manager involved has not made a number of successful employment offers, he or she would be wise to seek the assistance of an HR professional who has made dozens of offers.

There are at least three advantages to involving an HR professional in the offer. First, HR professionals are able to represent the salary offer from a more impartial and authoritarian place. They may say, "The offer is based upon our policies, our research on the prevailing wage, in comparison to others in the department, and those in similar positions across the organization." This presentation implies to the candidate that we are trying to be fair in our offer, that the offer is not arbitrary, and that we appreciate the candidate and what he or she will bring to the institution.

Second, if there has to be some salary negotiation, the HR professional has a better understanding of which factors can be considered. The HR manager is likely also able to find creative solutions, such as a different starting salary in exchange for a signing bonus (this may be just what is needed for a new hire trying to buy his or her first house). Other examples may be a virtual guarantee of professional development funds, or an offer to assist a spouse with updating his or her résumé to find employment at or near the institution. When a hiring manager is unsuccessful at getting more money for a candidate who seeks a better offer, the hiring manager looks less politically astute and less powerful in the eyes of the candidate. Having an HR manager involved shows that the manager is willing to fight for the candidate without damaging the manager's perceived political power or influence.

Last, the HR representative is also more knowledgeable about total compensation and can explain, defend, or represent the salary and benefits in the best possible light. In this case, the institution has the best chance of getting the candidate to accept the offer.

The general experience of an HR professional with the offer process and ability to handle unexpected negotiations should serve the institution well on these important occasions.

Still Recruiting: An Offer of Employment Is a Recruitment Process

Just as not every student accepts the offer of admission, and every student who mails in a deposit does not actually enroll in the fall, not every employee to whom we make an employment offer will accept it. Therefore, we must remember how we deliver the offer is an important part of the romanticized nature of the employment process. People will often remember when and where they were offered employment they accept or reject. Therefore, it is important to extend offers professionally, with the right decorum, and with the appropriate appreciation and sensibility for the particular candidate in mind.

PART FIVE

Completing the Search Process

CHAPTER 17

Closing the Search

AFTER THE FINALIST ACCEPTS AND SIGNS his or her employment offer or contract letter, it is time to close the search. While this phase of the search is largely administrative and procedural in nature, it is still an integral part of a successful search. The broad areas of closeout activities are related to the people and the process. Communicating with the candidates, the committee, and the campus community is the first step. Completing the paperwork and documenting the selection process helps to formally conclude the selection process and is the second and final step.

The committee is formally decommissioned, records are gathered, and the selected individual is transitioned from a finalist to a new employee with the following major closeout activities:

1. Debriefing the committee
2. Thanking the committee members for their service
3. Notifying other applicants that the position has been filled
4. Announcing the candidate to the campus
5. Gathering documents to be kept on file
6. Evaluating the success of the search process
7. Preparing for the candidate to come aboard
8. Assigning the new hire a liaison

Debriefing the Committee

At the committee's last meeting or via e-mail, you should ask the members to share their thoughts, feelings, and observations about the conduct of the search. Any lessons learned should be recorded and shared with the appropriate parties—HR or the *appointing authority*. This information will improve the search process, help the new hire become successful, or aid the college or university with recruiting future faculty and staff.

Thanking the Committee

The *appointing authority* should write a letter to formally thank the search committee members for their work. The appreciation can be given verbally as well, when possible. A nice touch to highlight the institution's appreciation for their service is to send actual thank-you letters—not e-mails—and a small token gift when possible, such as college or university paraphernalia—coffee cups, sweatshirts, or similar items. Such appreciation recognizes the significant amount of time invested in the process as well as of the importance of the work.

Notifying Unsuccessful Interviewees

Candidates who actually had an interview should be handled differently from those who were never a semifinalist or finalist. A personal touch should characterize the interaction with candidates who were interviewed in person or over the telephone or video. How this personal touch is carried out and who makes the contact will vary. Nonetheless, how these candidates are treated will make a difference in the reputation of the college and university as well as in its ability to attract future talent. Dejected applicants, just like disgruntled former employees, are usually quite vocal about their displeasure.

The committee chair, *appointing authority*, or HR, in that order of preference, should telephone finalists who were interviewed on campus to share the news that they were not chosen. Candidates who had interviews over the telephone should get either a phone call or a personal e-mail from the committee chair. Applicants who never became candidates for the position can receive the routine correspondence that comes from HR, or the standard nonselection form letter that may be generated by the committee or is sent automatically from the *applicant tracking system*.

Announcing the Candidate to the Campus

The *appointing authority* should send a letter or an e-mail to the campus community to announce the successful search and to share a short biography of the candidate with appropriate stakeholders. Sometimes the community of interest is the entire institution, or it may be a particular school/college or department—depending upon the nature of the position. One suggested protocol is to draft a short biography and get the new hire to approve its content. Nothing is more embarrassing for a new employee than to learn after the first day of employment that some of his or her personal information has been shared with thousands of people when it would have been the new hire's preference that this information be kept private—such as he or she was once a minor league baseball player or was a member of XYZ sorority.

The announcement to the community should be upbeat and include a personal touch. When the welcome note sent to campus—which was approved in advance—indicates the new colleague likes jogging, runners are likely to e-mail the new hire to tell him or her about jogging trails near campus. The welcome note can include the start date, where the office will be located, some initial work activities, and the new hire's contact information. Next, an invitation for community members to make a concerted effort to welcome the new colleague via e-mail, phone, or in person is always a nice touch. Candidates feel valued when they start building contacts and relationships before their first day of work.

Documenting the Search: Gathering Records

For professional and regulatory reasons, it is imperative that the records of the conduct of the search be kept in order. These documents are necessary for quality assurance and monitoring purposes, but also to comply with appropriate state and federal regulations and audit requirements. Most search committee records are held on file for two years to comply with federal regulations and three years for many states; the rules vary by state. Consult an HR professional or legal counsel as necessary.

Records are also kept in case anyone challenges the fairness of the search. Good records make for good defenses; poor records call unnecessary attention to an otherwise professional process. Here is a list of documents that should be kept on file:

- Approval form showing signatures (or electronic record indicating them)
- Names of committee members, chair, and staff assistant or other support personnel
- Position description
- Copy of advertisements and *position announcements*
- *Charge* to search committee
- Documentation of any recruiting and outreach activities
- Applicant list, noting semifinalist, finalist, and selected candidate
- Additional equal opportunity/AA documentation, as appropriate
- Any correspondence with candidates
- All applicants' application materials
- Copy of all correspondence between chair and committee (e.g., announcement of meetings, committee instructions, etc.)
- List of interview questions (e.g., telephone, committee, etc.)
- Screening instruments from all committee members (e.g., forms, matrices, rating sheets, etc.)

  o Interview evaluation rating sheets, etc.

  o Evaluations of other activities

  o Feedback from appropriate stakeholders

- Meeting minutes (see Exhibit #16: *Minutes of the Meetings: Keeping Track of Proceedings*, p. 78)
- Completed reference and background checks
- Copy of rejection letter sent to unsuccessful applicants
- Any other written notes about the search process
- Copy of offer letter
- Copy of acceptance letter
- Campus-specific documents or forms

Evaluating the Success of the Search

An informal or formal evaluation of the search is good practice. Documenting and recycling the good ideas and lessons learned generated during the process ensures that future searches are performed better. A simple phone call involving the committee chair, HR manager, and *appointing authority* (when appropriate) meets the standard. The discussion can include three questions: "What went well that we can replicate?" "What did not go well that we should change in the future?" and "What are other ideas about this search to which we should pay attention in the future?"

The HR manager and possibly the equal opportunity representative may also analyze and document the results of the recruitment efforts. From where did our candidates come? Which recruiting, networking, or advertising efforts produced the most and better candidates? This analysis, called a *yield ratio*, is used to determine which *sourcing* techniques produced the better outcomes. Applicant tracking systems (ATSs) are especially useful for this purpose because they ask applicants to disclose where they heard about the particular vacancy. The standard reports in the typical ATS help institutions to evaluate the relative success of their *sourcing* strategies. These reports are invaluable in supporting minority recruiting efforts as the comparison of which sources produced minority and majority applicants can be quite informative.

Preparing for the New Hire to Come Aboard

Preparing for the new hire to come aboard is an extension of the activities every organization undergoes with any new hire. However, sometimes in the excitement of a new hire, organizations miss some of the small details that make a difference. It is advisable to work with HR to ensure that the normal procedures are followed. These usually consist of a form or checklist to make sure things such as getting an e-mail account, a computer, and network access are secured as well as ensuring that benefits and employment forms are completed, relocation assistance is offered, or the new hire learns about employee discounts. While seemingly mundane, this is all important information for the new hire. It is a professional mistake for a candidate who was hired eight weeks earlier to arrive on campus the first day and many small details have been unaddressed. It makes the candidate feel as if he or she was not expected or valued. Starting the process early

does not have any downside (see chapter 18, *Welcoming a Colleague to Campus*).

Assigning a Liaison

Welcoming the new colleague to campus is designed to get him or her off to a good start. An integral part of this process is assigning a liaison or buddy to help the new hire with the transition. The liaison can be a coworker, an HR representative, or a member of the search committee. Sometimes the hiring manager serves in this capacity. The liaison might also actually be two persons since the needs of new hires are disparate. One category of need involves the details of the employment transition such as benefits, relocation, parking, where to rent or buy, and so on. The other is related to the professional and his or her work. Any informed person can offer the former assistance, though a professional in HR who is trained to help with this process might be the best choice. The latter should probably be a peer or another colleague who understands the "lay of the land." For a new faculty member having questions about research support, or a new administrator with questions about personnel policies and budgets, the liaison should be a peer.

In addition to new professionals' asking questions about their particular job, they will ask, "What is expected of professionals in general here?" "Where do administrators live?" "Is it okay for my family to come along to the college picnic with me?" "Will I be expected to join a particular civic group?" "Is a peer-reviewed publication in the first year a realistic expectation?" Because the *on-boarding* and orientation of new professionals is so delicate, a small bit of misinformation can steer a new professional in the wrong direction. Therefore, do not leave it to chance and allow anyone to be a liaison; choose wisely.

Allowing the department "busybody" who volunteers to host and give a community and campus tour to all new hires may or may not be a good decision—depending upon the individual's professionalism, opinions, and reputation. The next chapter provides detailed guidance on the process of getting the new colleague off to a good start. This time is an investment in future success and should be designed deliberately and taken seriously.

CHAPTER 18

Welcoming a Colleague to Campus

THE WELCOME MAT for the new colleague is rolled out the moment a candidate accepts the position, and it stays out until a week after the candidate has actually reported to work. Then, and only then, is the search officially over. *Appointing authorities* must remember that not every candidate who is offered a position will accept the offer, and not every candidate who actually accepts the position will come to work on your campus—similar to students who are offered admission and either accept or decline and either enroll or do not enroll. Often candidates will receive better offers from competitors—as they have likely applied for other positions if they were already in the job market when they expressed interest in your position. After all, if you think they are fantastic, others are likely to think so as well.

What you can prevent are candidates who do not report for work for reasons such as they do not feel welcomed, they get lost in the shuffle of relocating, they get wooed by others, or the institution makes mistakes in bringing them aboard. Being duly diligent and assisting new hires with making this difficult transition is the least the institution should do after it has spent a significant amount of time and money recruiting and selecting the candidate. While it may not appear to be the most fitting of analogies, it is as if the candidate says to the institution, "You spent a lot of time wooing me when we were dating, but now that I have said 'I do,' you have lost the romance and interest in me."

On-Boarding

Just as many students drop classes and move back home to go to the local community college or state university, new employees—such as newly minted 28-year-old assistant professors—might feel overwhelmed and unwanted on a large campus across the country and quit after only a few days on the job (see Vignette Y: *The One[s] Who Got Away*). It is essential to approach the task of bringing a new colleague aboard with as much vigor and professionalism as it took to recruit and select the candidate. This process, often called *on-boarding*, is essential to completing the search process.

Supporting and welcoming the new colleague consists of two sets of activities. The first is attending to the administrative and logistical activities that are involved with leaving one job and starting another, including possibly relocating. The second has to do with helping the individual—and potentially his or her family—with the transition on a personal and professional level. Starting a new job can be both a complex series of moving parts and a stressful time.

Many new hires need assistance in handling the details of finding a place to live, and organizations should assist in the process. Remember, the search is not over until the new hire starts working. (See *Relocation Assistance*, later in this chapter, for more information.) Regarding the second matter of assisting the new hire in his or her personal and professional identities, the liaison or buddy mentioned in the last chapter is an indispensable asset. While the liaison will provide guidance, assistance, and moral support in an informal or semiformal manner, the institution should have formal support programs as well. The *on-boarding* process should include an employee orientation program, usually conducted by the HR department, and an orientation to the job, usually conducted by the supervisor or designee.

Institutions should host separate employee orientations by class of employee, such as staff, administrators, and faculty, to ensure that each group gets the attention it deserves. Faculty orientation guests might include information from the sponsored research department or faculty senate leaders. Administrators might receive a presentation from the budget department and procurement offices. All employees should get an orientation from their supervisor to their duties, to their work spaces, and to their colleagues or team

VIGNETTE Y
The One(s) Who Got Away

Car in the City

On Valentine's Day, we hear the great news. Our superstar candidate who was our first choice has accepted our job offer and has faxed his acceptance letter to the provost's office. The conference call had answered a lot of his questions, including where to find an apartment in Boston. He did seem a little surprised to learn what the going rate was for places near campus.

After graduation he e-mailed the receptionist to ask if there were any roommate-locating services. He arrived on campus in August after driving for three days from Iowa. He was disappointed to find out that his new apartment did not come with a parking space, and that in the winter he would not be able to park on the street because of snow removal. Before classes he got lost downtown because of the difficulty of driving in such an old city with narrow streets. During the first week of classes, he received a parking ticket off campus because he is on the waiting list to get a permit to park on campus near his building.

On Columbus Day, he came into my office astonished to learn that his car insurance rate was now going to cost more than his car payment because the rates for Boston were three times higher than they were for Des Moines. At a faculty meeting, he joked that he might have to start sleeping in his car since he could not afford to pay for student loans, a car payment, car insurance, and an apartment in Boston. Since it was much easier to get to and from work on the subway than to have a car in the city, he said he was going to sell his car after the holiday. He drove home for the holidays but did not return. He accepted a one-year appointment at a local university near his hometown; he said it was for family reasons.

No Car, No Life

The southern California sunshine draws people from around the world. We were surprised that our new hire thought apartments in Los Angeles were cheap compared to the apartment she had in New York City while in graduate school. Usually, we get the opposite reaction. However, we were disappointed to learn later that before she selected an apartment, she was going to have to take her driver's test. She had never driven a car because she grew up in Manhattan. However, in Los Angeles, you cannot get anywhere without driving.

In June she called and told us that she passed her driver's test on the third attempt. The last we had heard was that she was buying a new car and was looking forward to moving out of the frigid northeast for balmy California. We were surprised again when she called to say that she decided that driving in L.A. traffic was not what she wanted to do. So she resigned her position in August, two weeks before she was due on campus for the start of the semester.

Not Like Me

We had thought it was a banner year. The faculty class of 2014 was the best in recent memory. They had come from impressive schools, had noteworthy publications, and had already garnered several earned awards. They compromised a diverse group including women, minorities, international scholars, and professors who research interests were in biotechnology, interdisciplinary studies, and several other cutting edge disciplines. However, by graduation all seven of them had left or announced their departure from the university. They all said the same thing in one form or another, "There wasn't anyone 'like me' on campus."

(continues)

(*continued*)

It seems that we thought that they would just fit in so we did not make a special effort to make them feel at home. They were accomplished professionals, had amicable personalities, and seemed to get along with everyone. They did not look or act any different than anyone else on campus. They seemed to fit in. In retrospect, I guess we should have made sure that they thought that the campus had as cordial and hospitable a culture as we had thought.

These vignettes highlight the importance of the transition activities to welcome new hires to campus. Helping people to relocate and transition is a much bigger deal for some than others. Committees, HR departments, and *appointing authorities* would be wise to be attuned to the needs, concerns, and preferences of their prized new hires. Remember, the search is not over until after the new hire has started work.

members. A structured orientation and *on-boarding* process designed to get the employee off to a good start is a best practice approach to ensure success. A final word of advice on this matter: orientation need not be a one-shot or one-full-day activity. It may consist of a series of short sessions to avoid giving the new hire information overload.

Relocation Assistance

What are some good places to live? Should I buy or rent? Where is the nearest dry cleaner? Is there a good bank? Where can I get a haircut? What do people mean when they say, "Go over to the Hill"? Where are the best primary schools? What does the college pay for in moving expenses? Do you know of any babysitters? Every employee has the same or similar questions. Why should every individual employee go through the same process alone and at his or her own peril? It is demoralizing for a new hire to spend a considerable amount of a new salary only to learn a few days after starting that university employees receive a 25% discount on the retail price of a particular service.

Many relocation experts, real estate agents, some local community economic development or tourism agencies, chambers of commerce, governments, and other civic organizations have new-resident services. The college or university should provide some referrals or services to help new hires get acclimated and settled into the community. If the employee never gets settled, he or she may not stay.

Fortunately, many relocation assistance companies provide their services to the college or university and employee free of charge. Similar to the commission services that travel agents used to enjoy, relocation agents are paid by providing referrals to local businesses. Therefore, they know most local businesses and have screened and evaluated many of them. The relocation expert is then in a position to offer a variety of choices to the new employee, such as names of the best movers, banks, or apartment complexes in the area. Whether the service is offered in-house—by HR— or outsourced to a relocation expert, new employees should get assistance with relocating as it might be a daunting process for many.

Welcoming Reception

Some organizations host an informal or semiformal lunch or gathering for the new person once he or she has been on campus a day or two. Attendees are often any or all of the following: members of the search committee, hiring manager, new coworkers, or anyone else who interacted with the candidate during the interview process. This is a great way to make the new person feel like a part of the team. While these sorts of activities are more likely to occur for more senior positions, the idea works for any position and is a nice gesture of goodwill to welcome new employees. An informal gathering at the local coffee shop can make any new employee feel special, and such gatherings can provide a sense of closure for the search committee as well. Welcoming receptions are an insurance policy toward retention.

Welcoming Activities

Here is a list of suggested *on-boarding* activities that can make the difference whether a new hire feels at home in his or her new institution:

- Welcome reception or gathering
- Invitation to lunch, coffee, or cocktails by committee members or coworkers
- Tour of campus (e.g., to include places to eat, get supplies and services, etc.)
- Introduction to key colleagues during first few days
- Meeting with president, provost, dean, or other officials soon after first day
- Announcement of new hire to campus via e-mail, newsletter, newspaper, faculty meeting, or similar venues
- Name listed in campus directory
- Invitation to employee gatherings, convocations, sporting events, etc., at the beginning of the year (whether or not they have started work—they could be in town house hunting)

- Gift certificate or discounts to local establishments (e.g., store, restaurant, sporting event, etc.)
- Gift of campus paraphernalia
- Welcome card or letter left in the employee's new office
- Invitation to your home the first week or two.

The goal for this process is to make the person feel welcomed and to get him or her off to a good start.

A Job Well Done

It has only been a few days and your new colleague is starting to use the campus lingo. Congratulations, the search committee process is finally over. The new hire is aboard and working. He or she has figured out where the parking lot is, where the bathrooms are, and whom to call with questions. The search umbilical cord can be severed. You have done a great job in finding, selecting, and welcoming a great colleague. Pat yourself on the back and congratulate your fellow committee members for a job well done.

PART SIX

Special Topics

CHAPTER 19

Special Topics

Acting and Interim Assignments

ACTING DESCRIBES AN APPOINTMENT wherein the person who normally holds a position is not available. There is no vacancy, just a temporary absence of the person who normally holds a position, so the person who is acting is literally *acting* on behalf of the normal officeholder. An example would be an acting president because the president is ill, out of the country, or on a sabbatical. Acting candidates are assumed to hold the full power and authority of a position for a limited time. *Acting* is often confused with *interim* and the two terms are often used interchangeably, though technically they are different.

Interim is the term describing a person appointed to a position temporarily until a permanent replacement is identified. It follows the literal meaning of an interval between points of time. The term also denotes a vacant position. While it is not definitive, the intent of most interim assignments is to manage the existing affairs of a position. Interim candidates are usually not expected to make any bold changes, chart new courses, or make policy decisions that are inconsistent with their predecessor's—assuming their predecessor left on good terms. They are usually charged with "holding down the fort" until a new professional is selected.

It is usually unstated that the interim appointee does not possess the full measure of authority that the regular person would hold. This explains why there is little expectation that the interim appointee will make bold personnel, budget, service, or other decisions that might conflict with an organization's strategy, operations, or policies. Yet, sometimes interims are charged with making certain changes that are in the best interest of the organization—such as reorganizing or making difficult personnel decisions—to prepare the organization for a new leader to begin with a fresh start. Examples include taking actions that are potentially unpopular or divisive, though necessary.

Often interim candidates are not expected to be candidates for the permanent position, though this is not always the case. The *appointing authority* may ask the interim candidate to accept the appointment with the understanding that he or she will not pursue the regular position when a search commences. Either way, the terms and conditions of the interim or acting assignment should be agreed upon and documented. Last, the interim process can be used as a training or probationary period for rising stars, for example, who will gain some experience in preparing for future opportunities. Or it can be a "try before you buy" option for administrators to give a promising individual a chance to prove that he or she is ready to take on new responsibilities. After an interim assignment is over, the individual may be appointed to the position in question without a search—if such appointments are allowed by campus policies—or a search will commence.

Diversity Tip: Interim assignments can be career-defining opportunities for talented professionals who are given the chance to prove themselves—sometimes ahead of their peers. Often these seemingly unimportant assignments create the pathway for some to learn critical skills that will give them an advantage for future positions. Organizations should ensure that a fair number of women and minority candidates are given equal opportunity to be placed into such positions, so they should examine the institution's patterns of making such appointments.

Internal Candidates

It is usually in the best interest of organizations to consider current employees as applicants, whether or not formal procedures exist to encourage this practice. Handling the applications and interviews of internal candidates is, however, a delicate matter. Dealing with the disappointment of such candidates often puts search committees in an awkward situation as the candidates may be friends of committee members. Internal candidates should be treated formally, evaluated with the same scrutiny as external candidates, and vetted thoroughly, including reference checks with their current supervisor.

False Search

When there are internal candidates for a position, organizations must take great care not to engage in a false search—that is, a search with a predetermined outcome. Such a search is both unethical and potentially illegal. If the school has procedures or policies for handling applications and interviews of internal candidates, the search committee must follow them to the letter. If no such procedures or policies exist, the committee must treat internal candidates as if they were external candidates to avoid any appearance of favoritism or unfairness.

Courtesy Interviews or Fake Interviews

It is indefensible to grant interviews to internal candidates who do not have any chance of being appointed. The *appointing authority* or committee chair must have the courage to look candidates in the eye and share the regrettable news. Further, such playacting by committees is a questionable use of time, resources, and ethics. Many people will make life decisions based upon the potential for employment (e.g., cancel family vacations; buy new clothes; pass up other interview or employment opportunities; or otherwise spend their time, effort, and money). Individuals should not be given an interview as a means of avoiding hurting their feelings (see *Internal Candidates*).

Checking References on Internal Applicants

Should search committees check on the current performance of internal candidates? Absolutely! Reference checking is required for screening external candidates and should be for internal candidates as well. Search

committees must evaluate internal candidates objectively. It is also regrettable to learn that an underperforming candidate who was placed on probation accepts a better position across campus for more money because the new supervisor failed to check references with the current supervisor. Additionally, experts advise that checking references also helps the new supervisor to learn the style, preference, needs, and capabilities of the new hire when speaking with those with whom he or she has worked. This knowledge is an asset for working with and managing the new hire in the future.

Decisions About Applications

Application Deadlines and Preferential Filing Dates
The *hiring authority* should follow relevant institutional policies in specifying the application deadline in his or her *charge* to a search committee. Human resources professionals disagree about whether to impose hard-and-fast application deadlines or to continue to accept applications until an offer has been made and accepted. Although the latter option may impede efficiency, it can also result in a larger and better pool of candidates. It is advisable to specify a preferred application deadline after which the screening process will be under way. This gives the committee the opportunity to consider exceptionally qualified candidates who may have been recruited into the pool or who heard about the position vacancy late (see Vignette Z: *Should We Consider Michael Jordan or Not?*). Institutions would be wise to err on the side of finding the best talent—effectiveness—in contrast to seeking administrative ease—efficiency.

Incomplete and Updated Applications
Should the search committee consider incomplete applications? Should it accept updates to applications after the deadline? The only rule is that all applications are handled in the same way. In keeping with relevant institutional policies, the HR department should develop a policy for handling incomplete and updates to applications. Organizations that prefer larger and richer applicant pools over a more efficient search process will have policies that help candidates during the application process. No organization should penalize applicants for letters of recommendation sent late or other actions beyond the applicants' control.

VIGNETTE Z
Should We Consider Michael Jordan or Not?

We placed an advertisement in January and started our search committee process; by March we had interviews with three superb candidates scheduled. The department chair had been speaking with a colleague across the country, and as they were discussing a variety of professional matters, she mentioned that the search was under way. Her colleague noted that a good friend of hers was interested in moving back east and had always been interested in the university. In addition, her friend was a Pulitzer Prize–nominated author.

Within a few hours, the esteemed author and scholar was on the phone speaking with the committee chair asking if he could put his "hat into the ring." The committee chair was not sure what to do, so, he called the department chair, who called the dean, who called HR. The advertisement clearly stated that the deadline for the position was February 15; however, this was one of the leading scholars in our field, in the prime of his career, and someone who grew up near our institution.

Wanting a different interpretation of the policy, the dean called the provost. In all of the commotion word was leaked to the search committee, whose members happened to be interviewing the first candidate later that day. The committee was in an uproar. Half the committee wanted to follow the rules and be "procedurally" correct and fair. The other half thought the university was being shortsighted and foolish for denying the department the opportunity to select the Michael Jordan of their profession.

What would you do? Expert advice is always to have preferential application dates instead of deadlines for all openings, which gives the institution the option to do what is in its best interest—that is, to review applications early, late, or in midstream. Those who argue that you must have a hard-and-fast deadline value administrative ease and perceived fairness (not necessarily actual fairness) as more important than making a good $3 million decision. Preferential hiring dates are also necessary if you are doing due diligence and recruiting candidates, not just advertising. Recruiting and networking gets the institution's tentacles out into unexpected places; this desirable process does not work in an orderly fashion—or within a time frame under our complete control—and the best candidates are not necessarily those who are actively looking for a job today.

The obligations of fairness include being fair to the institution. The institution should be allowed to consider the best possible candidates, not just the first candidates who hear about the position or the best candidates who are available in February. As long as all candidates are given notice that the process is open until an offer is made—as denoted in the advertisement—then all are subject to the same standard.

Publishing the Salary Range and Hiring Range

Compensation is both an art and a science so it is often confusing trying to decipher how much an organization is willing to pay for a position. Two compensation ranges come into play. First is the salary range, which is based upon what is the generally established value of a given position in the labor market. It is usually expressed as a percentage range around the average market value. Compensation experts and consultants receive years of training to learn how to do this scientifically.

For instructional purposes only, if the average market rate for a dean is $100,000 per year, and the institution's policy is a 40% range, then the salary range for the position is roughly $80,000 to $120,000.

The hiring range is almost always a subset of the salary range and reflects what an organization is willing to pay for a given candidate at this time, all things considered. All compensation attempts to balance internal equity and external equity—that is, to pay a fair salary in comparison to similar positions inside and outside the institution. Deans' salaries would be in the general proximity of vice presidents', executive directors', and others' with similar years of experience and responsibilities—internal equity. Our deans also should earn roughly the same as deans of peer institutions who work in communities similar to ours—external equity.

If our salary ranges are too low, we cannot attract applicants from other schools; if they are too high, we might get more applicants than normal. Rookies earn toward the bottom of the range, and veterans earn higher in the range. Deans of arts might be placed in the second quartile of the range, and deans of law and business might earn in the higher end of our hypothetical deans' range, in accordance with the equity of the external labor market for such positions.

Institutions may establish a hiring range to reflect what they will actually pay for a given position at the time, usually due to internal equity considerations. If the institution has four other long-serving deans earning between $90,000 and $105,000, then it is unlikely to use the full salary range and hire a new dean at more than $105,000. However, it may advertise a hiring range of $80,000–$110,000. Some institutions have internal policies that do not allow hires above the midpoint of the range; others do not pay a variance based upon discipline. The central point to acknowledge is that every institution varies in how it applies the art of compensation. Institutions must be clear in communicating via the ad whether the designated range is a hiring or salary range, because this not-so-subtle difference creates inherent implications for negotiation of salary offers.

Second, it is also a philosophical question of whether salary or hiring ranges should be published. Publishing tells would-be applicants what they might expect, and, therefore, it will encourage some and discourage others. However, it is deceiving to advertise a salary range with no intention of offering the full range to any candidate due to internal equity considerations. Likewise, it is unfair to candidates to note that the salary is negotiable or commensurate with experience when, in fact, the institution does not negotiate because of a collective bargaining agreement or budget

limitations, or in consideration of internal equity. Publishing ranges should be deliberate and thoughtful because of the signals that are sent. This area is fraught with potential pitfalls if the institution does not know what the correct market rate is for salaries at this time. This creates missteps in both advertising ranges and making offers. A poor first impression can sour an initial relationship. Laying the groundwork for a successful search prevents failed searches, and establishing competitive salaries is a key part of this process.

Benefits Briefs: Recruiting With Total Compensation

The selection process is a two-way transaction. While the institution is screening and evaluating candidates, candidates are screening and evaluating the institution as well. A chief consideration from the candidate's perspective is always the pay and benefits associated with any new position. Therefore, it is a good recruiting technique to familiarize all candidates who come to campus with your benefits package. This brief can be provided in written form, on a website, or as a verbal brief given by an HR representative. A 15-minute meeting can make the difference in an offer being accepted or not.

The governing principle is that total value of compensation includes benefits and *perquisites*. If the salary offered is lower than what the candidate expects or desires, then the benefits package becomes more important. Even if the salary is attractive, a poor benefits portfolio may lower the applicant's total compensation package. Therefore, applicants must be given a complete picture of their potential compensation to make a good employment decision.

Some items to include in your benefits brief include insurance (e.g., health, life, short- and long-term disability, etc.), retirement accounts, and various types of leaves. Do you offer sabbaticals and other administrative leaves, in addition to sick and vacation time? How about home-purchase programs, access to health and gym facilities, support of professional development activities, discount tickets to certain events, or other similar benefits? Also, many candidates are attracted to higher education institutions for their tuition assistance programs for employees and, sometimes, their family members.

Intangibles and *perquisites* may enrich the employment value proposition for candidates when they include benefits such as flexible work schedules, more generous leave accumulations, concierge services, work location, telework options, and even the amount of support available for professional development. Each organization uses different recruitment and retention programs, and managers should know what their options are before extending an offer to a potential employee (see chapter 16, *Making an Offer*).

Making the effort to ensure that the organization is attractive to candidates may make the difference between an employment offer being accepted or rejected. Benefits briefs are good tools for attracting candidates and should be incorporated into your hiring process. Many organizations put this information on the Internet, but do not make your candidates look for it; provide it up front to them as a part of your wooing of the candidate.

Recruitment Incentives

Recruitment incentives are designed to increase the odds that the selected finalist will accept an offer of employment. Many incentives are provided as onetime actions and may not be in the form of direct compensation. When a salary offer is less than expected or is less than the candidate currently earns, recruitment incentives provide needed leverage in salary negotiations. This recognizes the fact that pay is not the only reason people commit to a career in higher education.

Most organizations have a policy or general guidelines for the type of incentives they provide. Additionally, many recruitment incentives come with a retention clause that may require the new hire to stay with the organization for upward of three years to justify the extra effort and expense of certain incentives. Check with your HR or provost's office to find out more information about potential incentives.

Here is a sample list of some effective recruitment incentives:

- Hiring bonus
- Relocation stipend
- Moving expenses
- Guaranteed pay increase (in a contract)
- Research grant
- Discretionary expense budget (e.g., onetime expenditure, annual allotment, etc.)

- Professional development fund (e.g., onetime expenditure, annual allotment, etc.)
- Support staff assistance (access or dedicated support)
- Graduate assistants
- Research space
- Better office space
- Extra vacation leave (for one or more years)
- Sabbaticals (e.g., pre-tenure, additional, etc.)
- Delayed starting date
- Advanced standing toward tenure
- Additional benefits (e.g., life or disability insurance, retirement contributions, etc.)
- Tuition support (for employee and/or family members)
- Spousal employment
- Executive compensation (Consult with benefits counsel when considering this completely negotiable option due to its legality, complexity, and taxability.)

Such incentives are never automatic, are used as needed, and usually require several levels of approvals before they are granted. Seek guidance and approval before discussing such incentives with candidates. This is yet another reason to engage your HR colleagues in making offers.

Alternative Search Models

The website www.SearchCommittees.com has identified at least nine different search models used in higher education to select faculty and staff. The methods colleges and universities use vary considerably. The approach used to select a faculty member should differ from one used to select a president or provost. Similarly, the framework of the search committee process is often used to select custodians, administrative assistants, counselors, financial aid staff, and other support staff positions. However, it would be imprudent to use the complete search committee process in these instances, because the time, effort, and expense of the process are largely unnecessary. Nonetheless, many of the principles still apply.

Wise organizations will borrow ideas from the classic 16-step search committee process outlined in this book and use them selectively in their searches. For example, the "advise and consent" model is one where a committee is used only at the interview stage. An administrator screens and evaluates candidates down to a manageable number, and then invites members of his or her staff to assist with interviewing. The principles of shared governance, "two heads are better than one," reduction of bias, and a 360-degree perspective on the position are largely preserved when using and adapting the outline of the classic search committee model.

Some models take advantage of a targeted recruitment effort. In many of these cases, heavy recruitment and networking is undertaken to identify particular candidates. This practice can be advantageous for identifying minority candidates, or it can be intentionally or unintentionally discriminatory, depending upon how it is used. For this reason, equal opportunity officers should be involved in developing the policies and procedures concerning use of these models and may be involved in the approvals necessary to use them. The best advice is for HR professionals to lead the effort of codifying into policy the alternative models that are permissible on a campus, including the necessary approvals and safeguards.

Alternative models should not be used after a failed search has occurred and a committee is scrambling for options. Nor should they be considered without a basis in policy or campus tradition. When they are considered at the end of a search, they appear to be either illegitimate or the result of trickery. On these occasions, there is a perception that administrators are manipulating the process to pick a particular candidate, that favoritism is in play, or that someone is doing something wrong or unethical. To avoid these circumstances, the options for altering the search process should be documented in advance and published widely. A prudent course of action is to disclose whether alternative models are acceptable as a part of the *charge*, or require approval of alternative models to preserve the traditions of shared governance.

Search Firms

Search consultants and search firms provide very valuable services to colleges and universities and usually manage the entire search process in higher education on behalf of their clients. One of the main elements of their services is that they provide advice on the best methods of designing and executing a search. They tend to have their pulse on the industry and understand the markets and trends in higher education employment.

Another advantage of using a search firm is that they tend to have deep Rolodexes. They have good networks and are effective at recruiting talented professionals into the pool of candidates for a given vacancy. Gaining access to their Rolodex, professional advice, and assistance comes at a premium. The cost for their services varies by the type and level of position in question, but generally ranges from multiple tens of thousands of dollars plus expenses, to upward of 30% of the first year's salary for the position in question. Provost and presidential positions typically demand the high end of this range or a generally accepted market rate that is quite hefty.

While most search consultants, sometimes called *headhunters*, provide comprehensive support services, from defining a position to assisting the new hire with his or her transition, some offer à la carte services based upon the needs of the institution engaging their service. Examples of these are firms that can range from assisting in identifying and recommending a handful of qualified candidates for the institution to consider, to offering assistance with minority recruiting. Others may offer assistance in designing the search while some facilitate internal discussions to clarify the needs of a department or college. Search firms are typically used for executive, hard-to-fill, or highly technical positions.

Advantages of Applicant Tracking Systems

Applicant tracking systems (ATSs) and electronic approvals allow simplified access to data about position vacancies that is useful for analysis purposes. Historical information contained in an ATS, such as time taken from approval to hire, number of vacancies in the past year, searches filled with internal candidates versus external candidates in the last three years, and so on, can be used to streamline and improve internal processes. Tracking systems also contain the résumés of past applicants, giving access to a database of potential candidates. This is integral to the recruiting process when similar positions become available in the near future.

Labor Market Analysis

A labor market analysis is a review of the availability of potential employees by geographical area, discipline, or profession. Theoretically a labor market analysis should be conducted before one recruits and advertises for any vacancy, though in reality it is not routine for the average search. It is a necessity to complete some sort of analysis when trying to find candidates for hard-to-fill positions. The analysis provides information on the number of potential applicants in the labor pool from which you are about to recruit. If trying to find candidates for database administrator positions, it is good to know that they are in short supply in the mid-Atlantic region. This tells the hiring manager that he or she must be very aggressive in recruiting to find qualified candidates, since simple advertising may not be enough.

HR representatives should assist hiring managers in gathering information about a particular profession that will help determine the relative availability of potential applicants. There are a number of different indicators and sources of information about employment. General indicators are the state of the economy, the unemployment rate, and growth trends in a city, region, or state. Likewise, trends in a profession reveal critical information about the type of professionals being trained, entering, retiring, or changing positions and the job types (e.g., a chemist going into academe or industry). There are a number of different sources of data, such as the following:

- Departments of labor (i.e., federal and state)
- Bureau of Labor Statistics
- *Digest of Educational Statistics*
- Manpower Employment Outlook Survey
- Professional associations
- Trade associations

- Research institutes
- Minority PhD statistics
- Graduate programs in each discipline
- Almanac edition of *The Chronicle of Higher Education*
- Applicant database services*
- Job board databases* (e.g., CareerBuilder.com, Monster.com, etc.)
- Articles in industry or discipline newspapers and journals
- Professional opinions of leaders or other well-placed colleagues in the field
- Opinions of colleagues who have completed recent searches
- Opinions from search consultants, *headhunters*, and temporary agency personnel

Each of these sources can assist you in determining the number of potential candidates for a given field. Doing a little research and asking around before a search will save considerable time and effort. The following case study in Vignette AA: *An Eminent Scholar, Industry Star, and Superhero Required: A Labor Market Analysis Case Study* highlights a real-life example of thinking through the idea of market availability when recruiting.

---

*Many job boards now provide a service where they can forecast how many professionals by discipline are located in the general marketplace based upon applicants who have applied for positions over time. They can also tell you where these applicants are located based upon the address and ZIP code where candidates report they live when applying for different positions.

VIGNETTE AA
An Eminent Scholar, Industry Star, and Superhero Required
A Labor Market Analysis Case Study

A small engineering school wanted to hire an academic department head for its electrical engineering department and wrote an ad that listed the following criteria: (a) earned doctorate in the particular field; (b) substantial teaching experience; (c) three years of U.S. industry experience; (d) evidence of substantial scholarship (described in the actual ad as "professional eminence with credentials worthy of being appointed with tenure"); (e) administrative experience, preferably at the level of the new position; (f) experience in the accreditation process for the engineering discipline; and (g) other related criteria.

(continues)

(*continued*)

The ad was well written and described the needs of the institution accurately and completely; however, it did not reflect the reality of the marketplace at that time. First, relatively few individuals have doctorate degrees in any technical field. Second, many technical professionals would prefer to work in industry, where salaries are often as much as 400% of their academic counterparts'. Third, the industry experience implies that the only real experience is available in the United States. The ad clearly excluded Canadians and applicants from other countries whose industry standards often mirror U.S. standards. It also excluded professionals working for U.S. corporations abroad and professionals working for the government and the U.S. military, and it likely excluded many other attractive candidates.

Fourth, *substantial* evidence of scholarship implies that the ideal candidate be an associate or full professor currently, which means the individual is likely tenured elsewhere. This substantial and eminent requirement also means that the ideal candidate is *very competitive* and marketable. (Incidentally, the small engineering school is located in a city where there is a large, nationally prominent engineering university, which makes it hard to recruit eminent scholars to this smaller school.) Fifth, the type of administrative experience described in the ad basically requires the ideal candidate to hold the same sort of position elsewhere. Last, the requirement to have experience with the accreditation process of one of the engineering professional associations also limited the potential pool of applicants.

The analysis of this example went as follows: The *Digest of Education Statistics* indicated that only about 14,000 electrical engineering doctoral degrees had been awarded in the previous 20-year period (National Center for Education Statistics, 2013). Our first assumption was that an average career spans 30 years. Furthermore, those earning doctoral degrees in the last few years were likely not eligible since they would not have had at least 10 years of professional experience (three years of industry work experience and at least seven years of teaching experience at the associate professor level).

However, once you include the previous criteria, the potential pool of applicants almost vanishes. Three-quarters of the applicants are automatically excluded because eminence in scholarship implies at least the top 25% of all potential candidates—which now leaves a mere 3,500 candidates. Of the 3,500, you would have to assume that some did not have academic and industry experience, experience with the accreditation process mentioned, appropriate administrative experience, and so forth.

Of the low number of electrical engineering candidates left, a sizable number would not be willing to relocate to that particular part of the country, would not work for the salary (which was arguably not high enough to attract an eminent scholar), or were probably simply not in the job market at that time. The ad was well written but self-defeating. Therefore, it is no surprise that this school had searched for this position twice before but had closed each search without hiring a suitable candidate.

The following changes were recommended. The degree had to be in the particular *or* a related discipline, and teaching experience was required, not *substantial* experience (i.e., a candidate with 15 years' industry experience with appropriate research, publications, and management experience, but only a few years' teaching experience would probably be a suitable candidate). The criteria for industry experience could be a single criterion, eliminating a specific number of years *and* U.S. experience as requirements.

It was also recommended that the paradigm for evaluating administrative experience criteria be broadened. That is, the institution assumed the only experience that applied was as a department chair in an academic environment, thereby philosophically excluding industry administrative experience, or soft leadership/administrative experiences such as service as head of the faculty senate, or leading task forces, not to mention consulting experience for those with an exclusively academic pedigree. In conclusion, "experience in the accreditation process" was changed to "knowledge of" and that it be a *preferred* criterion, not a requirement. After the previous suggestions were used, the third search was successful. The prescriptive nature of the ad and the lack of market analysis had derailed earlier attempts at hiring a great candidate.

CHAPTER 20

Legal, Ethical, and Regulatory Issues

Diversity, Equal Opportunity, and Affirmative Action Myths and Mix-Ups

Diversity

DIVERSITY IN AN EMPLOYMENT context refers to the employment of a broad mix of people who reflect the general demographic characteristics of an organization's community, customer base, industry, and interests. A diverse organization recruits, selects, promotes, and retains professionals based upon their contributions to the organization above all other considerations, a true meritocracy. A progressive diversity posture recognizes and promotes the irrefutable business case that the best organizations are ones that use the inherent richness of people from many different backgrounds because their unique skills, values, and perspectives give the organization a competitive advantage in the marketplace to respond to a broad range of organizational challenges and opportunities. Diversity is not a legal requirement; it is a business imperative for success.

Equal Opportunity

Equal opportunity refers to the legal framework provided by a series of state, federal, and sometimes local laws and regulations that attempt to create a level playing field for all applicants and employees where candidates have a fair chance of succeeding regardless of their background. Equal opportunity laws exist in a number of areas, including gender, race, ethnicity, religion, national origin, disability, marital or veteran status, sexual orientation, political affiliation, or genetic predisposition—depending upon in which jurisdiction a college or university is located. Specifically, organizations are prohibited from discrimination against employees who are members of these *protected classes* of individuals. One of the primary roles of HR professionals or *diversity advocates* who assist in the hiring process is to ensure that the search is conducted within the context of these legal parameters. Seeking

the advice of these professionals when there are questions in this area is prudent for any hiring manager.

Affirmative Action

Affirmative action (AA) refers to the legal mandate to pursue an aggressive recruiting strategy that attempts to provide equal opportunity for certain groups of applicants who have traditionally not had access to such opportunities. The groups that are targeted in an AA recruiting strategy are those the organization has identified as having been underrepresented in the populations the organization employs. The organization then establishes goals determined from this analysis and in comparison to the available workforce. The legal basis for AA programs at the national level was established in 1972 and comes from the president's Executive Order 11246, as amended. Many states and local governments have also codified AA requirements by either executive order or legislative action.

According to the *Code of Federal Regulations*,

> The goal of any affirmative action plan should be achievement of genuine equal employment opportunity for all qualified persons. Selection under such plans should be based upon the ability of the applicant(s) to do the work. Such plans should not require the selection of the unqualified, or the unneeded, nor should they require the selection of persons on the basis of race, color, sex, religion, or national origin. (*Uniform Guidelines to Employee Selection on Procedures*, 1978)

Executive Order 11246 requires that institutions put forth a "good faith effort" in the recruitment and selection process. Seeking assistance of HR or AA personnel in this process is a basic expectation of a professional search. The following AA recruitment and selection activities are recommended by the *Uniform Guidelines on Employee Selection Procedures* (1978).

Procedures

- Establish short- and long-term goals for selecting available qualified persons.
- Establish and use a recruitment program designed to attract said applicants.
- Organize, design, and redesign work to provide broad opportunities for all to enter and progress in a chosen career field.
- Validate selection procedures to ensure that they have no adverse impact on *protected class* applicants.
- Ensure that the selection process leads to an applicant pool that includes qualified candidates from targeted minority groups.
- Establish a career development program that provides opportunities for employees to grow beyond entry-level jobs.
- Review the success of your AA program.

Hiring managers should work with their HR department to learn whether the employment process in their organization is governed by an AA plan. Furthermore, to meet the mandates of the law, many organizations have an AA plan. Search committee chairs should familiarize themselves with the institution's AA plan or ask the HR or EEO/AA/diversity officer to brief them and their committee on the pertinent parts of this plan.

Many experts argue that a best practice approach to recruitment is to embrace the tenet of a diverse workforce, which is likely to produce a workplace that looks like the communities it serves. By embracing the inherent differences in people and celebrating their unique talents, organizations create an inclusive place to work for all and a desirable organization with which to do business. The ideals of a diverse workplace are particularly appropriate in the 21st century, especially given increasing globalization and a more mobile workforce.

Inclusion

Inclusion implies that all members—majority and minority—feel that they are full members of a community, that they are empowered to participate in the group, and that they are valued and appreciated just as much as every other member of the community. Mere presence and participation are not sufficient for inclusion; being a valued part of the whole is the essential criterion.

Americans with Disabilities Act

In the 1990s, legal protection for those with physical or mental disabilities expanded greatly. As a result, the search process is subject to any applicable state laws forbidding disability discrimination and to the Americans with Disabilities Act (ADA), as amended, which prohibits discrimination in hiring against otherwise qualified individuals who can perform the *essential functions* of a job, with or without *reasonable accommodation* (see Exhibit #3: *Identifying Essential Functions*, p. 26).

The ADA raises many questions for employers. Among them: Which physical or mental conditions constitute a "disability" under the law? What are the "essential functions" of a job? What accommodations for a disability are reasonably required in each individual case? What information about an applicant's physical or mental condition can be sought and relied on at various stages of the search process?

Employers can and should require every employee to be qualified to perform the essential functions of a job. Furthermore, they are free to select the most qualified applicant. Nonetheless, they must select applicants on the basis of job-related factors, not the presence or absence of any disability—that is, they should select on the basis of a candidate's abilities, not the presence of a disability.

Red Flags

Red flags are perceived information about a candidate that would disqualify or eliminate him or her from further consideration. An example might be an unexplained gap in employment, a bad reference, or questionable credentials. Any potential *red flag* concern should be investigated thoroughly and verified. Too often supposed *red flags* are identified and used to eliminate well-qualified candidates without substantiation. A gap in employment might be a typographical error, maternity leave, or a religious sabbatical. One poor reference out of 10 could be a biased former colleague, or the candidate could have grown professionally since that time. Questionable credentials can be verified easily if an effort is made to contact the degree-granting institution. Unclear information from a résumé can be verified with a simple phone call or during an interview or a reference check.

A word of caution about *red flags*: they are often thrown onto the table at search committee meetings to raise doubts about candidates whom an individual member does not like. Some experts highlight this maneuver as a common tactic to undermine women and minority candidates (Moody, 2010). *Red flags* that are not presented with clear agreed-upon evidence, fact, or verification should not be a screening consideration.

Red flags can also be used as a stealth tactic that points out the deficiencies of a candidate, but the deficiency is not an agreed-upon criterion by which other candidates are measured. For example, a history candidate in African American history *may* not be credentialed to teach the general survey course on American history. While this may or may not be true, the preference was not a stated requirement for the position, nor was it noted in the advertisement for a professor of African American history. In this case, the "nice to have" criterion is used to disqualify the candidate who happens to be the most qualified person in the pool. In this case the candidate has two degrees in African American history, instead of a degree in American history with an emphasis in African American history (see *Evaluating Organizational Fit: Defining and Documenting Fit*, p. 108).

Red flags are worthwhile words of caution when used appropriately. However, the factor illuminated as a *red flag* must be factual, evidence based, and verified; otherwise, it should not be used to sidetrack the committee's deliberations. Nor should a *red flag* be used to conceal bias.

Confidentiality

Confidentiality is a fundamental requirement of any professional search. First, candidates expect that their pursuit of a position will be confidential until they become a finalist so they do not jeopardize their current employment. This expectation is grounded in case law where individuals have the expectation that their privacy will be preserved. Therefore, search committees are sworn to secrecy and must not reveal the candidates in their pool before, during, or *after* the search. Second, if a college or university does not conduct confidential and professional searches, it is not likely to be effective in attracting professionals willing to work at the institution.

Confidentiality also extends to the reference-checking process. Many search committee members wrongly think it is acceptable to "call around" to their professional network to ask about a candidate under consideration (see Vignette U: *Calling a Friend: Oops Goes the Reference Check*, p. 116). This process is discourteous to the candidate and is fodder for *libel and slander* lawsuits. Individuals should give you advance permission to conduct an informal or formal reference and background check. Individuals should also be given the courtesy of knowing that you are checking their background so they can notify their references to expect your call.

Immigration: Non–U.S. Citizen Applicants

Organizations often receive résumés from individuals who are not U.S. citizens but have a desire to work in the United States. Because their eligibility to work in the United States depends upon their visa status, immigrants must apply to the federal government to gain permission to work in the country. Immigration issues are most common when organizations are hiring new college graduates who have student visa status (also known as an F-1 visa), which restricts their ability to gain and maintain employment eligibility.

Foreign national graduates who study in the United States and wish to stay and work after graduation must gain employment from an organization that agrees to sponsor them for a visa—usually an H-1B visa. Typically, recent graduates on F-1 visas can automatically remain in the United States for 12 months after graduation completing what is called OPT (Optional Practical Training) if they have secured employment directly related to their major field of study. Students in science, technology, engineering, and math (STEM) fields may be eligible for 17 months of OPT. During this 12- or 17-month period, graduates can then apply for an H-1B visa. The U.S. Citizenship and Immigration Services website, www.uscis.gov, has a great deal of information about immigration issues. However, many different visa categories and legal parameters affect an immigrant's eligibility to work; therefore, committee chairs/hiring managers should work with their HR manager or legal counsel when considering applicants who are not U.S. citizens.

Scholars who have been in the country for a while and are on H-1B visas must maintain such visa status for at least six years before they can apply for permanent residency. Becoming a resident alien allows a foreign national to remain and work in the United States indefinitely. However, while on an H-1B visa, the individual must maintain the sponsorship of an employer. Therefore, a candidate who has an H-1B visa and wishes to change employers must obtain sponsorship of a new employer before being hired or retained. A layman's generalization of the technical requirement of an H-1B visa is that the institution must demonstrate that the candidate is the most qualified person available. The standard for permanent residency is that there are no qualified Americans available to work in the area. Due to the technical nature of immigration law, committees should work with their HR manager and/or legal counsel when considering applicants with some sort of visa status.

Appendices

APPENDIX A
Position Authorization Form

1. DEPARTMENT	2. POSITION #	3. RECRUITMENT #

4. APPOINTING AUTHORITY (Name, Title, and Department)	5. DATE

6. OFFICIAL TITLE OF POSITION	7. WORKING TITLE

8. APPOINTMENT TYPE

FACULTY	RANK	ADMINISTRATIVE STAFF	PROFESSIONAL STAFF	CLASSIFIED STAFF
☐ Tenured	☐ Professor	☐ 12-Month	☐ 12-month	☐ Permanent
☐ Nontenure Track	☐ Associate Professor		☐ 9-month	☐ Project Appointment
☐ Fixed-Term Contract ☐ Other	☐ Assistant Professor ☐ Instructor ☐ Lecturer ☐ Other	☐ Other	☐ Other	☐ Other

9. ANTICIPATED STARTING DATE	10. FTE (Full-Time Equivalent) %

11. FUNDING SOURCE (Institution, Grant, Foundation, Auxiliary, etc.)	FUNDING ACCOUNT NUMBER

12. POSITION TYPE ☐ Existing Position ☐ New Position	13. ANTICIPATED SALARY RANGE $ _____ to $ _____	

14. NAME OF FORMER INCUMBENT	15. LAST DAY WORKED

16. RECRUITMENT	17. HR USE ONLY
☐ INTERNAL	Salary Range
☐ EXTERNAL	Hiring Range
☐ ONGOING	Title
	Job Family
	Role Code
18. DEPARTMENT HEAD APPROVAL (Budget Authority) Date	CONTROLLER Date
19. DEAN OR DIRECTOR APPROVAL Date	VICE PRESIDENT Date
20. HUMAN RESOURCES Date	PRESIDENT (if necessary) Date

APPENDIX B

Northwest Virginia College
Temporary Staff Authorization Form

Name _____   ☐ [check if current or former NVC employee]

Date _____

Position Title _____   Rate of Pay _____ per _____

Department _____   Supervisor _____

Term of Temporary Assignment: from _____ to _____

STATUS	TYPE	BUDGET	FUNDING SOURCE
☐ Full-Time	☐ Exempt	☐ Budgeted	☐ Account Numbers
☐ Half-Time	☐ Nonexempt	☐ Not Budgeted	
☐ Part-Time	☐ Other	☐ External Funding	

Justification: Provide any necessary explanation or justification in the space provided. Attach any additional documents to this form, such as job description, letters, requests for special arrangements, as necessary.

_____

_____

Federal law requires that all personnel complete an I-9 Employment Eligibility Verification form within 72 hours of commencing employment. Please ensure that your temporary person reports to HR within this time frame.

_____   _____

Director/Department Head   Date   **Dean/Vice President (if necessary)** Date

_____   _____

Director of Human Resources   Date   **President (if necessary)**   Date

APPENDIX C
Position Analysis Questionnaire (PAQ)

This device is used to help incumbents and their managers delineate the most important duties, tasks, and responsibilities for a given position. The by-product of this process is a job/position description.

Part One

NAME: _____

DEPARTMENT: _____

SUPERVISOR'S NAME: _____

SUPERVISOR'S TITLE: _____

PRESENT JOB TITLE: _____

PROPOSED TITLE: _____

1. DESCRIPTION OF MAJOR DUTIES: List the three to five most important duties, responsibilities, tasks, or functions of the job to be classified/reclassified *and* the percentage of time spent on those duties. Provide general overview descriptions grouped into major areas.

a.

b.

c.

d.

e.

2. PERIODIC DUTIES: Activities performed annually, quarterly, seasonally, or on some other recurring basis (do not include duties already noted).

3. SPECIAL OR COLLATERAL DUTIES: List any other duties or tasks that have not been noted and are very important for this particular job.

4. SPECIAL KNOWLEDGE, SKILLS, ABILITIES, AND/OR OTHER (check all that apply).

☐ Uses special machines or equipment? List _____

☐ Responsible for financial transactions, budgets, or cash? List _____

☐ Collects data, generates reports, etc.?

☐ Special amount of physical activity required?

☐ High degree of contact with public/customers?

☐ Does position supervise other positions? What positions? _____

☐ Does position work independently or with little or no supervision?

☐ Does position have independent decision-making authority? What areas? _____

☐ Responsible for originating policies, procedures, plans, or programs?

☐ Responsible for expensive equipment or supplies? Such as? _____

☐ Difficult working conditions?

☐ Is special/unique knowledge or education required? What area(s)? _____

☐ Can you learn this job by doing, or by on-the-job-training?

☐ Must one have experience before ever attempting this job? How much?_____

5. What is the most difficult, demanding, or important part of the job?

6. What are some of the indicators that work has been performed well (e.g., reports, completed jobs, widgets made, satisfied customers, new programs/policies, number of sales, or deadlines met)?

7. What are the areas you consider to be the technical parts of the job (e.g., must have specific skills in a particular area, or be able to handle other specific responsibilities)?

8. Has the job changed in the last one to three years; if so, how?

9. Summarize or provide a synopsis of the position in two to three sentences.

Part Two
Supervisor's Classification Questionnaire

1. Give an overview/synopsis of the position in question.

2. Please comment on the employee's statements on the Position Analysis Questionnaire (indicate any additions, deletions, modifications, or differences in emphasis or opinion).

3. What do you consider the most important or difficult duties and responsibilities of this position?

4. What level of supervision and attention does the supervisor expect to give to this position?

5. If this position became vacant, please describe the qualifications you think the successful candidate would have to possess. (Do not describe the *person* in the position now. Describe the *requirements of the job/position*, not a person!)

6. Assuming you have hired a new person in the position with the qualifications described, how long would it take for this qualified person to learn to do the job effectively (75% effectively)? (Circle one)

1–5 days   1–2 weeks   3–4 weeks   1–3 months   6–12 months   More Time

7. Compare this position to other positions within your organization. (Compare positions or jobs, not people!)

This *position* is similar to or a peer to what positions? _____, _____

This *position* is senior to what positions? _____, _____, _____

This *position* is junior to what positions?_____, _____, _____

8. What title do you feel is most appropriate for this position? _____

9. Other comments or observations about this position?

10. Are you aware of any positions that are similar to this position (inside or outside of the institution)?

11. Please provide any other information you feel would be helpful in classifying this position properly.

12. What professional resources can be used as resources in comparing this position (e.g., books, websites, etc.)?

APPENDIX D

Position Announcement Template

Search College

COLLEGE OF BUSINESS * PO BOX 8087 * RICHMOND, VA 23223 * (804) 836-6964

POSITION VACANCY

Search Committee College is a diverse community and seeks to assure equal opportunity through a continuing and effective Affirmative Action program.   www.searchcommittees.com

Search Committee College is a graduate school of the art and science of professional human resources practices and enrolls thousands of students annually. It is located in a historic community on the banks of the James River. About 100 miles from Washington, D.C, Virginia Beach, and the Shenandoah Valley, perfectly situated in the middle of nowhere but close to places you would actually want to be.

APPENDIX E
Charge for Dean of Research

The newly created position of dean of research will have primary responsibility for managing the office of research and external grants. In my view, the major responsibilities for this position will be as follows:

- establish research infrastructure that will liaise with entities such as the colleges and schools of the university, grant writers, governmental relations, and other appropriate operations of the extension facility;
- chair the Institutional Review Board (IRB) committee;
- ensure that the university meets its research targets;
- ensure that all researchers comply with all university policies; state, federal, and grant agency policies; and procedures and regulations;
- adequately support extension research activities; and
- develop internal policies, procedures, protocols, and guidelines.

In addition to these duties, my priorities for this new office are to elevate the university's profile in the larger research community. Most internal and external constituents have no idea about this new position and its role, yet most constituents feel strongly that we need such a position. The new dean will have to be a good ambassador for the role and function of the office and be able to articulate the vision to internal and external audiences. Therefore, the IRB committee chair should gather the input of the following people—vice president of external relations, director of grants, senior vice president of extension services, and the university's chief research officer—as the committee completes the position profile.

In a straw vote, the faculty senate had differing opinions about the type of leader we needed in this position. Half voted for a "rainmaker" type for the dean's position, and the other half preferred someone who would "make the trains run on time." The dean's council strongly preferred the latter. I would prefer the former, someone who would be entrepreneurial, garner significant external support, and create a vibrant new research culture at the university.

Interviews

After finalists are selected, there should be a series of interviews with all key stakeholders. These should include me, the dean's council, the vice president of external relations, the executive council of the faculty senate, department heads, and members of the research office.

Advertising

This should be a national search with advertisements in all of the appropriate journals, including *Journal for University Research*. Internal candidates are encouraged to apply, and nominations should be forwarded to the committee chair. The committee is encouraged to recruit highly qualified individuals from peer or more selective universities as well.

The Process

- The position should be open for six or more weeks to receive applications and nominations and to recruit promising applicants.
- I will assist with reference checks for the final candidate.
- Two rounds of interviews are acceptable. One round can be conducted via telephone or videoconference. As a matter of protocol, all internal candidates who are qualified should be offered at least a first-round interview. I would like them to be considered to identify their potential to grow into this position or other positions that may be created within this new division.
- No later than April 1—earlier is desirable—please make your recommendation in the form of a slate of two to four finalists with their strengths and weaknesses delineated. Please do not rank finalists; provide only a summary of the candidates' strengths and weaknesses.
- I will meet with the committee in person to discuss your recommendation.

APPENDIX F
Diversity Topics

A good professional search incorporates elements that produce a rich, diverse, robust, rigorous, and fair search by design. A search that does not have crisp and clear selection criteria is not rigorous, so it will not produce the ideal candidate because applicants are judged against the wrong standard. Fluid selection criteria also provide room for personal preferences and bias to creep into the process. A poorly designed recruitment strategy causes organizations to fish in old ponds that produce a limited variety and inadequate mix of applicants. Such an approach does not produce a diverse set of applicants. Networking activities fall prey to the same limitation if they do not reach out to different communities. For these and countless other reasons mentioned throughout this text, a thorough search creates the environment that inherently produces a fair search.

Elements that support a diverse search have been incorporated throughout this text, just as they would be through any credible search process. As noted earlier, a successful, professional, and diverse search happens as a part of the process, not in addition to the process (see *Diversity Success Does Not Require Extra Effort*, p. 13). Nonetheless, this text provides an expert guide to conducting a diverse search. Key diversity topics discussed in this book can be located in the index. They are presented in bold type.

Glossary

Advertising: a process that announces a position vacancy through various printed and online media to those who are in the market for employment.

Affirmative Action: the legal mandate to pursue an aggressive recruiting strategy that attempts to provide equal opportunity to applicants from underrepresented groups.

Applicant Tracking Systems: Web-based software designed to announce vacancies, take online applications, prescreen candidates, and serve as a communication portal with applicants and a database of potential candidates for future openings.

Appointing Authority (also *Hiring Authority*): person who has both the budgetary and personnel authority to establish and hire for a position. This person may or may not be the direct supervisor of the position being hired (i.e., a vice president who has the authority for all positions in his or her division when a director is the supervisor of the position in question).

Background Check: a pre-employment screening approach in which a job candidate grants permission to the hiring organization to verify the accuracy of information provided on a résumé and/or job application (e.g., criminal records, credentials, education, Social Security number, driver's license history, past employment, references, credit reports, etc.).

Behavioral Interview: an interview approach that asks candidates to describe how they behaved in a past situation with the expectation that past behavior is the best predictor of future performance.

Case Study/Scenario Question: an interview question without a right or wrong answer designed to evaluate how a candidate processes information, solves problems, makes decisions, or responds to difficult or ambiguous situations.

Charge (also *Committee Charge*): the set of written and verbal instructions that the appointing authority gives the search committee at its initial meeting regarding conduct of the search, including the nature and needs of the position in question, the selection process, and the kind of applicant that is desired.

Committee Charge (see *Charge*).

Cultural Competency: understanding, appreciating, and being able to interact effectively with people from different cultures, backgrounds, and socioeconomic statuses.

Diagonal Selection: appointing search committee members from across the organization and at different levels to get a 360-degree view of the position and its requirements.

Diversity Advocates: usually volunteers who support their institution's diversity efforts by providing training, monitoring, and support in cultural diversity and equal opportunity selection techniques to search committees and other groups.

Dissenting Opinion (also *Minority Report*): a confidential letter to the appointing authority from a committee member or members who disagree with the recommendation of the committee.

Diversity: in an employment context refers to employment of a broad mix of people that reflects the general demographic characteristics of an organization's community, customer base, profession, and interests.

Employment Branding: generally the reputation of an organization and its perceived qualities and characteristics related to its hiring policies and practices, compensation and benefits, and treatment of its employees. This perceived reputation helps or hinders the organization's ability to attract, recruit, and retain employees. An example of an employment brand at work is, "Google is known to be a great place to work."

Employment Landing Page: refers to a section on an institution's website that is designed to attract and retain employees by highlighting the advantages of working at the institution. Such sites typically include information about recruiting policies, benefits, pay, career opportunities, and similar propaganda with pictures and videos of attractive people smiling and enjoying themselves that encourage applicants to apply for jobs. Employment landing pages are similar to websites that are designed to attract applications for admission.

Equal Opportunity: the legal framework provided by a series of state, federal, and sometimes local laws that attempts to create a level playing field for all applicants and employees for positions wherein candidates are given a fair chance to succeed regardless of their background.

Essential Functions: groupings of tasks, duties, and responsibilities that are meaningful descriptors of the job without which the job would be different—that is, if you remove an essential function, the job becomes fundamentally a different job. Delineating essential functions is a requirement of the Americans with Disabilities Act (ADA), as amended.

Ex Officio Member: a Latin phrase roughly translated as "by virtue of office (position)." For the purpose of searches, it means nonvoting members who, by virtue of their responsibilities, are appointed to serve on search committees, such as an HR manager, equal opportunity officer, or a designated representative. Ex officio members provide a variety of support skills to search committees, such as advice, consultation, training, and administrative and logistical assistance.

Fit (also *Organizational Fit*): a description of whether a candidate's makeup, style, and personal and professional characteristics are congruent with the views and values of an institution, specifically its mission, vision, goals, and ways of doing business. These preferred characteristics should be documentable, observable, and/or measurable and widely agreed upon for them to be valid criteria with which to screen and evaluate candidates. Otherwise, they can be a guise for bias, discrimination, personal preference, or other irrelevant and unfair assessments, which are a distraction from the true knowledge, skills, abilities, training, experience, and know-how of candidates.

Headhunters: third-party recruiters often retained when normal recruitment efforts have not proven successful. Though their methods are different from those of search consultants, they are often confused with them.

Hiring Authority (see *Appointing Authority*).

Inclusion: a concept that implies that all members—majority and minority—feel as if they are full members of a community, and they are empowered to participate in the group as equals who are valued and appreciated just as much as every other member of the community. Mere presence and participation are not sufficient for inclusion; being a valued part of the whole is the essential criterion.

Information Interview Questions: fact-based questions used to gather or clarify pertinent information necessary to evaluate candidates.

Interviewing Committee: committee chosen to actually evaluate semifinalists/finalists in person, over the telephone, via teleconferencing, or through some other personal contact (see *Search Committee, Selection Committee*).

Job Description (also *Position Description*): document that summarizes and records the duties, responsibilities, requirements, and related factors of a position.

Job Analysis (also *Position Analysis*): a process of gathering detailed information about the duties, tasks, and responsibilities of a position, the results of which are documented in a job/position description.

Job Analysis Interview: conversation led by a trained person to interview a series of incumbents and supervisors to uncover and detail the requirements of a particular position.

Job Analysis Questionnaire (also *Position Analysis/Classification Questionnaire*): an inventory-type instrument used to uncover detailed information about the work performed, work conditions, equipment used, and other characteristics of a position through the use of standardized questions and checklists of typical characteristics, from which job descriptions are drafted (see Appendix C).

Minority Report (see *Dissenting Opinion*).

Negligent Hiring: a legal concept that makes an employer liable for hiring an employee who is either unfit or unqualified for a position and who subsequently causes physical harm to others' body, property, or organizational reputation. The tort doctrine states that the employer "knew or should have known" that that employee was a danger or potentially harmful and would have found out such facts if it had performed an adequate background check.

On-Boarding: orientation activities (e.g., relocation, transition support, orientation, and initial training) that help an individual transition into employment and enable the employee to get off to a good start.

Opportunity Hire: allows institutions to appoint a well-qualified candidate without a search when there are compelling business-related reasons to do so. Such occasions should be rare and should occur only in the most exceptional circumstances that are in the best interest of the institution, such as in the case of an eminently qualified faculty member with national/international stature, a trailing spouse, to promote diversity, to achieve certain previously defined academic objectives, or for similar strategic reasons.

Organizational Fit (see *Fit*).

Panel Interviews: interviews with a group of stakeholders versus with one decision-making authority. A search committee is a classic interview panel.

Perks (see *Perquisites*).

Perquisites (also known as perks): fringe benefits and other tangible and intangible incentives that entice employees to work somewhere and remain employed (e.g., parking spaces, particular offices, flexible schedules, club or association memberships, etc.).

Position Analysis/Classification Questionnaire (see *Job Analysis Questionnaire*).

Position Announcements: printed or electronic fliers or brochures that contain advertisements that provide detailed information about a particular position opening and the company where it is located (see Appendix D).

Position Authorization (also *Position Requisition*; also *Request to Recruit*): usually a form, routed to various offices inside an institution, that seeks authorization to commence a search and hire for a position whether it is newly created or a vacancy. The form authorizes both the position and the budget to support the position (see Appendices A and B).

Position Description (see *Job Description*).

Position Requisition (see *Position Authorization*, also *Request to Recruit*).

Protected Classes: Refers to groups identified federal, state, or local law— including gender, race, ethnicity, religion, national origin, disability, marital or veteran status, sexual orientation, political affiliation, or genetic predisposition— who are covered by anti-discrimination laws.

Reasonable Accommodation: a modification of a job to allow an otherwise qualified person to perform the job.

Recruitment: the active process that seeks to cultivate applicants from the universe of possible qualified applicants, whether or not they are actively in the market for an opportunity at a particular point in time.

Request to Recruit (see *Position Requisition*, also *Position Authorization*).

Screening Committee: a group of subject matter experts charged with culling the applicants down from a large number to a more manageable number for consideration by a search committee or hiring manager.

Search Committee: a group of individual stakeholders from various areas and levels within an organization that come together in a structured and coordinated manner to screen, evaluate, and recommend potential candidates for employment (see *Interviewing Committee, Selection Committee*).

Selection Committee: search committee that has the authority to select, rather than recommend, candidates for hiring. An example is when all faculty members of a department select a department head (see *Interviewing Committee, Search Committee*).

168 — SEARCH COMMITTEES

Situational Interview: contains questions that ask candidates how they might respond to a hypothetical scenario.

Sourcing: identification and cultivation of potential candidates through proactive or reactive recruiting, networking, and advertising techniques.

Staff Assistant: an administrative or professional employee who is assigned to support the activities of a search committee and provide administrative and logistical support for the conduct of the committee's work.

Task Inventory: a list of the major activities a job entails that is often used to evaluate a position or to create a position description. Inventories are often purchased from vendors to help organizations review and classify positions appropriately.

Telephone Interview (also *Video Interview*): a screening technique to gather additional information from applicants, clarify information found in the résumé, and otherwise assist in screening applicants. Telephone interviews are usually conducted in small groups using conferencing equipment and are generally shorter and simpler question-and-answer sessions than traditional on-site, face-to-face interviews. Video interviews are similar and differ only with the use of cameras that allow the committee and candidate actually to see one another during the interview.

Video Interview (see *Telephone Interview*).

Work Sample: a screening technique that uses actual work activities to evaluate a candidate's knowledge, skills, and abilities for a given job. Work samples are the most valid and reliable screening technique because they depend on actual work a candidate would be expected to perform on the job.

Yield Ratio: details the relative success of that particular *sourcing* activity compared to other activities. It contains a number of components, including how much it costs to advertise, recruit, or network for applicants; the number of applicants generated by the source; and a comparison of the proportion of interview and job offers accepted by a source.

References

American Council on Education & American Association of University Professors. (2000). *Does diversity make a difference? Three research studies on diversity in college classrooms.* Washington, DC: Authors.

Bertrand, M., & Mullainathan, S. (2003). *Are Emily and Greg more employable than Lakisha and Jamal? A field experiment on labor market discrimination.* National Bureau of Educational Research Working Paper 9873. NBER Digest.

Board of Regents of the University of Wisconsin System. (2010). *Benefits and challenges of diversity in academic settings* (2nd ed.). Retrieved from http:// wiseli.engr.wisc.edu/docs/Benefits_Challenges .pdf

Burke, M. E., & Schramm, J. (2004). *Getting to know the candidate: Conducting reference checks.* SHRM Research Report. Alexandria, VA: Society for Human Resource Management.

Chua, R. Y. J. (2011). Innovating at the world's cross-roads: How multicultural networks promote creativity. *Harvard Business School Working Paper 11*(85).

Chun, E., & Evans, A. (2007). Are the walls really down? Behavioral and organizational barriers to faculty and staff diversity. *ASHE Higher Education Report, 33*(1). San Francisco: Jossey Bass.

Chun, E., & Evans, A. (2013). *The new talent acquisition frontier: Integrating HR and diversity strategy in the private and public sectors and higher education.* Sterling, VA: Stylus.

Deloitte. (2011). Only skin deep? Re-examining the business case for diversity. Human Capital Australia. Retrieved from http://www.deloitte. com/assets/Dcom-Australia/Local%20Assets/ Documents/Services/Consulting/Human%20 Capital/Diversity/Deloitte_Only_skin_deep_ 12_September_2011.pdf

The Doors. (1967). People are strange. On *Strange Days* [record]. Hollywood, CA: Elektra.

Ford, R. L. (1993). *Interview guide for supervisors* (4th ed.). Washington, DC: College and University Personnel Association.

Global diversity and inclusion: Fostering innovation through a diverse workforce. (2011). *Forbes Insights.* Retrieved from http://images.forbes. com/forbesinsights/StudyPDFs/Innovation_ Through_Diversity.pdf

Gurin, P. (1999). Expert report of Patricia Gurin. *Michigan Journal of Race & Law, 5*(1), 363–425.

Herring, C. (2009). Does diversity pay? Race, gender, and the business case for diversity. *American Sociological Review, 74,* 208–224.

Hochel, S., & Wilson, C. E. (2007). *Hiring right: Conducting successful searches in higher education.* San Francisco: Jossey-Bass.

Hong, L., & Page, S. E. (2004). Groups of diverse problem solvers can outperform groups of high-ability problem solvers. *Proceedings of the National Academy of Sciences of the United States of America, 101*(46), 16385–16389.

Horwitz, S., & Horwitz, I. (2007). The effects of team diversity on team outcomes: A meta-analysis review of team demography. *Journal of Management, 33*(6), 987–1015.

Hurwitz, M. (2011). The impact of legacy status on undergraduate admissions at elite colleges and universities. *Economics of Education Review, 30*(3), 480–492.

Kaplan, M., & Donavan, M. (2013). *The inclusion dividend: Why investing in diversity and inclusion pays off.* Boston: Bibliomotion.

LaCorte, E. (1998). Educating and empowering selection committees. *CUPA Journal, 48*(2), 5–10.

Lee, C. D. (2001). *Search committees: A tool kit for human resources professionals, administrators, and committee members.* Knoxville, TN: College and University Professional Association for Human Resources.

Lee, C. D., & Bradley-Baker, L. R. (2012). Successful recruitment and hiring strategies. In M. A. Chisholm-Burns, A. M. Vaillancourt, & M. Shepherd (Eds.), *Pharmacy management, leadership, marketing and finance* (2nd ed., pp. 418–432). Sudbury, MA: Jones and Bartlett.

Lee, J. A. (2010, June). Students' perceptions of and satisfaction with faculty diversity. *College Student Journal, 44*(2).

Madera, J. M., Hebl, M. R., & Martin, R. C. (2009). Gender and letters of recommendation for academia: Agentic and communal differences. *Journal of Applied Psychology, 94*(6), 1591–1599.

Marchese, T., & Lawrence, J. F. (2006). *The Search committee handbook: A guide to hiring administrators.* Sterling, VA: Stylus.

Mathis, R. L., & Jackson, J. H. (2003). *Human resource management* (10th ed.). Mason, OH: South-Western.

Milem, J. F. (2003). The educational benefits of diversity: Evidence from multiple sectors. In M. J. Chang, D. Witt, & J. Hakuta (Eds.), *Compelling interest: Examining the evidence of racial dynamics in colleges and universities* (pp. 126–169). Redwood City, CA: Stanford University Press.

Moody, J. (2010). Rising above cognitive errors: Guidelines to improve faculty searches, evaluations, and decision-making. Retrieved from http://www.diversityoncampus.com

National Center for Education Statistics, Digest for Education Statistics. (2013). *Annual Reports Program.* Retrieved from http://nces.ed.gov/surveys/annualreports/digest.asp

O'Rourke, S. (2011). *Placing diversity in the academic mission: Institutional strategies for faculty diversity.* Higher Education Recruitment Consortium (HERC). Webinar and PowerPoint slides.

Page, S. E. (2007). *The difference: How the power of diversity creates better groups, firms, schools, and societies.* Princeton, NJ: Princeton University Press.

Rivera, L. A. (2012). Hiring as cultural matching: The case of elite professional service firms. *American Sociological Review, 77*(6), 999–1022.

Slater, S. F., Weigand, R., & Zwirlein, T. J. (2008, May 15). The business case for commitment to diversity. Harvard Business School Case, Business Horizons, BH276-PDF-ENG.

Smith, D. G., Gerbick, G. L., Figueroa, M. A., Watkins, G. H., Levitan, T., Moore, L. C., . . . & Figueroa, B. (1997). *Diversity works: The emerging picture of how students benefit.* Washington, DC: Association of American Colleges and Universities.

Smith, D. G., Turner, C. S., Osei-Kofi, N., & Richards, S. (2004, March/April). Interrupting the usual: Successful strategies for hiring diverse faculty. *The Journal of Higher Education, 75*(2), 135–160.

Steinpreis, R., Anders, K. A., & Ritzke, D. (1999). The impact of gender on the review of the curricula vitae of job applicants and tenure candidates: A national empirical study. *Sex Roles, 41,* 509–528.

Sullivan, J. (2000). *Diversity recruiting: The compelling business case.* Retrieved from http://www.ere.net/2000/01/14/diversity-recruiting-the-compelling-business-case/

Topa, G., Brown, M., & Setren, E. (2013, June). Do informal referrals lead to better matches? Evidence from a firm's employee referral system. *Federal Reserve Bank of New York Staff Reports.* Retrieved from http://www.newyorkfed.org/research/staff_reports/sr568.pdf

Uniform Guidelines on Employee Selection Procedures, Policy Statement on Affirmative Action (1978); 43 FR 38295, 38312, Aug. 25, 1978; 29 C.F.R. part 1607.17-4.

Vicker, L., & Royer, H. (2006). *The complete academic search manual: A systematic approach to successful and inclusive hiring.* Sterling, VA: Stylus.

Watson, W., Kumar, K., & Michaelsen, K. (1993). Cultural diversity's impact on interaction process and performance: Comparing homogeneous and diverse task groups. *The Academy of Management Journal, 36*(3), 590–602.

Diversity, Selection Bias, and Search Committee Bibliography

Alger, J. (1999, Spring). When color-blind is color-blind: Ensuring faculty diversity in higher education. *Stanford Law and Policy Review, 10*(191).

Antonio, A. L. (2000). Faculty of color and scholarship transformed: New arguments for diversifying faculty. *Diverse Digest, 3*(2), 6–7.

Antonio, A. L. (2003, November/December). Diverse student bodies, diverse faculties: The success or failure of ambitions to diversify faculty can depend on the diversity of student bodies. *Academe, 89.*

Baez, B. (2000). Race-related service and faculty of color: Conceptualizing critical agency in academe. *Higher Education, 39*(3), 363–391.

Bielby, W. T., & Baron, J. N. (1986). Sex segregation and statistical discrimination. *American Journal of Sociology, 91*, 759–799.

Biernat, M., Manis, M., & Nelson, T. (1991). Stereotypes and standards of judgment. *Journal of Personality and Social Psychology, 66*, 5–20.

Brayboy, B. M. J. (2003). The implementation of diversity in predominantly white colleges and universities. *Journal of Black Studies, 34*(1), 72–86.

Casadevall, A., & Handelsman, J. (2014). The presence of female conveners correlates with a higher proportion of female speakers at scientific symposia. *mBio, 5*(1), 1–4, doi: 10.1128/mBio.00846-13

Chun, E., & Evans, A. (2009). *Bridging the diversity divide: Globalization and reciprocal empowerment in higher education.* San Francisco: Jossey-Bass.

Cole, S., & Barber, E. (2003). *Increasing faculty diversity: The occupational choices of high-achieving minority students.* Cambridge, MA: Harvard University Press.

Coleman, A. L. (2001). *Diversity in higher education: A strategic planning and policy manual.* Washington, DC: College Board.

Deaux, K., & Emswiller, T. (1974). Explanations of successful performance on sex-linked tasks: What is skill for the male is luck for the female. *Journal of Personality and Social Psychology, 29*, 80–85.

Dovidio, J. F., & Gaertner, S. L. (2000). Aversive racism and selection decisions: 1989 and 1999. *Psychological Science, 11*, 315–319.

Dowdall, J. A. (2007). *Searching for higher education leadership: Advice for candidates and search committees.* ACE/Praeger Series on Higher Education. Westport, CT: Praeger.

Eagly, A. H., & Karau, S. J. (2002, July). Role congruity theory of prejudice toward female leaders. *Psychological Review, 109*(3), 573–597.

Georgi, H. (2000). *Is there an unconscious discrimination against women in science? Who will do the science in the future?* A Symposium on Careers of Women in Science. Washington, DC: National Academic Press.

Glazer, N. (2003, Summer). The black faculty gap. *Public Interest, 152*, 120–128.

Goldin, C., & Rouse, C. (2000, September). Orchestrating impartiality: The impact of "blind" auditions on female musicians. *The American Economic Review, 90*(4), 715–741.

Hale, F. W. (Ed.). (2004). *What makes racial diversity work in higher education.* Sterling, VA: Stylus.

Heilman, M. E. (1980). The impact of situational factors on personnel decisions concerning women: Varying the sex composition of the applicant pool. *Organizational Behavior and Human Performance, 26*(3), 386–395.

Hurtado, S., Milem, J., Clayton-Pedersen, A., & Allen, W. (1999). *Enacting diverse learning environments: Improving the climate for racial/ethnic diversity in higher education.* San Francisco: Jossey-Bass.

Kayes, P. E. (2006). New paradigms for diversifying faculty and staff in higher education: Uncovering cultural biases in the search and hiring process. *Multicultural Education, 14*(2), 65–69.

Ketcham, B. (2005). *So you're on the search committee.* Herndon, VA: The Alban Institute.

Knowles, M. F., & Harleston, B. W. (1997). *Achieving diversity in the professoriate: Challenges and opportunities.* Washington, DC: American Council on Education.

Martell, R. F. (1991). Sex bias at work: The effects of attentional and memory demands on performance ratings for men and women. *Journal of Applied Social Psychology, 21*(23), 1939–1960.

Moody, J. (2004). *Faculty diversity: Problems and solutions.* New York: Routledge.

Reviewing applicants: Research on bias and assumptions. (2006). Women in Science & Engineering Leadership Institute, University of Wisconsin System. Retrieved from http://wiseli.engr.wisc.edu/pubtype.php.

Ridgeway, C. L. (2001). Gender, status, and leadership. *Journal of Social Issues, 57,* 637–655.

Schreiber, M. N., Juedes, D. R., Norlin, E., Rhodes, G., & Whitmire, E. (2000, September). *Diversity web sources in higher education.* Chicago: College & Research Libraries News.

Smith, D. G. (2000). How to diversify the faculty: Get beyond the myths and adopt new hiring practices if you want to add significant numbers of minority group members to the faculty. *Academe, 86*(5), 48–52.

Springer, A. D. (2004). *How to diversify faculty: The current legal landscape.* Retrieved from http://www.aaup.org/Legal/info%20outlines/legaa.htm

Stainback, K., & Tomaskovic-Devey, D. (2012). *Documenting desegregation: Racial and gender segregation in private-sector employment since the Civil Rights Act.* New York: Russell Sage Foundation.

Steinpreis, R., Anders, K. A., & Ritzke, D. (1999). The impact of gender on the review of the curricula vitae of job applicants and tenure candidates: A national empirical study. *Sex Roles, 41,* 509–528.

Trix, F., & Psenka, C. (2003). Exploring the color of glass: Letters of recommendation for female and male medical faculty. *Discourse & Society, 14,* 191–220.

Turner, C. S. V. (2002). *Diversifying the faculty: A guidebook for search committees.* Washington, DC: American Association of Colleges and Universities.

Valian, V. (1999). *Why so slow? The advancement of women.* Cambridge, MA: MIT Press.

Valian, V. (2005). Beyond gender schemas: Improving the advancement of women in academia. *Hyapatia, 20*(3), 198–213.

Vedantam, S. (2005, January 23). The bias test: You may be more prejudiced than you think. *The Washington Post Magazine,* 1–12.

Vonhof, J. (1999). *Pastoral search: The Alban guide to managing the pastoral search process.* Herndon, VA: The Alban Institute.

Weems, R. E. (2003). The incorporation of black faculty at predominantly white institutions: A historical and contemporary perspective. *Journal of Black Studies, 34*(1), 101–111.

Wenneras, C., & Wold, A. (1997). Nepotism and sexism in peer-review. *Nature, 387,* 341–343.

Williams, D. A. (2013). *Strategic diversity leadership: Activating change and transformation in higher education.* Sterling, VA: Stylus.

Wilson, R. (2002, July 12). Stacking the deck for minority candidates? *The Chronicle of Higher Education, 48*(44), A10–A12.

About the Author

Dr. Christopher D. Lee is a self-described HR evangelist and a leading authority on the search committee process. He believes that artful application of progressive HR principles and practices is the answer to most organizational challenges. His background includes having served as the chief HR officer for four institutions of higher learning—Georgia Highlands College (formerly Floyd College), Southern Polytechnic State University, Bates College, and the Virginia Community College System. He has taught as an adjunct professor of HR at several institutions during his career, including Lewiston-Auburn College of the University of Southern Maine and the University of Richmond. Chris was an American on Education (ACE) fellow, and was placed in the provost's office of Northeastern University during his 2003–2004 fellowship year.

He is a former question writer for the PHR (Professional in Human Resources) and SPHR (Senior Professional in Human Resources) examinations administered by the Human Resources Certification Institute (HRCI). He is the author of numerous HR-related articles and chapters, and three books, including *Performance Conversations: An Alternative to Appraisals*. He recently completed the manuscript for his fourth book, tentatively titled *Performance Questions: 7 Answers, 30 Minutes, Unlimited Results*.

Chris's first book, *Search Committees: A Tool Kit for Human Resources Professionals, Administrators, and Committee Members*, earned the 2001 Kathryn Hansen publication award from the College and University Professional Association for Human Resources (CUPA-HR). Since then, he has been an invited contributor to the second edition of the seminal work in the field, *The Search Committee Handbook* by Ted Marchese and Jane Fiori Lawrence; he has provided search committee training to more than 1,000 HR professionals; and he has consulted with dozens of colleges and universities on the search committee process. He is the founder of the website www.SearchCommittees.com, an online repository of hundreds of resources and training materials on the search process designed to train and empower search committees.

Chris has presented at conferences and consulted with clients in the United States, Canada, Australia, and South Africa on search committee or performance management–related topics. A graduate of Auburn, Golden Gate, and Georgia State universities, he is also certified as a Senior Professional in Human Resources. Additionally, Chris is a retired lieutenant colonel in the U.S. Marine Corps Reserves. He can be reached at Chris@SearchCommittees.com.

Index

Key diversity topics discussed in this book are pesented
in bold type.

Notes

* The role of the EEO/diversity/AA officer is detailed across a number of entries including the following: xiv, 12, 17, 21, 29, 30, 34, 44, 46, 54, 65, 66, 74, 81, 150, 154, 159, 167